How to Do Everything
Mac

About the Author

Dwight Spivey is a software and support engineer for Konica Minolta, where he specializes in working with Mac operating systems, applications, and hardware, as well as color and monochrome laser printers. He teaches classes on Mac usage, writes training and support materials for Konica Minolta, and is a Mac OS X beta tester for Apple. Dwight lives on the Gulf Coast of Alabama with his wife Cindy and their two beautiful children, Victoria and Devyn. He studies theology, draws comic strips, and roots for the Auburn Tigers in his ever-decreasing spare time.

About the Technical Editor

Guy Hart-Davis is the author of more than 40 computer books, including *How to Do Everything: iPod & iTunes, Fourth Edition*, and the forthcoming *Mac OS X Leopard QuickSteps*.

How to Do Everything
Mac

Dwight Spivey

New York   Chicago   San Francisco   Lisbon
London   Madrid   Mexico City   Milan   New Delhi
San Juan   Seoul   Singapore   Sydney   Toronto

The *McGraw·Hill* Companies

Cataloging-in-Publication Data is on file with the Library of Congress

McGraw-Hill books are available at special quantity discounts to use as premiums and sales promotions, or for use in corporate training programs. To contact a representative, please visit the Contact Us pages at www.mhprofessional.com.

How to Do Everything: Mac

1234567890   DOC DOC   0198

ISBN   978-0-07-150272-6
MHID   0-07-150272-6

Sponsoring Editor
Roger Stewart

Editorial Supervisor
Janet Walden

Project Manager
Vastavikta Sharma,
International Typesetting
and Composition

Acquisitions Coordinator
Carly Stapleton

Technical Editor
Guy Hart-Davis

Copy Editor
Bill McManus

Proofreader
Manish Tiwari

Indexer
Kevin Broccoli

Production Supervisor
James Kussow

Composition
International Typesetting
and Composition

Illustration
International Typesetting
and Composition

Art Director, Cover
Jeff Weeks

Cover Designer
Pattie Lee

Cover image used by permission from Apple Inc.

*To my beautiful wife Cindy, who valiantly and lovingly held down the fort while I
was busy slaying dragons.
To my angels, Victoria and Devyn—Daddy can play again, guys!
To my mom and dad, my sister and brother-in-law, and my nieces and nephews, for
your love and encouragement.
To my God, through whom all things are possible.*

Contents at a Glance

Contents

Acknowledgments

This is the first book I've ever written, and I couldn't have been blessed with a better team than these wonderful folks!

Roger Stewart and Carly Stapleton: you two are amazing. Roger, the patience you exhibited as my first editor was beyond all my expectations. Carly, your help throughout the entire process has been wonderful and you made it seem effortless. My experience with you both makes me look forward to my next writing project.

Thank you, Neil Salkind, with all my heart. I'll never be able to adequately express my appreciation for your help as my agent in making one of my biggest dreams come true.

Guy Hart-Davis was my technical editor for this project. I was very pleasantly surprised when I found out that someone of his caliber was connected with my first book. Thank you, Guy, for your guidance and professionalism. Your gentle correction and expert advice was invaluable.

Thanks to Bill McManus, Janet Walden, and Vastavikta Sharma for their help in the editing process. I would also like to extend my heartfelt appreciation to the rest of the editing and production staff who made this book possible.

A very special thanks goes to Jerri Ledford and James Kenny. James, thank you for steering me to Jerri, and for giving me so much support. Jerri, your help in getting me signed on with Neil and Studio B was the catalyst in getting this book published, and your professional help is beyond any measure of gratitude that I can extend. Again, thank you both so very much.

Introduction

Congratulations are in order! Chances are good that if you've purchased this book you either own or soon will own a Mac, and that is always a good thing. If you are using a computer for the first time, your experience will be light years beyond that of your friend or family member who started out with a PC. If you are a seasoned PC user, the Mac is so elegant and so simple to use in comparison to what you're used to that the way you work with, and what you expect from, a computer will change forever. Some people have a hard time understanding how someone could get so excited about a *computer*, and their puzzlement is understandable. It's hard to get pumped about the average PC, but we're not talking about that; we're talking about a Mac! I've seen many a person shrug their shoulders and laugh at the notion that all computers aren't equal, only to have them sit in front of a Mac and watch them as they "ooh" and "aah" with each click of the mouse. Welcome, my friend, to computing as it was meant to be experienced.

What Makes a Mac a Mac?

A Mac is as much about getting the job done as it is about having a great time doing it. Macs are built for speed, looks, durability, functionality, and plain old "coolness." Nobody designs a better computer, inside and out, top to bottom, than Apple—period.

Macs are well known for the stability and dependability of their hardware, as well as their software's legendary ease of use. What makes the Mac so reliable and easy to use is the fact that it is all Apple all the time. Apple designed every aspect of your Mac, from the physical shell that houses all of its components, to the minutest detail of its interface (the stuff you see on your computer screen).

PC manufacturers use a hodge-podge of parts from third-party manufacturers when they build their computers, and the cheaper the parts the more likely the PC's reliability should be questioned. The cliché that "you get what you pay for" applies perfectly here. Apple doesn't manufacture every single part that goes into your Mac, but they work very closely with any third-party manufacturers to be sure the compatibility and dependability of the product matches the high standards Apple and its customers have come to expect.

If one didn't know better, one might think the term "ease of use" was coined to describe Apple's operating system. While nothing in this world is perfect, Apple's Mac OS X, which is the key element of every Mac sold, comes the closest to reaching that status in the realm of computer operating systems. Apple goes to great lengths to make sure that the environment you work in is every bit as functional as it is beautiful. There was a time several years ago when Apple's lead in the area of user interfaces seemed to wane, but the latest versions of Mac OS X have once again widened that gap with their competition.

Apple has what is arguably one of the most loyal customer bases of any company in the world. The fervency with which Mac fans follow Apple's every move is a testament to the quality Apple infuses into every product they release, particularly their Macintosh line of computers.

What You'll Learn from This Book

One of my hopes is you will learn that a computer can be much more than just a device to create spreadsheets and read email. In *How to Do Everything: Mac* you will discover that your Mac can handle anything from the most mundane job to the most exciting, and can complete them both with equal amounts of elegance and ease.

Here are but a few things you will learn to do with this book: surf the Internet, read email, write school reports, create spreadsheets, make your own movies, share your photos with the world, listen to music, synchronize contacts with your PDA or cell phone, stay on time by making custom calendars, video chat, print documents, back up your computer, add external devices to your Mac, download items from the Internet, and much more.

My other hope is that you'll enjoy the process of learning how to use your Mac, and that *How to Do Everything: Mac* plays a large and helpful role in that process. I strived to write this book with your enjoyment, not just your education, in mind.

Part I

Get Started with Your Mac

Chapter 1

Welcome to the World of Mac!

How to...

- Understand the difference between consumer and professional Macs
- Discover the different parts of your Mac
- Set up your Mac
- Find out which version of the Mac operating system your Mac has
- Start, restart, and turn off your Mac

When Apple first introduced the iMac to the world in 1998, their goal was to provide a powerful yet user-friendly computer that the average person could not only afford but use without having to own a degree in computer engineering. The iMac was the first in Apple's line of consumer Macs, which soon expanded to include the eMac and the iBook. The popularity of the consumer Macs was undeniable then, and is even greater today. There was once a time when Apple was associated mainly with creative professionals, such as graphic artists, musicians, and the Hollywood crowd, but that time has passed. While Apple remains the computing company of choice in those circles, they have extended their reach into all expanses of computing, from the home to the laboratory.

Macs for Consumers

Macs come in two varieties: consumer and professional. Apple saw the need to divide its computer offerings in order to accommodate not only the artists and movie directors of the world, but also the average person who wanted a computer that just worked correctly right out of the box.

What's the Difference Between a Consumer and Professional Mac?

Some people may be put off by the term "consumer Mac," thinking that it somehow denotes an inferior machine, but that is certainly not the case for the audience it is intended for. On the contrary, today's consumer Mac is a powerhouse of technology. The main difference is that consumer Macs are loaded, while professional Macs are loaded for bear!

As evidenced by the iMac's built-in monitor, the Mac mini's incredibly small size, or the MacBook's built-in camera, Apple's consumer products are intended to be easy to use, incredibly stylish, and, above all, affordable. Their main function is to be an extension of their users' everyday lives—or as Apple terms it, iLife. Most people who use computers simply need to send emails, surf the Web, download and edit pictures and video, play games, listen to music, and perhaps burn a DVD or two. Consumer Macs are more than capable of handling these tasks that are becoming a bigger and bigger part of our lives with each passing year.

Professional Macs are designed for maximum computing power, and most people probably won't need power of this magnitude. The professional Mac is meant to be upgradeable and expandable to the extreme. Tons of RAM (memory), outrageously fast video cards, and lots and lots of hard drive space are required for demanding tasks such as movie editing, rendering of huge graphics files, or compiling thousands of lines of code, tasks the vast majority of us will never have a real need for. However, should you choose to purchase a professional Mac, rest assured that while built for the highest end of computing needs, they are quite adept at handling your average everyday computing chores.

How to Do Everything: Mac focuses on the consumer choices that Apple provides, but since consumer and professional Macs both use the same operating system, Mac OS X, most of the items and functions mentioned in the book are available for both. Professional Macs typically ship with the base operating system and minimal applications, while the consumer Macs are usually loaded with software, such as Front Row and Photo Booth, that is geared more to the average computer user.

Which Macs Are for Consumers?

A quick trip to Apple's website, www.apple.com/mac, shows that they don't break up their products along consumer and professional lines, but rather according to whether the product is a desktop machine or a notebook (a.k.a. laptop). The iMac and Mac mini would be classified as consumer desktop machines, while the MacBook would be the lone consumer notebook offering.

iMac

The iMac is the quintessential consumer Mac. Whether you're new to the Mac community or a dyed-in-the-wool Mac fan, everyone has heard of the iMac and will instantly recognize its famous design styles. The iMac has evolved into its present-day form while maintaining the all-in-one design and functionality that made it famous. The built-in monitor and speakers make for an incredibly clean look and feel, without the clutter of wires associated with most desktop computers.

Photo by Robert Nelson reproduced under Creative
Commons Attribution Share Alike 2.0 License

Mac mini

The Mac mini is a tiny mite that's mighty! It's easily the most affordable Mac that Apple offers, and is a miniscule 6.5 inches square and 2 inches wide. While much smaller than its consumer siblings, it still packs a wallop with up to a 1.83 GHz Intel Core Duo Processor and a possible 2GB of RAM. While the Mac mini does boast a very low price point and small footprint, it doesn't ship with a keyboard, mouse, or monitor. If you don't already have a monitor, mouse, and keyboard, you will have to add them to the cost of your Mac mini, making it perhaps not the best bargain.

Photo by Chris Lawrence reproduced under Creative Commons Attribution Share Alike 2.0 License

MacBook

The MacBook is basically a portable iMac. All the capabilities of the iMac are in this small, portable unit, sacrificing only the large screen sizes of the desktop-anchored iMac. The ability to take your Mac wherever you go is a bigger draw than a large screen size for many users, so the MacBook is a very popular choice.

Photo by Jared C. Benedict reproduced under Creative Commons Attribution Share Alike 2.0 License

Intel Processors

Everyone is familiar with the little jingle that plays at the end of most Intel commercials. If you are a new Mac user, you probably assume that all computers have always used Intel processors, but that's certainly not the case. Apple used PowerPC processors (jointly developed by IBM, Motorola, and Apple) for years with their computers. The PowerPC processors were powerful workhorses and had speed to burn, so why did Apple change? That's a good question, but I'll bet some of you asked a more obvious one, like…

What's a Processor?

The term "processor" is simply short for "microprocessor," which is also known as a CPU (central processing unit). The processor is the brain of your Mac, where all the information your Mac receives or transmits goes to or comes from. Processors handle most of the millions of calculations your Mac has to perform.

Why Did Apple Choose Intel?

The PowerPC processors had served Apple well for a very long time, so why did Apple drop them for Intel? The short and sweet of it is that the PowerPC was getting to the point in its development where it couldn't meet the performance commitments made by IBM. Apple had to be certain of its long-term ability to meet the high performance demands of its customers, and thus they were forced to seek other options. Intel was able to meet those demands, and then some, and the rest is computing history.

How Does an Intel Processor Benefit You?

Let me count the ways! The announcement by Apple that they were including Intel processors in the Mac sent shockwaves through the computing industry and media. The biggest question was whether Apple would make Mac OS X, the operating system your Mac uses, available for installation on third-party PCs, and the resounding answer was "No!" However, we did find out that it was possible to install Windows on your Mac. As a matter of fact, Apple has even provided a way to facilitate this, called Boot Camp, which Chapter 18 explores. Now, why would you want Windows on your Mac? You bought a Mac to get away from Windows! That's also something I'll discuss in Chapter 18.

Other benefits of having an Intel processor are that more developers have become interested in the Mac, because it is much easier for them to bring their applications to the Mac platform than ever before. This can only be a good thing. Also, alternative operating systems such as Linux can be installed on your Mac, although Apple doesn't officially support this (meaning that they supply Boot Camp for installing Windows but offers no such utility for installing Linux or other operating systems as of this writing).

Explore Your Mac

When you buy a new car, it's always a good idea to familiarize yourself with the location of its controls so that you can operate the car safely and confidently. A similar concept applies to your new Mac. In order to use your Mac efficiently and with much less frustration, you should know where to insert CDs, where to connect printers and cameras, and even where to plug in the power cord (which is a pretty important thing to do, by the way).

What Are All These Ports (and Other Items) For?

Macs all come with the same basic port configurations, but do sport a few differences. Ports are the "mysterious" openings located on the side or back of your Mac.

Ports are used for connecting external devices to your computer, and as you can see by looking at your Mac, their sizes and shapes vary greatly depending on what type of device you are connecting. Universal Serial Bus (USB) connectors aren't the same size and shape as FireWire or Ethernet connectors for the obvious reason of preventing you from mistakenly connecting a USB cable into your Mac's FireWire or Ethernet ports. Thankfully, Apple has included ports for each of these connection types, and a few more.

USB ports are generally used for connecting devices such as your keyboard and mouse, small printers, digital cameras, scanners, and the like. USB is the most commonly used of the ports and comes in two versions, or speeds: 1.1 and 2.0. Version 2.0 is much faster than version 1.1, and is backward compatible, meaning a device that has only a 1.1 port can connect to another device via a 2.0 port and work just fine.

FireWire is a blazingly fast connection type used primarily for connecting digital video cameras and external hard drives. There are currently two speeds, or types, of FireWire: FireWire 400 and FireWire 800. Both are more fully discussed in Chapter 19.

Ethernet is what you use to connect a Mac to your network, if you're not using a wireless connection. It's also very fast and is how your Mac communicates with other devices on your network, as well as the rest of the world via the Internet if you use a broadband Internet Service Provider (much more on this topic in Chapter 5).

Other common ports are the headphone/audio out ports, which are what you use to connect (you guessed it!) headphones and external speakers.

Now let's take a look at each of the consumer Macs to see where all these ports, and other items, reside on your particular model.

iMac

The iMac has the most ports of the three consumer models. As shown in Figure 1-1, it has three USB version 2.0 ports, two USB version 1.1 ports (located on the keyboard), two FireWire ports (one each of the 400 and 800 versions), one 10/100/1000Base-T (Gigabit) Ethernet port, an audio in/optical digital audio in port, a headphone out/optical digital audio out port, and a Mini-DVI port (for connecting additional monitors or a projector). A built-in iSight camera, microphone, and slot-loading CD/DVD drive round out the list (see Figure 1-2).

Mac mini

The Mac mini sports a surprisingly large number of ports for such a small device. As Figure 1-3 shows, it includes ports for FireWire, Gigabit Ethernet, USB 2.0 (four ports), video out (DVI), audio in/optical digital audio in, and headphone out/optical digital audio out. There is also a slot-loading CD/DVD drive on the front panel of the Mac mini (see Figure 1-4).

MacBook

MacBooks come with an iSight camera and microphone built right in, along with a slot-loading CD/DVD drive (see Figure 1-5). Available ports include FireWire, Gigabit Ethernet, Mini-DVI, audio in/optical digital audio in, headphone out/optical digital audio out, and two USB version 2.0 ports (see Figure 1-6).

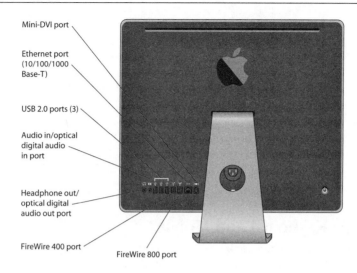

Mini-DVI port

Ethernet port
(10/100/1000
Base-T)

USB 2.0 ports (3)

Audio in/optical
digital audio
in port

Headphone out/
optical digital
audio out port

FireWire 400 port

FireWire 800 port

FIGURE 1-1 Rear view of the iMac showing its available ports

Set Up Your Mac

When it comes to setting up your Mac in a workspace, there are several factors that you should consider. While these factors may not seem very important at first glance, you will appreciate their significance once you've hunkered down over your Mac for a couple of hours.

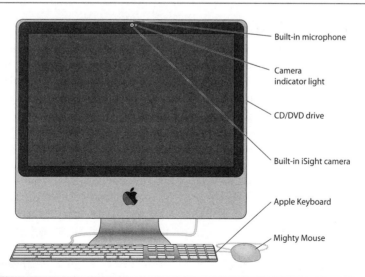

Built-in microphone

Camera
indicator light

CD/DVD drive

Built-in iSight camera

Apple Keyboard

Mighty Mouse

FIGURE 1-2 Front view of the iMac

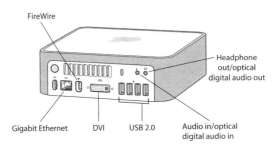

FireWire

Headphone
out/optical
digital audio out

Gigabit Ethernet   DVI   USB 2.0   Audio in/optical
digital audio in

FIGURE 1-3   Rear view of the Mac mini

Hook Up Your Keyboard and Mouse

Without a keyboard and mouse connected, you won't be going far on your Mac's first test drive, unless you have a MacBook, of course. Macs only use keyboards and mice that have wired USB connectors or that are wireless.

Connecting wired keyboards and mice is as simple as finding an available USB port on your Mac and plugging in the device's USB connector. That's it! Apple's keyboards have USB ports on them so that you can easily connect your mouse to the keyboard, saving valuable cable length for the mouse.

Wireless keyboards and mice aren't tough to set up, either. You have to install batteries into the devices before they will work, though. Once you install the batteries, it's up to the Mac to discover the keyboard and mouse when it starts up. If it does not do so, consult the documentation that came with the mouse or keyboard for assistance.

Connect to a Power Source

I'm sure some of you are rolling your eyes and saying, "I know how to plug in my computer! This guy must think I'm an idiot!" Well, I assure you I certainly do not think that. You were bright enough to purchase this book, so I'm certain you're capable of connecting the power cord from the Mac to an electrical outlet. However, there is more to think about than just getting power to your Mac.

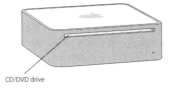

CD/DVD drive

FIGURE 1-4   Front view of the Mac mini

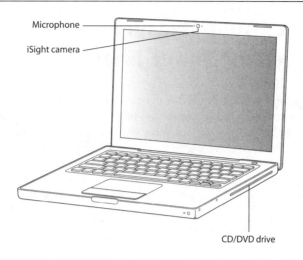

Microphone
iSight camera
CD/DVD drive

FIGURE 1-5   Front view of the MacBook

A surge protector is a "must have" for any Mac. A surge protector keeps your computer safe from "spikes" in the electrical lines that can harm your Mac's internals. If the voltage is suddenly increased in your power lines, the rush, or surge, of electricity may be too much for your Mac to handle, and the electrical components of your Mac will be cooked. The surge protector is able to "absorb" these unexpected increases in voltage, protecting your Mac from almost certain death.

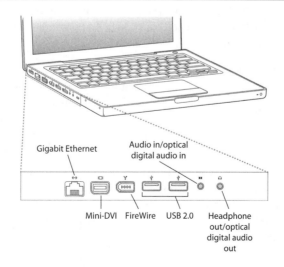

Gigabit Ethernet
Audio in/optical digital audio in
Mini-DVI   FireWire   USB 2.0   Headphone out/optical digital audio out

FIGURE 1-6   Side view of the MacBook

Keep Your Mac on Even when the Power Is Off

Very few things can make you pull the follicles right out of your scalp quicker than the power shutting off in your home or office while you're in the middle of an important project with your Mac. When the power goes out, the work you haven't saved will be lost forever.

This nightmare scenario can be avoided with the purchase of a UPS. I don't mean you have to buy your own shipping company; I'm referring to an uninterruptible power supply. A UPS looks like a large surge protector, with many outlets so that multiple devices can plug into it. The UPS contains a battery that it will switch to almost immediately when utility power is disconnected. Your Mac can run off of this battery power for several minutes, giving you the time to safely save the files you are working on.

MacBook users won't have to worry about this kind of issue since they have batteries in their Mac already.

TIP   *The old adage "You get what you pay for" applies here. Typically, the higher the price you pay for a surge protector, the better the protection you will receive. Costlier surge protectors generally are able to absorb larger voltage increases than lower-cost units are able to absorb.*

Set Up Your Working (or Playing!) Environment

The space you choose to work in is just as important a decision as any other regarding your computing experience. Your Mac doesn't much care where you put it, but you will. Here are just a few things to consider when setting up your work area:

- **Environment**   Make sure that the room you choose to work in is well lit and cool. The upside of good lighting is obvious, even though many people do find it easier to focus on a monitor if the light is not quite so bright. Find a "happy medium" that allows you to comfortably focus on the screen while supplying ample light for reading and seeing other objects. The temperature of the room is important because it will rise considerably when the computer is running, particularly if you are in relatively close quarters.

- **Desk**   When using a laptop, you can pretty much lounge anywhere you like with your Mac. However, if your Mac is a Mac mini or iMac, you will be tied to your desk. Be sure that your desk is large enough and sturdy enough to accommodate the sizes and support the weight of your computer and whatever peripherals you choose to connect to it, such as a printer or scanner.

■ **Seating** When selecting a chair, make sure it is comfortable and supportive. If your chair is so plush that your posture is almost doubled over, you might want to get something slightly more firm. If the seat is so hard your legs fall asleep after five minutes, you might want to consider cushioning up a bit.

TIP   *Make sure your chair isn't too high or too low. This is very important when it comes to using your keyboard and mouse. Be sure that your forearms are parallel to the desktop to keep from placing too much strain on your wrists, elbows, neck, and back.*

If you really want to get the skinny on proper posture, check out www.ergonomics.org for more information on the subject than I ever knew existed (see Chapter 5 first for help with connecting your Mac to the Internet).

Start It Up!

Let's get the ball rolling, already! Turning on your Mac for the first time requires knowledge of only one thing: where the power button is, of course. If you have an iMac, the power button is located on the left rear panel of the monitor. The Mac mini's power button is on the back of the unit, and the MacBook's is found above the right side of the keypad. Just push the power button and away you go.

Use the Setup Assistant

When you turn your Mac on for the very first time, you are greeted in several languages before being presented with the Setup Assistant. Apple provided the Setup Assistant to make it easy for a Mac newbie to set up a user account, set the computer's time, register their product, and perform several other tasks that get your Mac ready to go as quickly and simply as possible. If you prefer to not go through the Setup Assistant, you can quit it at any time by pressing ⌘-Q (simultaneously pressing the COMMAND and Q keys) and then choosing Skip from the available options.

What's All This On My Screen?

Once your Mac has completed booting up, the first thing you see is the Finder and the default desktop picture. The Finder is the Mac user's best friend, and is an application you will use more frequently than any other. The Finder never stops running (although it can be restarted) and its sole function is to help you navigate the files and folders on your Mac. I will go into much more detail about the Finder in Chapter 3. For now I will keep things simple until you familiarize yourself with your current surroundings. The following list explains what you're seeing on your freshly booted Mac (see Figure 1-7):

■ **Menu bar** The menu bar is the topmost part of your screen that holds several menus: the Apple menu, the Finder or application menu, status menus, and the Spotlight menu (the small magnifying glass in the upper right corner).

FIGURE 1-7   Your first look at the Mac OS X desktop

- **Desktop**   The desktop is the first thing you see when you boot up and is where your desktop (or background) picture resides. The desktop can also contain files and folders. More details about the desktop are provided in Chapter 2.

- **Dock**   The Dock is the area at the bottom of the screen that contains icons for frequently used applications, folders, or ongoing processes. These icons are actually shortcuts to the real items. See Chapters 2 and 3 for more information on the Dock.

- **Window**   Windows are used when browsing your computer for files, applications, or folders. They also contain their own sets of menus and shortcuts. Chapter 2 covers windows in more depth. A window doesn't open by default when your Mac first comes on; I opened the one in Figure 1-7 for illustration purposes.

I'll delve into much more detail regarding these items in subsequent chapters.

How Do I Drive This Thing?

The next step is to figure out how to actually maneuver in this strange new land. If your Mac is an iMac, it came with an input device called a mouse (see Figure 1-8), which comes standard with most desktop computers. You use the mouse to point at an item and then click on it with

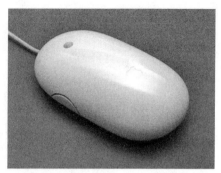

Photo by Fritz Saalfeld reproduced under Creative
Commons Attribution Share Alike 2.0 License

FIGURE 1-8   Your iMac's mouse

one of the mouse's buttons to perform an action. Your mouse has two buttons, though on a
Mighty Mouse (which is what comes with your iMac) it appears as if you have only one large
button. The standard clicking technique to select (highlight) an item that the mouse is pointing
at is to click the left side of the mouse (left-click) once with your index finger. To open an item,
left-click the item twice (double-click). To move an item, left-click the item and hold the button
down, pull the mouse in the desired direction to move the item to its new location, and then
release the mouse button. To see a menu of options for an item, click the right side of the mouse
(right-click) with your middle finger.

If you have a Mac mini, you have to purchase a separate keyboard and mouse, which are
obviously your primary input devices.

TIP   *Although I recommend using Apple's line of keyboards and mice for use with your Mac
mini, you're not required to do so. When buying a keyboard and mouse for your Mac
mini, just be certain that they use USB connections, not PS2. Another item to be aware
of is that Mac keyboards have two* COMMAND *keys, the icon for which looks like this:* ⌘.
The ⌘ *keys are located on either side of the* SPACEBAR. *When shopping for a keyboard,
keep these keys in mind.*

MacBooks use an entirely different technology called a trackpad (see Figure 1-9), but it
works on the same principle as a mouse. To use a trackpad, place a finger on the pad and move
it around on the surface; you will see the pointer on your screen move along with your finger.
To select an item that you are pointing at, click the trackpad button once; to open the item,
double-click the trackpad button. To simulate a right-click with the trackpad, hold down the CTRL
(CONTROL) key on the keyboard while clicking the trackpad button. You can use a USB mouse
with your MacBook if you prefer that instead of the trackpad.

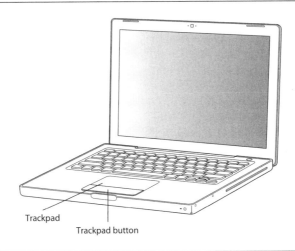

Trackpad

Trackpad button

FIGURE 1-9   Your MacBook's trackpad

What Version of the Mac OS Do You Have?

Even in today's computer-centric world, if you were to ask most people what OS their computer uses, they would stare at you as if you were a seven-and-a-half-foot-tall Wookiee who just stepped off a Corellian Engineering Corporation YT-1300 freighter and pulled the ears off the nearest gondar (just a little *Star Wars* lingo to keep the geeks interested). Actually, most people would simply ask…

Um, What Exactly Is an OS?

Great question, and thanks for playing!

OS stands for "operating system," which is the software that makes your Mac work. Without an operating system, a computer is just a pile of cables, chips, and silicon. If your Mac were an aircraft carrier, its operating system would be the crew and you would be the captain. The operating system carries out your commands, opening files, surfing the Web, sending email, scanning and printing, and swabbing the deck (okay, that last one was just to see if you were paying attention). There are lots of operating systems in the world of tech, but only one that comes natively with your Mac: Mac OS X. That's pronounced "Mac OS *Ten*," the Roman numeral, not "Mac OS *Ex*," the letter. Other operating systems will work with your Mac, as mentioned earlier in our discussion of Intel processors, but that's a topic for later (Chapter 18).

While there are other operating systems out there, Mac OS X is generally regarded as the cream of the crop. No other operating system combines the ease of use, stability, and high level of security that Mac OS X provides out of the box, and it's the best-looking operating system around. The Mac experience is legendary and, while sometimes overblown by a few Mac zealots, is by far the best bang for your computing buck. Some might argue that a "free" operating system, namely Linux, is better due to the obvious: it's free! However, that old adage of "you get what you pay for" rears its ugly head again. Don't get me wrong, Linux fans! Linux has come light years from where it was just a short while ago, and I would encourage any experienced computer user to give it a go, but it can't hold a candle to the seamless ease of use that Mac OS X affords. This is mainly due to the fact that Mac OS X is developed by engineers who are paid to make it the best of the best, and Linux is developed largely by volunteers.

How to ... Check the Version of Mac OS X You're Using

To check what version of Mac OS X your Mac is running, simply choose Apple | About This Mac (in other words, click the Apple menu in the upper-left corner of your screen and click About This Mac in the drop-down menu). The resulting window shows you what version of Mac OS X you currently have installed. Knowing the version of your operating system can be very helpful should you need to troubleshoot any issues in the future.

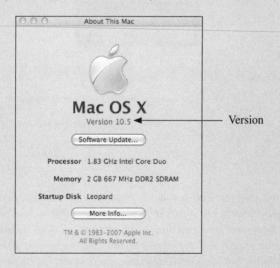

Notice that the version of Mac OS X used for this book is Mac OS X 10.5, otherwise known as Leopard. Apple loves to name the different versions of Mac OS X after big cats. Mac OS X 10.4 was called Tiger, 10.3 was Panther, 10.2 was known as Jaguar, 10.1 was dubbed Puma, and 10.0's nom de plume was Cheetah.

Restart, Shut Down, and Put to Sleep Your Mac

Your Mac may need to be restarted from time to time (for various reasons that will be covered in later chapters), or you may just want to turn it off when you've finished your work. Do you need to turn off your Mac every time you quit using it? No. Putting the Mac to sleep is a great way to give your Mac a rest until you need to use it again.

Restart Your Mac

To restart your Mac, choose Apple | Restart. You are asked if you are sure you want to restart. Since you're new to this sort of thing, go ahead and click the Restart button. The screen appears as though it's being turned off, but instead of turning completely off it goes dark for a few seconds before beginning the boot process again.

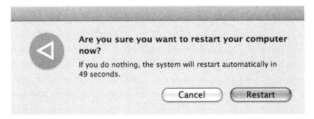

 *When you are asked whether you really want to restart or not, be sure to click the Cancel button if you do not want the Mac to restart. If you don't make a choice, the Mac automatically restarts after two minutes. Some applications do not allow the system to restart until you specify what it should do with the documents you're working on, but others allow the system to quit them without hesitation, losing any information you haven't saved.*

Shut Down Your Mac

To shut down, or turn off, your Mac, choose Apple | Shut Down. You are asked if you are sure you want to shut down, just like when you restart. As before, go ahead and click the Shut Down button. When the screen goes completely black, you have shut down successfully.

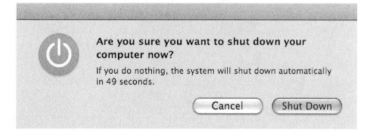

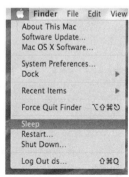

CAUTION

Continuing with the similarities between the restart and shutdown functions, when asked whether or not you truly want to shut down, be sure to click the Cancel button if you're not ready to turn the system off. If you don't make a choice, the Mac automatically shuts down after two minutes and you lose whatever work you haven't saved. Some applications do not allow the system to shut them down until you specify what to do with the documents currently being worked on, but others allow the system to quit them without so much as an "hasta la vista."

Put Your Mac to Sleep

While this procedure sounds like you may need to take your Mac to the veterinarian, it's really not all that dramatic. As a matter of fact it's actually a good thing.

To put your Mac in sleep mode, choose Apple | Sleep (it's getting pretty easy to decode these Apple menus, isn't it?). The screen on your Mac will go dark, but it will not shut down. Sleep mode saves energy and allows the Mac to come back up to a working state much faster than does a cold boot (turning the Mac back on after it's been shut down). When your Mac is in sleep mode, it is still on but using a very minimal amount of power. Another plus to sleep mode is that all your applications and documents are still open and running, exactly the way you left them before your Mac took a siesta.

TIP *Don't worry if you left your Mac on for a while and came back to see a black screen; your Mac has put itself to sleep. Mac OS X will go to sleep on its own after a period of nonuse. To bring the Mac back up, just push any key on the keyboard or click a mouse button.*

Summary

Apple's lineup of consumer Macs includes some of the best computers available for home users or office professionals, and with Intel processors they can even run Windows. Now that you've set up your Mac and are successfully up and running, you're ready to jump right into the fun stuff!

Chapter 2

Getting to Know Your Mac

How to…

- Discover your keyboard
- Understand what a GUI is
- Make sense of the menus, icons, and windows
- Know the difference between a file and a folder
- Use hard disks, CDs, and DVDs
- Get further help from your Mac

Everyone likes to know what they are doing right out of the gate, but when it comes to new things, this is impossible. The frustration of learning something new is only made all the more complicated when that something new is a computer. People who haven't used a computer or don't know very much about them are usually frightened of them. In Chapter 1 I used the illustration of familiarizing yourself with the controls of a new car before you drive it. That same illustration applies for this chapter, but I want to go back a little further, to when you first learned to drive. Remember how excited and scared you were? You had some idea what the pedals and steering wheel were for, but until you got your feet and hands on them and discovered the intricacies of their operation, you were probably very timid. Those feelings are what most people have when they use a computer for the first time.

This chapter will help you discover how to efficiently "work the pedals" of your Mac so that the rest of your learning experience will be a much more comfortable one. Now, what if that car you first learned to drive with wasn't your dad's pickup truck or mom's Oldsmobile, but a brand new Porsche? That's what it feels like to use a new Mac for your first computing experience (but you'll need a small electric fan to get that "wind in your hair" effect)!

A Very Brief Word about Keyboards

"What could be so complicated about a keyboard?" some more experienced readers might be asking. Well, for a new computer user, plenty! Sure, the letters and numbers on some of the keys are obvious, but today's keyboards have lots more than letters and numbers. Depending on which Mac you have, Apple's keyboards have keys for ejecting CDs and DVDs, setting the Mac's speaker volume, and even increasing and decreasing the monitor screen's brightness level. Consult the documentation that came with your Mac to discover any special keys that may be native to your particular model.

It's GUI, Not Sticky

It's time to get to know your surroundings a little better. Discovering what all those pictures and folders on your computer's screen are is the next step in getting familiar with your Mac. Those things are part of your Mac's GUI (pronounced *goo-ee*), which is an acronym for *graphical user interface*.

What's a GUI?

A GUI is all of those pictures and symbols you see on your Mac's screen. Everything on that screen is a component of the GUI. GUIs have been around for a very long time, and they are the real reason that computers have become so integral to the daily lives of millions of people over the past couple of decades. "Back in the day" you could make your computer do things only by typing commands into it via your keyboard (hand cramps aplenty!). I don't know about you, but I can't see my grandmother hunkered over her desk, typing a couple hundred lines of programming code into her computer via her keyboard, just so she can print her shopping list. Thanks to GUIs, all she has to do is open a text editor program by pointing her mouse to that program's icon and clicking it, typing her list, and then clicking the Print icon. GUIs have made life for the average computer user light years better than it once was.

Discover Your Inner GUI

Let's take a look at all the elements that make up your Mac's GUI and find out what their basic roles are.

Icons

Icons, a few examples of which you can see in Figure 2-1, are the small pictures you see nearly everywhere on your Mac. These pictures represent objects on your Mac and, if designed properly, are usually very descriptive of that object. For instance, icons for text documents typically look like a piece of paper, iPhoto's icon includes a camera and a photo of a palm tree, Printer Setup Utility's icon looks like a printer, and so on.

Menus

Menus, which are essentially lists, simply give you multiple options in one location (see Figure 2-2). Menus are great ways for application programmers to save space on your screen, keeping it clean from clutter by arranging similar options in a single place. For example, when you click the Apple

FIGURE 2-1   Examples of icons

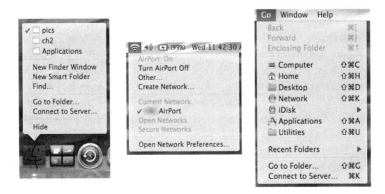

FIGURE 2-2   Examples of menus

menu at the top-left corner of your screen, you are presented with many options, all originating from the same locale. When you choose one of the options, the menu disappears.

Windows

Windows, like the one shown in Figure 2-3, allow you to see what files, folders, applications, utilities, and other whatnots are inside your Mac. There are lots of options when it comes to

FIGURE 2-3   A typical window

viewing windows, which I will cover in detail in Chapter 3. You can move windows to any position on the screen and resize them, making them as large or as small as you prefer, so you can arrange and resize multiple windows to see all of their contents simultaneously.

The Dock

The Dock (see Figure 2-4) is the bar you see at the bottom of your screen that contains icons for shortcuts to applications, folders, and disks. You can customize the Dock to contain whatever applications, files, and folders you use the most. The Dock is always present, but you hide it, resize it, or move it to a different position on the screen. Using the Dock greatly decreases the time you spend opening common applications and disks, and makes viewing ongoing processes, such as viewing the progress of a print job, a snap. More information on the Dock is presented in Chapter 3.

> **TIP** *Did you notice the icon of the really friendly-looking fellow on the left side of the Dock? The picture used for this icon is known as Happy Mac. This icon represents the Finder, and this is the only place you will find it on your Mac. Clicking this icon brings the Finder to the forefront of everything else, which can be very handy if you've got multiple windows open at once and you need to get back to a starting point.*

Files and Folders

Many people confuse the terms "file" and "folder" when it comes to computers in general. A *file* is an individual document (spreadsheet, text file, illustration, picture, movie, and so forth) on your Mac, while a *folder* is a container for multiple files. Folders on a Mac are used just like folders in a filing cabinet, but unlike filing cabinet folders, they can hold as many files (documents) as you see fit to put in them. Folders are your Mac's primary method of organization.

A Map of Your Desktop

Now that you have a basic idea of what the typical items in a GUI are, Figure 2-5 gives you a little tour of the desktop.

FIGURE 2-4   The multitalented Dock

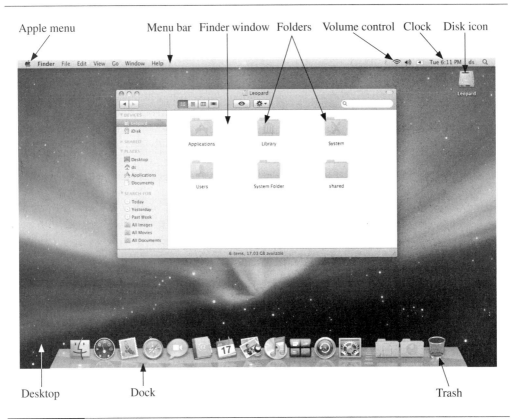

Apple menu   Menu bar   Finder window   Folders   Volume control   Clock   Disk icon

Desktop   Dock   Trash

FIGURE 2-5   Desktop 101

Hard Disks, CDs, and DVDs

Hard disks (also known as hard drives), CDs, and DVDs are just different methods of storing information, or data.

Your Mac comes with an internal hard disk that it uses to store the operating system files that run your Mac, the applications you use, the documents you create, and pretty much everything else on your Mac. Hard disks are not removable like CDs and DVDs, but are capable of holding a great deal more information than CDs and DVDs and generally enable you to access that information faster than you can access information on CDs and DVDs. Your Mac's hard drive is upgradeable should you ever feel you need more space. See Chapter 19 for more on upgrading and adding hardware to your Mac.

Most people think of CDs and DVDs as disks that house their music and movies, and your Mac can certainly use them for that, but your Mac also can use them to save, or back up, your data. Software companies usually send their applications or games to customers using CDs or DVDs.

FIGURE 2-6   CD and DVD icons

As a matter of fact, your Mac came with a set of installation disks that are most likely DVDs. Your Mac has a built-in CD/DVD drive, called either a SuperDrive or a Combo drive, in which you can insert these types of disks. Figure 2-6 shows what CD and DVD icons look like on your Desktop and in your Finder. If your Mac came with a SuperDrive, you can play (or "read") and copy files to (or "burn") both CDs and DVDs, but if your system has a Combo drive, you can play both CDs and DVDs but only burn CDs (and not DVDs).

Lost Already? Get Help from Your Mac

While your Mac is well known for being the easiest-to-use personal computer in the world, it's still a computer, and by that very definition can still be complicated and confusing. Even the geekiest of the geeks has to occasionally get help from someone somewhere, whether they will admit it or not. While I obviously recommend that you consult this very book for most of your basic questions, from time to time you may not have immediate access to your trusty *How to Do Everything: Mac* book. For those tragic times when you find yourself in that predicament, your Mac will come to the rescue! Apple has a handy help feature built right into the operating system called … well, Help.

The menu of every application includes Help, and that's fine if you need to access information about that particular application. However, if you just want general Mac Help, you must be in the Finder, and then select Help from its menu.

Remember our earlier tip: to get to the Finder really quickly, just click the Happy Mac icon on the leftmost side of the Dock.

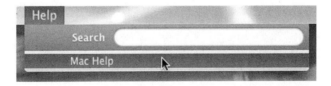

The default Help screen displays some commonly asked questions, and you can also search for specific topics by typing in some keywords in the search field. Help then displays a list of help topics that match your keywords, ordered by their possible relevance. Double-click the topic that most closely relates to your search needs.

You can also browse the Index for topics that interest you. Click the Index link in the upper right corner of the Help window, then click the letter that corresponds to the name of your subject.

TIP   *Try to be as specific as possible with the keywords you search for. The more specific you are, the better Help will be able to narrow the number of topics it displays.*

Summary

Now that you're familiar with the most basic of the basic GUI concepts, you should have enough confidence to begin some serious exploration of your surroundings. Jump into Chapter 3 and put some of your new discoveries to work.

Chapter 3

Cruisin': Navigating Your Mac

How to...

- Use the Finder
- Understand the files and folders that come with your Mac
- Add and delete files and folders
- Use the Trash to manage deleted files and folders
- See the contents of files...without opening them!
- Search for files and folders
- Use the Dock
- See all the windows you have open
- Use multiple desktops with Spaces
- Discover the Dashboard and Widgets

Now that you've become somewhat chummy with your new pal, your Mac, it's time to get a bit more acquainted. Learning how to navigate the files and folders that populate your Mac is vital to using your computer with efficiency and confidence. However, you're about to discover more than just getting around your file system. There are several Mac basics covered in this chapter, but if you've never used a Mac before, you're about to see that even the basics on a Mac are cooler than most upscale features on other operating systems.

Discover the Finder

As mentioned in Chapter 1, the Finder is your best friend when it comes to using your Mac. The Finder has been with the Mac since its inception in 1984, although it has weathered many changes in that span of time. Let's jump in!

To get started, you need to know how to open and close Finder windows. Finder windows are accurate of their namesake, as they allow you to find, or see, items on your Mac's hard drive. As often is the case with any operating system or application, there is more than one way to perform an action—in our case, open a new Finder window. The easiest way is to simply click the Finder icon in the Dock, and a new window will pop up almost instantly (unless you already have a Finder window open, in which case that window will be brought to the forefront). Another way to open a Finder window is to choose File | New Finder Window.

By default, Finder windows are arranged exactly as shown in Figure 3-1. The items identified in Figure 3-1 are described in the following section.

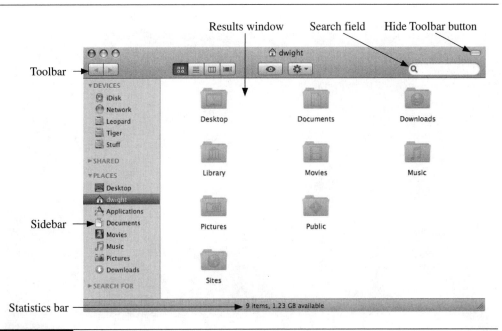

FIGURE 3-1   A typical Finder window

I'm sure the red, yellow, and green buttons in the upper-left corner of the Finder windows have gotten your attention by now. These buttons allow you to change the state of your Finder windows. To close a window, click the red button. To minimize a window, click the yellow button, which places the window in the Dock. To automatically resize the window, click the green zoom button. A second way to minimize a window is by double-clicking the title bar of the window.

> **TIP**   *Did you notice the cool "genie" effect when you minimized your window? If you ever feel like impressing your PC-using friends, try showing them a couple of neat tricks you can do when minimizing windows. Hold down the SHIFT key when clicking the minimize button, and the window "pours" itself very slowly into the Dock (see Figure 3-2). SHIFT-clicking the minimized window in the Dock causes the image to be "poured" back out.*

Get Around in a Finder Window

Let's explore the typical Finder window so that you are familiar with how to get around in it easily and quickly. Look to Figure 3-1 for the placement of the following items in the Finder. Some of these items are customizable, but we won't get that far until Chapter 4.

■ **Toolbar**   The toolbar gives quick access to frequently performed tasks. You can hide the toolbar by clicking the small oval (Hide Toolbar) button in the upper-right corner of the Finder window.

FIGURE 3-2 The "genie" effect is a neat way to minimize windows.

- **Sidebar** The sidebar provides fast access to items such as drives, folders, and network devices.
- **Search field** Perform quick searches for items in a particular drive or folder by typing your search words in the search field.
- **Results window** When you click an item in the sidebar, its contents are displayed in this window.
- **Statistics bar** When you click an item in the sidebar or results window, the statistics bar shows you how many items are contained inside of it and the remaining amount of space on your hard drive.

TIP *Is the default size and shape of the Finder window not to your liking? You can change that by clicking and dragging the bottom-right corner of the Finder window and molding it into whatever size and shape you want.*

Choose the Right View for You

As mentioned, the results window in the Finder shows you the contents of an item you have clicked in the sidebar. The default view of the results window displays those contents as icons. If Icon view isn't your cup of tea, you're in luck; there are three other options for viewing items in your Finder: List view, Column view, and Cover Flow view.

To switch between views, click one of the four View icons in the toolbar of your Finder window.

List view does just what its name implies; all items in the results window are arranged in an ordered list. The order of the list is up to you. By default, the items are listed alphabetically in descending order, but you can change this order by clicking the column header. You can also order the items by the date they were modified, or by the size of the files.

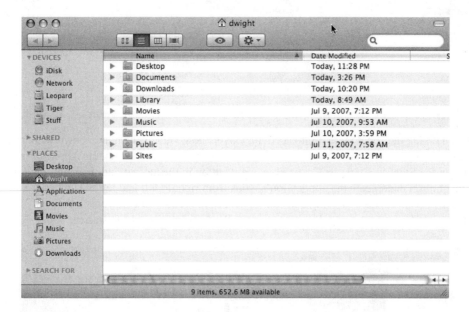

Column view is my personal favorite but it can take a little getting used to, especially if you've used another computing platform such as Mac OS 9 or Microsoft Windows. When in Column view, each time you click a drive or a folder, a new column opens to display the information contained in that drive or folder. If that drive or folder contains other folders, click one of them and you will see a new column that displays its contents, and so on. If you click a file while in Column view, a new column shows you a preview of that file. As examples, if the file is an MP3 music file, you can listen to the song by clicking the play button in the Preview column, or if it's a movie file, you can watch a miniature version of the movie in the Preview column.

When taking the "cool factor" into account, Cover Flow view is the hands-down winner. To get the full effect of Cover Flow view, open a new Finder window and click the Applications shortcut in the Sidebar. Click the Cover Flow view button in the toolbar and then click-and-drag the slider button underneath the application's icons from right to left and left to right over and over again. Go ahead; quit gawking and call the rest of the family to come check this out. We'll wait for you before we continue. Pretty neat, huh? Well, we're just getting started!

Sometimes you may have so many items in a folder or disk that the results window can't display them all. In those cases, the Finder adds a scroll bar and a set of up and down arrows (see Figure 3-3) that allow you to move up and down the window to see the entire contents of the window. If you are in Column view, you may even get scroll bars and arrows below the columns, as shown in Figure 3-4. To use the scroll bar, just click-and-drag it in the direction you want to go. To use the arrows, just click the arrow that corresponds to the direction you want to go.

Set Finder Preferences

One thing you are about to discover about Macs is that, like a famous hamburger chain once told us, you can have it your way. We all have preferences in how we like to perform our daily routines, and your Mac allows you to let your preferences be known for quite a bit of its functionality. The following is a list of the tabs in the Finder preferences pane with a brief description of the

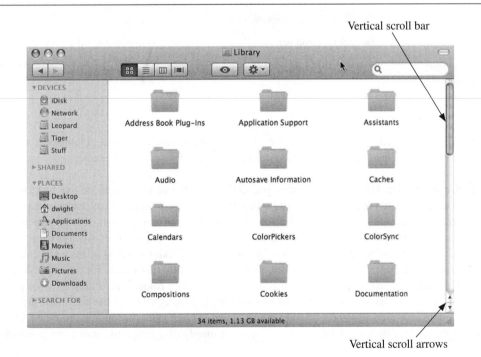

Vertical scroll bar

Vertical scroll arrows

FIGURE 3-3   A scroll bar and scroll arrows in a Finder window using Icon view

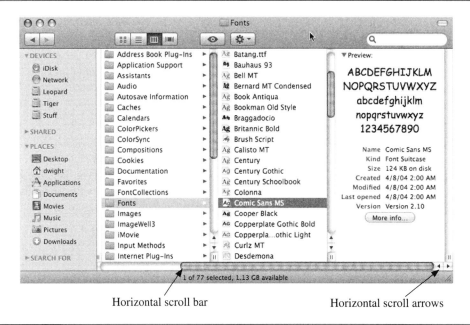

Horizontal scroll bar   Horizontal scroll arrows

FIGURE 3-4   A scroll bar and scroll arrows in a Finder window using Column view

preferences found on each tab. Check out how they all work and make whatever changes, if any, that suit you best. To open the Finder preferences pane, choose Finder | Preferences.

■ **General**   The General pane allows you to choose what items to show on the desktop, such as hard drives, CDs/DVDs, or servers you may be connected to over your network (more on that way down the road in Chapter 15). You can also choose which folder you want new Finder windows to automatically open in. If you check the "Always open folders in a new window" check box, an entirely new Finder window opens each time you open a folder. Spring-loaded folders is a great feature that makes for even speedier browsing and file arranging. When you drag a file over a folder and hold it there for a few seconds (you can adjust the time by moving the Delay slider at the bottom of the General preferences pane), the folder will "spring" open and you can just drop the file right in. This isn't much of a feature if you are simply dragging a file into a single folder, but if you need to move the file to a folder that may be deeply embedded in several other folders, using spring-loaded folders is a huge timesaver.

■ **Labels**   Labels are really helpful for organizing information. Labels don't change your files' or folders' contents in any way; they just allow you to assign a color to each file and folder so that you can group them by whatever designation you give the colors.

■ **Sidebar**   The Sidebar preference pane lets you choose whether to show certain items by default in the sidebar of Finder windows. The options are pretty self-explanatory.

■ **Advanced**   From here you can choose whether to show extensions assigned to your filenames and whether you should be prompted with a warning each time you try to change an extension or empty the Trash. Most files have an extension that tells the user and the Mac what applications are associated with that file or what kind of file it is. Those extensions are hidden on the Mac by default because you can usually tell what applications go with a file by its icon, but you can choose to always show the extensions anyway by checking the "Show all file extensions" check box. Since these extensions can be changed, whether by accident or on purpose, you're given the "Show warning before changing an extension" option. Checking this box simply enables a message that warns you every time you try to empty the Trash. This is the Mac's way of making absolutely sure that you wish to empty the Trash. Checking the Empty Trash Securely box simply means that your trash is gone for good when you empty the Trash. You may think that would be the case without having to check such a box, but it's not. More on that topic later in this chapter in the section "Delete Files and Folders."

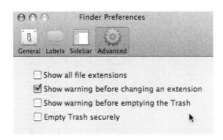

Get Information about Your Files and Folders

Sometimes you may need to know how large or small an item is, whether you have permissions to access the item, and many other types of information that at first glance may seem to have no real use for the typical user but in fact is very important to have available if you ever need it. To get this valuable information for any item on your Mac, either right-click or CTRL-click the item's icon and choose Get Info from the shortcut menu. Another method of getting this information is to select the item and then choose File | Get Info.

The Get Info window that opens gives you a veritable cornucopia (I've always wanted to say that!) of information about that particular item, as shown in the example in Figure 3-5.

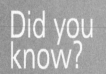

Your Wish Is My ⌘!

There is yet a third way to open the Get Info window, but I wanted to show this to you separately since it relates more to the general usage of your Mac than just to getting information.

I'm sure you've noticed the ⌘ character by now, either on your keyboard (the keys on either side of the SPACEBAR) or next to selections within menus. This is called the Command character and has been a part of Apple computers since the first Mac was released in 1984. The ⌘ key is most useful for giving commands to your Mac via the keyboard, which often is quicker than pointing and clicking with your mouse to choose a command from a menu.

In the instance of getting information for a file or folder, instead of using one of the aforementioned techniques, click the item once to select it, then press and hold the ⌘ key and the I key simultaneously. This technique is called a *keyboard shortcut*, and when spoken or read is "COMMAND-I" or ⌘-I.

The ⌘ key can be used in conjunction with lots of other keys to perform different tasks. Click a menu in the menu bar and you will see that many of the selections in the list have corresponding keyboard shortcuts to their right. Try to get in the habit of using these keyboard shortcuts. Once you have a few of the more common shortcuts memorized, you will use your Mac much more efficiently.

Yes, there is life beyond the mouse!

FIGURE 3-5 A "veritable cornucopia" of information

Discover and Use Mac OS X's Files and Folders

Now that you are more familiar with how to move about your Mac, it's time to find out what all these files and folders are that populate your newfound friend.

Open a Finder window and click the icon for your hard drive in the upper-left corner. In this section, we are primarily concerned with the folders you see in the results window. Let's take them one at a time:

■ **Applications** The Applications folder is where your Mac stores all of its applications and utilities. This is typically the folder you use to install other applications you may pick up along the path of your Mac journey. There is another folder that resides in the Applications folder, called Utilities, that contains utility applications. These applications are tools that you will only have to use once in a blue moon to add devices to your Mac, run network diagnostics, and the like.

NOTE *The Applications folder isn't the only place you can keep applications. When you install an application as an administrator (one of the user accounts, discussed in Chapter 4), you have the right to put an application anywhere you want. If you want that application to be available to all users of your Mac, you would be wise to follow conventional wisdom and use the Applications folder; otherwise, feel free to install it anywhere that is convenient for you. The reason all users of the computer may not be able to access the application when you install it anywhere other than the Applications folder is that the users may not have permission to access that other folder. Chapter 4 also provides more information about permissions.*

■ **Library**   This folder holds tons of information that your Mac, and the applications you have installed, uses, such as printer and scanner drivers, settings preferences, desktop pictures (a.k.a. wallpaper, for all you former Microsoft Windows users), screensavers, and so forth. All the items in the Library folder are for system-wide use, meaning that any item in this folder is accessible to all user accounts for the Mac.

CAUTION   *There are several Library folders in Mac OS X. The Library folder at the root of the hard disk (/Library) is the one just discussed. There is also a Library folder inside the System folder, and each individual user account on the Mac has its own Library folder. If you have an item—a screensaver, for instance—that only you are to have access to, don't install that screensaver in the system-wide Library folder (/Library/Screen Savers); place it in your individual Library folder (Your User Account Name/Library/Screen Savers). I'll discuss user account permissions in greater depth in Chapter 4.*

■ **System**   Never, never, never touch this folder! Don't even click it to see what's inside or your hard plastic mouse will turn into a real live wiggly one with red beady eyes and a skinny tail, right there in your hand! Okay, maybe that's a slight exaggeration, but if you like your Mac to actually remain stable and useable, you will heed my advice to leave this folder be. The System folder is Apple's own playground, and unless you are a super-duper mega-geek, it's best to not venture here.

■ **Users**   This is the folder where all of your personal preferences, emails, and other various and assorted sundries are contained. If it pertains to you and you alone, this is where it resides. The Users folder holds individual folders for each user account on the system. The Users folder contains so much information that it merits having its own subsection!

The Users Folder, In Depth

Each user account has its very own folder in the Users folder, and those folders are chock full of other subfolders that are of utmost importance to the owner of that account. The following list discusses each of those subfolders in turn:

Desktop

■ **Desktop**   This folder literally holds all the things you see on your desktop. The Desktop folder is the actual physical location of those files on your hard drive.

Documents

Documents This folder is actually empty until you put something in it. Apple was simply kind enough to create a folder for you to keep all your important documents in, like tax filings, receipts for items you've purchased online, and the like.

Downloads

Downloads This folder is the default location for all the files you download from the Internet.

Library

Library This is the Library folder that should be closest to your heart, for this particular one contains all that is "you" about your Mac. All of your personal preferences are in this one folder, such as what desktop picture you prefer, which Finder view you like most, whether you want to be prompted when emptying the Trash, what login picture you use for your user account, your email server information, all your favorite websites, and much, much more! Thankfully, the vast majority of what takes place in the Library folder is handled by Mac OS X itself, and the user typically has very little interaction with it.

Movies

Movies This is another of the empty folders Apple was nice enough to create ahead of time for you. Apple assumed that you would at some point save video files on your Mac, whether they are home movies or movie trailers. This is the place to store your moving picture shows.

Music

Music Everybody's got an iPod, right? Well, no, not everyone, but we all like to listen to music. iTunes is the default application for listening to and buying music on your Mac, and the Music folder is where iTunes stores all those melodies.

Pictures

Pictures When you connect your digital camera to your Mac, iPhoto can import your photos to the computer. Those imported pictures live in this folder.

Public

Public This folder is where you place files you'd like to share with other users of the Mac. If you have a file in the Desktop folder of your user account, other users cannot access it. You would need to move the file to the Public folder, or place a copy of it there. There is a folder inside of Public called Drop Box. Other users put files they may wish to share with you into the Drop Box folder.

Sites

Sites You may want to create your own webpage or host a personal website. If so, this is a convenient location for all the files you may need.

Create, Rename, and Delete Files and Folders

Your Mac comes with tons of files and folders as part of the default operating system, but now it's time for you to make, modify, and unmake your own.

Create Files and Folders

Creating folders is almost too easy! To create a folder, simply right-click or CTRL-click an empty space on your desktop or in an existing folder and choose New Folder from the shortcut menu. Or if you want to get fancy with your newly found keyboard shortcut skills, use ⌘-SHIFT-N. Your new folder appears and is called "untitled folder."

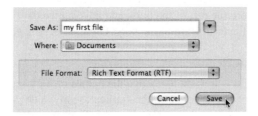

FIGURE 3-6   A standard Save dialog box

Notice that the name of the folder is highlighted in light blue; your Mac is waiting for you to give your new folder a name, so just type anything you like (typically something that's descriptive of the folder's contents).

TIP

There are some characters that are off-limits for folder and file names. These characters are colons (:) and periods at the beginning of the name (.). Some applications may also not allow slashes (/) in their filenames.

Creating files is a little more involved. You can create files from all kinds of sources, but for demonstration purposes we'll stick with something very simple. Not only are you creating a file for the first time, but you are also making your first foray into opening and using an application! Trust me, this won't hurt a bit. Open a new Finder window and double-click the Applications folder. One of the most basic applications on your Mac is called TextEdit; find it in the Applications folder and double-click its icon to open it. When TextEdit opens, you are automatically presented with a blank page. Simply type **hello, world** and choose File | Save (or press ⌘-S). The Save dialog box opens, shown in Figure 3-6; this is where you give your file a title (I called mine "my first file") and tell your Mac which folder to save it in.

By default, your Mac saves the new file in the Documents folder of your user account's home folder, which is located at *Hard Drive* | Users | *Your User Account* | Documents. Your home folder is where your personal information is stored on your Mac, such as application preferences, iPhoto and iTunes libraries, Internet downloads, and so on. Each user account has a unique home folder.

You've just created your first folder and file, and learned how to open and use an application! My work is done! Please ignore the rest of the book and have a nice day!

What's that? Still there? Eager to learn more, huh? Great, then let's get back to it.

Rename Files and Folders

Somewhere down the road you may want to change the names of files and folders you've created. Instead of reopening a file or folder in the application in which you created it and saving a copy with a new name, you can simply rename the item. To change the name of an item, click its name to select it, pause for just a second, and then click the item's name again and the name will be highlighted in light blue. Simply type in the new name of your file or folder and then press RETURN or click elsewhere on the screen to apply the name. If you just want to change a portion of the item's name, click anywhere in the text and you will see a flashing cursor in the place you clicked. You can then click-and-drag over the portion of the text you want to change, to highlight it, and type new text, or you can move to the place in the text you need to change by pressing the appropriate ARROW key on your keyboard and then edit the name as you would in a word processor. Practice this technique on the new file and folder you recently created.

Delete Files and Folders

If you're a pack rat and love to keep everything you've ever acquired, you would be wise to not carry this over into your computing habits. Otherwise, soon your Mac's desktop will resemble that of my dad's, with so many file icons on the desktop that the desktop picture can barely be seen! (Love you, Dad!) Your Mac comes with a hard drive, but the space on that hard drive is finite. So how do you free up the space on your hard drive? By deleting all the old jokes your former army pals or office mates sent you via email, trashing the old recipe file for the green bean casserole you hate, and getting rid of the game demo you downloaded that expired six months ago.

There are two steps to actually deleting files from your Mac. The first step is to move the file to the Trash, and the second step is to empty said Trash.

The most common way of moving files into the Trash is to simply drag-and-drop them onto the Trash icon on the far right side of the Dock, as shown here. You can also right-click or CTRL-click a file and choose "Move to Trash" from the menu. The Trash icon changes from empty to holding what appears to be a piece of crumpled paper, indicating there are now files in the Trash.

To empty the Trash, right-click or CTRL-click the Trash icon in the Dock and choose "Empty Trash" from the menu. If you see a message asking if you're sure you want to empty the Trash, click OK to continue or click Cancel to halt the action. If that window does open and you choose to click OK, your Mac makes a sound like it's crumpling paper and the Trash icon changes back to its empty state. Once you've emptied the Trash, you've completed deletion of the file.

Until you empty the Trash, the file you placed in it can still be retrieved. To get a file from the Trash, click the Trash icon. A Finder window opens, displaying the contents of the Trash. Just drag the file from the Trash window and place it in the location desired.

Create Aliases

No, we're not about to learn Apple's version of international espionage, but rather how to create an easy way to get to a file or folder you frequently use. An alias is basically a shortcut to a file or folder that is elsewhere on your Mac.

Did you know?

A File Deleted from the Trash Is Still on Your Hard Drive

Be aware that performing the steps to delete a file from the Trash does not completely remove all traces of the file you deleted from your hard drive. You have only told your computer to make the space that the file occupies on your hard drive available to be written over with new data. The file itself is still there and can be accessed by a hacker with the right tools. Someone who knows what they are doing can still retrieve sensitive files such as tax returns or credit card numbers even after you've deleted them. But never fear, the Mac is here! The way to permanently delete these files from your hard drive is to use the "Secure Empty Trash" command:

1. Move the files you wish to delete to the Trash like before.

2. Choose Finder | Secure Empty Trash. Your Mac will ask you if you're sure you want to permanently remove the file from the system.

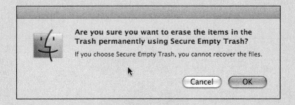

3. Click Cancel if you change your mind. There is no turning back once you click OK!

Let's say you have a file you are working on for a project, and you've placed that file several folders deep on your hard drive for organizational purposes. Instead of having to drill through the multiple folders every time you want to access the file, create an alias for that file and place it on your desktop. From then on, when you want to access the file, just double-click the alias and the original file will open in the appropriate application.

To create an alias, right-click or CTRL-click the file or folder you want to create the alias for, and choose "Make Alias" from the menu (or select the file and press ⌘-L). A new duplicate icon of the original file is created and the name of the file is appended by the word "alias." Notice the new icon has a small arrow in its bottom-left corner; this is another indicator the icon is an alias.

hello, world   hello, world alias

Place the alias wherever you like so that you have easier access to the original file, folder, or application.

Look! Quick! It's Quick Look!

Quick Look, not to be confused with QuickTime (discussed in Chapter 10), is an oh-so-cool way to view your files—without actually opening them. Talk about revolutionary! You can browse an entire document without once starting up the program that created it.

Open a Finder window and navigate to a folder containing the document you want to review. Select the file and then either click the Quick Look icon (looks like a small eye; see Figure 3-7) in the Finder's toolbar or press the SPACEBAR to open Quick Look.

Figure 3-8 shows a file as viewed with Quick Look. Scroll through all the pages using the scroll bar, or view the file in full screen by clicking the arrows at the bottom of the Quick Look window.

FIGURE 3-7   The eye of Sauron sees all! (A little reference for the "Lord of the Rings" fans in the audience)

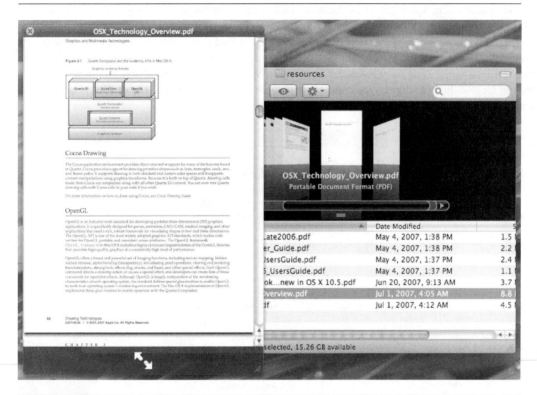

FIGURE 3-8   Taking a Quick Look at a file

Search for Stuff on Your Mac

Anyone who's ever used a computer has lost a file at some point. Opening folder after folder in search of that elusive file can be incredibly frustrating and a huge waste of time. Thankfully, Apple saw fit to equip Mac OS X with the best search features of any operating system available. There are two ways to search your Mac for files: Spotlight and Find.

Search Using Spotlight

Spotlight is a lightning-fast search utility that searches your entire hard drive, including every type of file on it, for the search criteria you specify.

To search using Spotlight, click the blue circle containing the magnifying glass that's in the upper-right corner of your screen. If you are looking for files containing the words "hello, world," type those words in the text field. Spotlight will find every single file on your system that includes "hello, world," whether that file is a text file, a saved iChat session, an email, a movie file, picture, song, or whatever. Of course, a Spotlight search could potentially render tons of hits, so the Mac divides the results into categories and Top Hit (the file or files your Mac considers most likely to be what you are searching for).

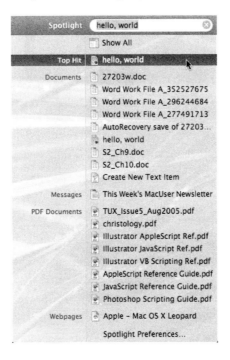

Once you've found the file you are looking for, you can either double-click it in the Spotlight list to open it or hold your mouse over the entry and your Mac will show you where the file is located.

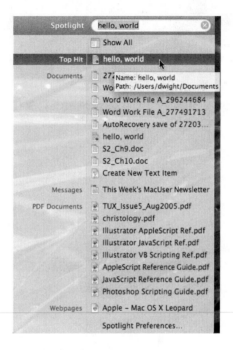

Search Using Find

The Find feature is just as fast as Spotlight, but is much more useful for searching specific locations for files. If you don't know the name of a file or where you may have saved it, but can remember some of the text contained in the file, Spotlight may be your best option. However, if you do know what folder or hard drive contains the file, Find is better than Spotlight since you can narrow your search to just that location. Using Find avoids the potential for Mac OS X to return a huge list of search results, the vast majority of which may be completely irrelevant.

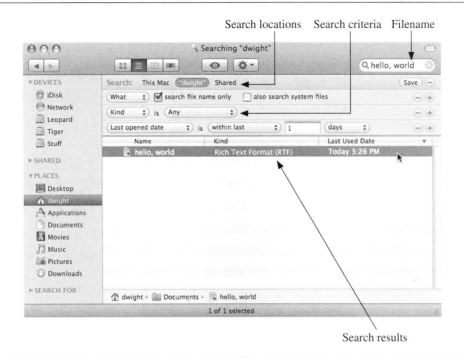

FIGURE 3-9   A typical Find window with search results

To search for files using Find, you must be in the Finder, so click the Finder icon in the Dock. Now choose File | Find, or just press ⌘-F. At first glance the Find window looks like a standard Finder window, but a closer inspection reveals the search functions (see Figure 3-9). Choose the location in which you wish to search for the file in the search locations section of the window, and then modify the search criteria, such as what date the file was created or what kind of file it is (text, music, images, etc.). You may add or remove search criteria by clicking the + or – signs next to them. Type the information you are searching for in the text field located in the upper-right corner of the window (note the magnifying glass icon), and the results will display beneath the search criteria.

I Wanna Dock!

Up to this point you've had minimal experience with the Dock, which is one of the more striking and versatile user interface elements of Mac OS X. The Dock, shown in Figure 3-10 in its default configuration, is more than just a decoration for the bottom of your screen; it's a tool that makes using your Mac more fun and efficient.

| FIGURE 3-10 | The Dock in all its default glory |

Add, Move, and Delete Icons in the Dock

Most people use the Dock to access the applications they use most often. The Dock already has icons for several applications in it by default. You can rearrange these icons by clicking and dragging them to the position you prefer. Go ahead and try it. Isn't it cool how the other icons slide over to make room for the icon you're moving? You can also add or remove application icons to or from the Dock as you see fit. To add an application icon to the Dock, open the Applications folder at the root of your hard drive and drag-and-drop its icon onto the Dock.

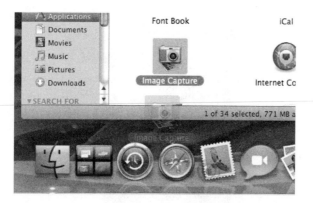

The original application remains in the Applications folder; you've only created an alias for that application's icon. This means that removing the application's icon from the Dock does not harm the original application itself. To remove the icon, just click-and-drag it out of the Dock, and you will see a neat little "POOF!" as it disappears.

The Icons Aren't Just There for Show

The application icons in the Dock can do more than just open their respective applications.

You can tell whether an application is running or not by looking at its icon in the Dock. See the glowing dot under the Finder icon in Figure 3-10? That dot indicates the Finder application is up and running; each application that you have running displays a glowing dot beneath its icon in the Dock, even if the application's windows are hidden from sight.

Some applications, such as iTunes and System Preferences, allow you to access some of their functions from the Dock. Right-click or CTRL-click the application's icon and, if that application supports this functionality, you see a menu with several more options outside of the standard group.

Access Files and Folders from the Dock

Notice the divider line between the blue Documents folder and the icon to its immediate left (System Preferences by default), looking toward the right side of the Dock in Figure 3-10; this line separates the Dock into two sections. The left section is where all your application icons are kept, and the right side is where you can place icons of files and folders you access often. For example, open a Finder window, open the Users folder, and drag the icon for your home folder to the right side of the Dock and drop it next to your Trash icon. However, be careful not to drop it *in* the Trash! Now you have quick and easy access to your home folder. These folder icons are called stacks. Click the home icon, or stack, that's now in the Dock and a menu similar to this one pops up.

You can now select anything that is in your home folder from this menu. Very convenient! If you do the same with your Applications folder, any of your applications can be launched easily enough from the Dock without having to put an icon for each one in the Dock.

Apple has included the Downloads stack in the Dock by default, which is an alias for the Downloads folder in your home directory. Any time you download something from the Internet or save an attachment from your email application, the item is automatically stored in the Downloads folder. The Downloads stack in the Dock will bounce once to notify you that download of the item is complete. Click the Downloads stack to access items in your Downloads folder. Using the Downloads stack will help keep your desktop nice and clean.

Did you notice the way the list of subfolders "fan out?" When you have lots of folders (too many to comfortably fit into the "fan"), they don't fan out, but rather are arranged in a grid.

You can choose to open a stack with either a fan or a grid configuration by clicking-and-holding the mouse button down on the stack until the configuration menu pops up. Put your mouse pointer over the View As menu and choose Fan or Grid from the list.

Set Preferences for the Dock

The Dock allows you to set preferences that enable you to use or modify the Dock to your liking. Does the Dock tend to get in your way? Hide it! Move it! Shrink it! Disable it! No, no, you can't disable it (why would you want to?), but the other three options are easy to do with the Dock's preferences. To open the Dock preferences pane, shown in Figure 3-11, choose Apple | Dock | Dock Preferences.

Let's go over the options in the Dock preferences pane:

- **Size** Use the slider to make the Dock take up the full length of your monitor or to make it really, really small.

- **Magnification** If you choose to make your Dock small, you may not be able to see the icons very well. Turning Magnification on (by checking the box next to it) causes the icons to enlarge as you move your mouse over them. You can select how large the icons magnify by adjusting the Magnification slider.

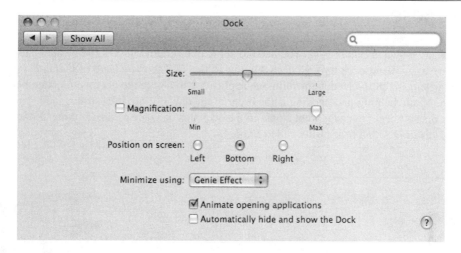

FIGURE 3-11 The Dock preferences pane

- **Position on Screen** The Dock doesn't have to stay at the bottom of the screen; you can choose to move the Dock to the right or left side of the screen by clicking the appropriate radio button.

- **Minimize Using** I discussed the Genie Effect that you see when minimizing windows earlier in the "Discover the Finder" section of this chapter. To change the effect when minimizing windows, choose Genie Effect or Scale Effect from this pop-up menu. Scale Effect causes the entire window to "shrink" proportionally into the Dock.

- **Animate opening applications** Have you noticed that when you click the icon of an application in the Dock, the icon bounces up and down as the application opens? Checking or unchecking this box enables or disables these bouncing icons.

- **Automatically hide and show the Dock** If you don't like the Dock on your screen at all, then check this box; the Dock then "hides" below your screen. Don't worry, it's not gone forever! To retrieve the Dock, bring your mouse pointer all the way to the bottom of the screen and hold it there until the Dock "pops" back up.

You can access many of the options in the Dock preferences pane, shown here, by right-clicking or CTRL-clicking the gap, or empty space, in the Dock.

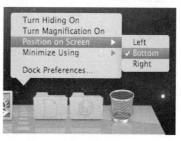

Expose Exposé

Let's say you've got lots of applications open and there are windows on top of windows on your screen, as shown in Figure 3-12. You need to get to one certain window in one application, but you have to hunt-and-peck through each window to find it. Then you have to start copying and pasting elements from one document in one application to a separate document in another application. Again, hunting-and-pecking is the order of the day. Calling it frustrating and time-consuming doesn't begin to cover what a pain in the neck this is. Once again, it's Mac OS X to the rescue, this time with a little utility called Exposé.

FIGURE 3-12   A jumbled mess of windows

You can prompt Exposé to clear up all the clutter of multiple open windows in one of three ways:

■ **Press F9** Exposé arranges all the open windows neatly on your screen so that you can view them all at once. As you move your mouse over each window, the window highlights and the name of the application it belongs to is displayed (see Figure 3-13). Just click the window you want and it will be brought to the fore.

■ **Press F10** Exposé displays only windows that relate to the application you are currently using (see Figure 3-14). You can just click the one you are looking for to bring it to the head of the class.

FIGURE 3-13   F9: All the unruly windows have snapped to attention.

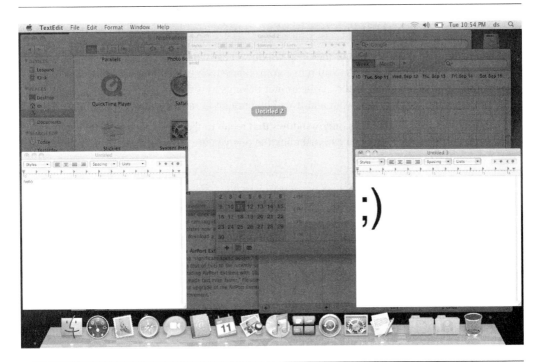

FIGURE 3-14   F10: Only windows for the application you are working in are displayed.

■   **Press F11**   Exposé sweeps clean your desktop (see Figure 3-15). All the open windows on your desktop scram out of the way. This is helpful if you need to see a file on your desktop in a hurry. Pushing F11 a second time brings back all the open windows to their original positions.

FIGURE 3-15 F11: There's that elusive desktop!

To change which keys you press to perform the preceding Exposé actions, choose Apple |
System Preferences, and then click the Exposé & Spaces icon. The options in the Exposé &

Spaces preferences pane allow you to change the default shortcut keys for the different Exposé functions.

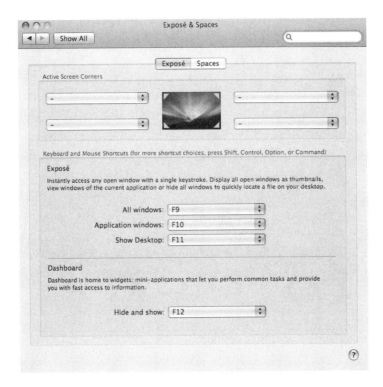

Spaced Out!

Spaces is one of the most recent, and most useful, additions to Mac OS X. Spaces "divides" your Mac's workspace into multiple areas, or spaces, one for each task or work type that you decide. You can create a space for your spreadsheet work, another for browsing the Web, a third for listening to music, and yet another for watching a movie. Having multiple spaces keeps your desktop organized and keeps you focused.

Create Spaces

Open the Exposé & Spaces preferences pane and click the Spaces tab at the top of the pane (see Figure 3-16).

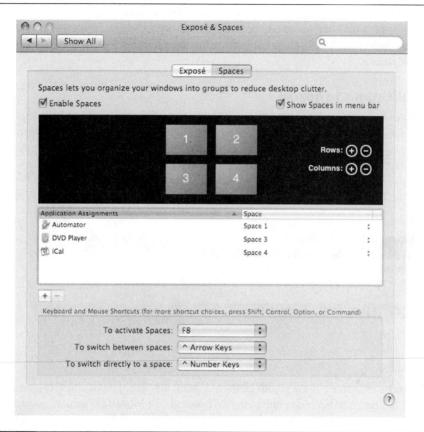

FIGURE 3-16 The Spaces tab of the Exposé & Spaces preferences pane

Checking the "Enable Spaces" check box turns on the Spaces functionality for your Mac, while checking the "Show spaces in menu bar" check box places the number for the space you are currently using in the menu bar.

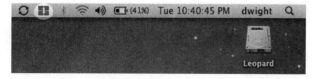

You can easily switch between spaces by clicking the Spaces number in the menu bar and selecting a different space number from the resulting list.

The default number of spaces is four, but you can add or subtract from that number at your discretion. Click the + or − buttons to add or remove rows and columns. You can have no less than one and no more than four rows or columns, allowing a minimum of two spaces and a maximum of sixteen.

Assign Applications to Spaces

The Application Assignments section of the preferences pane allows to you assign an application to open only within its assigned space. Click the + or − button under the Application Assignments section to add or remove applications from the binding list. When you add an application to the list, its default space is 1. To assign a different space, click its listing in the Space column of the Application Assignments section and choose the appropriate space number from the list. You can also set the option to Every Space, keeping the application available in each space you use.

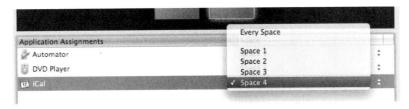

Switch Spaces

Jumping from space to space is easy with keyboard shortcuts. The default shortcuts are listed in the Exposé & Spaces preference pane in the "Keyboard and Mouse Shortcuts" section of the Spaces tab. Unless you change the default settings, to scroll through the spaces, you hold down the CTRL key and press the RIGHT ARROW or LEFT ARROW key. To go immediately to a certain space, hold the CTRL key and click the number corresponding to that space. The first time I did this I had all 16 spaces enabled and populated and was zipping through them all as fast as I could press the RIGHT ARROW key! I know that's childish, but don't begrudge me a little fun! Careful, though, you can get a pretty mean blister if you're not a professional.

Organize Spaces

Press the F8 key, or click the Spaces icon in the Dock, and you see a grid showing all of your spaces and their respective contents. Did you mistakenly open a document in one space but need to get it to another? No problem! Click-and-drag the document you want to move from the space it's in to the space you want it to be, just like the example shown in Figure 3-17. Sweet!

FIGURE 3-17   Move, moving, moved!

Run Widgets from the Dashboard

You've seen that pressing the F8, F9, F10, and F11 keys can cause your Mac to do some pretty nifty cartwheels, but pressing F12 may top them all. With once press of the F12 key, a whole new world of widgets opens up on your Mac, and this world is called the Dashboard. The Dashboard allows your Mac to run very small, but sometimes very powerful, applications called widgets. With widgets, you can perform common tasks, get information in a flash, and even play games simply by pressing the F12 key. There are widgets available for just about any task you can imagine. The default set of widgets that comes installed with Mac OS X will help you check your local weather, see how your stocks are performing, convert measurements, browse the Yellow Pages, consult a dictionary, see the status of a flight, and even translate common languages.

Dashboard Basics

If you haven't done so already, push the F12 key and let's dive in. Double-clicking the Dashboard icon in the Applications folder will also open the Dashboard. The upside to using the F12 key is that if you keep pressing it over and over, you'll get that *Wayne's World* zoom-cam effect as the Dashboard opens and closes repeatedly. "Party time!" "Excellent!" When you open the Dashboard, you are promptly greeted by your default set of open, or running, widgets (see Figure 3-18).

To see other widgets you have installed, click the circle containing the + symbol that's in the lower-left corner of the screen, and the widget bar opens, as you can see in Figure 3-19. If you see a small arrow on the left or right side of the widget bar, there are more widgets installed than can be displayed at once; just click the arrow to see the rest of the widgets.

To close the widget bar, click the circle on the left that contains the *X*.

Open and Close Widgets

To use one of the widgets in the widget bar, click its icon and it will open in the Dashboard. The newly opened widget quite literally "splashes" onto the screen. You can typically click the outer edges of a widget and drag it to whatever position on the screen you prefer it to reside. To close

FIGURE 3-18 Your first look at Dashboard widgets

an open widget, all you need do is click the *X* in its upper-left corner and it will appear to be "sucked" into oblivion. You see the *X* in the corner only when the widget bar is open.

Set Preferences in Widgets

Many widgets allow you to modify them to suit your needs. For our example, we'll use the Weather widget.

Chances are pretty slim that the default city used in your Weather widget is the one you live in, so you might want to change that. The default city is chosen by the Weather widget according to the time zone you selected when you first turned on your Mac and used the Setup Assistant. When you hold the mouse pointer over the Weather widget, you see a small circle with an *i* in the lower-right corner (see Figure 3-20); click it. When the widget "flips over," you can see the default city in the upper-left corner (see Figure 3-21). Type in the name of your city or its ZIP code, and then click the Done button in the bottom-right corner (see Figure 3-22). As you can see from Figure 3-23, your city's weather conditions are now displayed.

FIGURE 3-19   The widget bar is open for business!

Find More Cool Widgets Than You Can Shake a Stick At

As mentioned earlier, there are lots of widgets out there just waiting for you to discover them. Apple has a great website that contains more than 3000 widgets created by third-party developers and even by regular Mac users like you and me. To get to this site, open the Dashboard widget bar

FIGURE 3-20   Click the Info (*i*) button

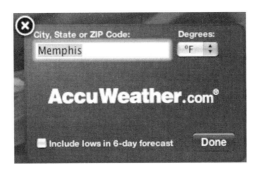

FIGURE 3-21   Weather widget's default settings

FIGURE 3-22   Making the Weather widget yours

FIGURE 3-23   Your local weather conditions are now available at the click of a button.

and click the Manage Widgets button that's above the upper-left side of the bar. Click the More Widgets button in the widget management window, and Safari (your Mac's default web browser) opens to the Dashboard home page. The wonderful world of widgets is now your oyster.

Summary

In this chapter, you learned a bit about how things generally work in Mac OS X. From getting familiar with the Finder, adding and removing items in the Dock, and sorting multiple windows, to using Spaces, you've come a long way from your first cautious steps as a young Macling! Chapter 4 will show you how to customize your Mac to suit your personal tastes.

Chapter 4

Stylin' and Profilin'! Customizing Your Mac

How to...

- Give your Mac a more personal touch
- Choose a screen saver
- Set your monitor preferences
- Create user accounts for each person that uses your Mac
- Change settings for user accounts
- Set Parental Controls

Your Mac is the best-looking and easiest-to-use computer on the planet, both on the outside and the inside (Mac OS X) right out of the box. Apple has done a fabulous job with the Mac's interface and color schemes, and each iteration of Mac OS X just gets better than the last. But there is a way to make your Mac look even better: customize it to suit your tastes. There are several elements of your Mac's interface that you can change so that they appear and behave how you prefer them to. To some this may seem like fairly trivial stuff, but most of us work better in surroundings we personally enjoy.

Tailor Your Environment

The first modifications you normally make when you buy a new home are those that will make the biggest and fastest impact, such as painting walls and installing new carpeting or hardwood floors. Since your Mac is your new "cyber-home" for the foreseeable future, let's stick to the same philosophy and go for the changes that will pack the most punch.

Choose a Desktop Picture

Nothing makes more of an initial visual impact than the desktop picture you use. Mac OS X's default background already looks great, but eventually you will want to customize it to your liking.

The desktop picture (a.k.a "wallpaper" to current and former Microsoft Windows users) can be anything you want. The options are only restricted by the format of the file you want to use for your desktop picture, which will typically be JPEG, PICT, or TIFF.

To change the desktop picture, choose Apple | System Preferences, click the Desktop & Screen Saver icon, and then click the Desktop tab. Alternatively, if you're one of those folks who likes doing things the easy way, simply right-click or CTRL-click the desktop and choose Change Desktop Background from the menu. Apple has stocked Mac OS X with pictures and patterns you can choose from, as you can see in Figure 4-1. You can even use your own pictures by clicking the + button in the lower-left corner and browsing your Mac for the folder that contains the picture you want, or by scrolling down the folder list and selecting a picture from your iPhoto library (learn all about iPhoto in Chapter 11).

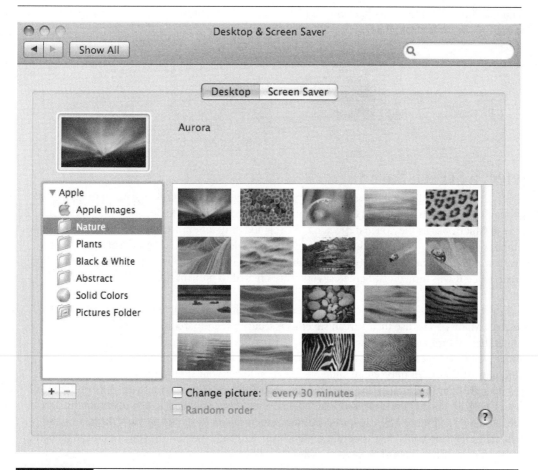

FIGURE 4-1   Desktop pics o' plenty!

If you wish, your Mac can actually change the desktop picture for you automatically. Check the "Change picture:" check box at the bottom of the Desktop & Screen Saver preferences pane and choose how often or in what manner you want the picture to change from the pop-up menu to the right. Check the "Random order" check box if you want the Mac to choose randomly which picture to display from the folder you've selected.

If the picture you want to use for your desktop picture does not fit well on your screen, you can change the way the picture is shown. In the upper-left corner of the Desktop tab is a small preview of the picture you currently have selected. Just to the right of that preview is a pop-up menu that allows you to adjust the way the picture is displayed on your screen. Simply choose the option you prefer from that menu.

Select a Screen Saver

Screen savers are really neat to watch, but beyond that they don't provide the same functionality in today's world of LCDs (liquid crystal displays, the screen display technology used by your iMac or MacBook) as they once did when CRT (cathode ray tube) monitors dominated the computing landscape. "Back in the day," images or text that appeared continuously on a CRT screen would "burn in" on the monitor, causing a negative of the image or text to show up on the screen when it was turned off. Screen savers were created to prevent this "burn in," but LCDs don't experience this problem.

Screen savers may seem to be merely decorative in the 21st century, but that's not entirely the case. Many people use their screen saver as a security feature, requiring a password to be entered before turning the screen saver off. Screen savers can also be informative, by providing news updates and reminding you of appointments. You can even set up your screen saver preferences to show an impromptu slide presentation using your iPhoto library.

Open System Preferences and click the Desktop & Screen Saver icon to open its preference pane. Click the Screen Saver tab and you will see a list of preinstalled screen savers on the left side, as shown in Figure 4-2. Click any of these screen savers to see its preview display on the right side, enabling you to see what the screen saver will look like before you commit to using it.

The Screen Saver tab offers several options for your screen savers:

- Check the box next to "Use random screen saver" to let your Mac pick a screen saver randomly.

- Use the "Start screen saver" slider to tell your Mac after how many minutes of being idle it should start your screen saver.

- Click the Test button to see exactly what the screen saver will look like while it's running.

- Click the Options button to customize the screen saver. Most screen savers allow you to customize the way they work. If a screen saver doesn't allow you to customize it, the Options button is grayed out so that you can't click it.

- Check the box next to "Show with Clock" to have the time displayed on the screen with your screen saver.

FIGURE 4-2   Previewing screen savers in the Desktop & Screen Saver preferences pane

■ Click the Hot Corners button to select tasks for your Mac to perform when the mouse pointer is held in one of the corners of the screen for a few seconds. For instance, click the Hot Corners button, click the pop-up menu that represents the lower-left side of the screen, select Start Screen Saver, and then click OK. Move your mouse pointer to the bottom-left corner of your screen and hold it there; your default screen saver will start up. Using Hot Corners allows you to tell your Mac to perform one of the available tasks with one move of the mouse, instead of having to open multiple windows to get to that task. The example given lets you start the screen saver instantly without having to wait for it to start at the designated time.

Customize the Finder Window Toolbar

The toolbar in a standard Finder window offers some useful features, but Mac OS X allows you to add or remove items in the toolbar, further streamlining your Mac to your needs.

Open a new Finder window and then choose View | Customize Toolbar. A drop-down panel, like the one shown in Figure 4-3, gives you instant access to a plethora of previously hidden functionality. Let's quickly examine each of the available items:

- **Back** Go back and forth between folders you've already viewed.
- **Path** Shows the path to a particular file on your hard drive.
- **View** Select between List, Icon, Cover Flow, or Column view.
- **Action** Highlight a file or folder in the Finder, and then click Action to display a list of available commands for that item.
- **Eject** Click to eject a disc, close a disc image, or disconnect from a server.
- **Burn** Click to burn a disc (CD or DVD).
- **Customize** A shortcut to the customization panel.

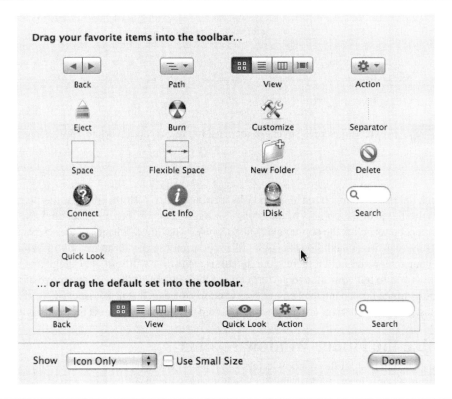

FIGURE 4-3 Yes, this is indeed a plethora of functionality!

- **Separator, Space, and Flexible Space**   Separates items in the toolbar.

- **New Folder**   Creates a new folder in the drive or folder currently displayed in the Finder.

- **Delete**   Places a selected file or folder in the Trash.

- **Connect**   Use to connect to a server on your network.

- **Get Info**   Click to view a file's or folder's information.

- **iDisk**   Connects you to your iDisk, assuming you have a .Mac account (discussed in Chapter 14).

- **Search**   Adds a search field to the toolbar.

- **Quick Look**   Click a file to highlight it, and then click the Quick Look icon to view the file without opening the application that created it.

The default toolbar items are Back, View, Quick Look, Action, and Search. You can drag the entire default set from the customization panel to the toolbar to reset the toolbar to its original state. You can also drag-and-drop an item anywhere in the toolbar, and you can remove it by dragging it off the toolbar altogether.

Next, select how you would like the items in the toolbar to be displayed. Click the Show pop-up menu in the bottom-left corner of the customization panel, and then choose one of the three options. You can also change the size of the icons in the toolbar by checking the Use Small Size check box.

When you're finished customizing the toolbar, click the Done button. From now on, every Finder window will use your new setup.

Personalize Your Icons

Mac OS X provides beautiful, top-flight icons, but it also gives you the freedom to use your own icons should the notion strike you. Aside from being purely ornamental, custom icons can actually be useful to help categorize files and folders that share some common trait. You can create your own icons, download new icons from Internet websites, and mix and match icons already on your Mac. For more information about icons, tools to make your own icons, and downloading icon offerings from other "Mac heads," visit The Iconfactory at www.iconfactory.com (see Chapter 5 to see how to set up your Mac for the Internet, if you haven't done so already).

To personalize an icon, follow these steps:

1.   Find an item that uses the icon you want to use for your files or folders, click it to highlight it, and then open the Get Info window (choose File | Get Info or press ⌘-I) for the item.

2.   In the Get Info window (see Figure 4-4 for an example), click the icon in the upper-left corner and choose Edit | Copy (or press ⌘-C). You've just copied the icon to your Mac's clipboard, which is a hidden storage area for items you are copying. Close this item's Get Info window.

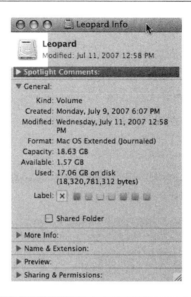

FIGURE 4-4 Click the icon in the upper-left corner to edit or copy it.

3. Find the item whose icon you desire to change, and open the Get Info window for it, as in Step 1.

4. Click the item's icon in the upper-left corner of the Get Info window and choose Edit | Paste or press ⌘-v.

5. Close the Get Info window, and the item should now display with its new icon.

NOTE *By this point, you should be catching on to how to perform the most common tasks, so hereafter you won't always be given a detailed description of how to perform these tasks.*

Use the Appearance Preferences Pane

To make still more changes to the way Mac OS X looks and acts, open System Preferences and click the Appearance icon. The Appearance preferences pane allows you to change many more settings to further personalize your Mac; most of these settings are self-explanatory.

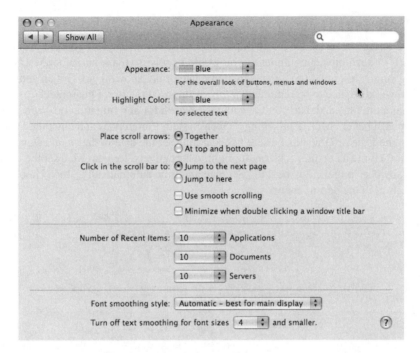

One option whose function isn't self-explanatory is "Number of Recent Items." To understand what this option refers to, click the Apple menu and hold your mouse over Recent Items to see the last several applications, documents, and servers you have frequented. You can change the number of items displayed for each of these categories by changing its corresponding setting in the Number of Recent Items pop-up menu.

Another vague option is "Font smoothing style." Basically, this just allows you to change the way fonts are displayed on your screen. For example, font smoothing can cause smaller-size text to be more difficult to read, so this option enables you to turn off font smoothing for that particular size.

Set the Basic Settings

Some things are just so basic you almost want to skip over them to get to the next astounding Mac OS X feature, but these settings are more important to your overall Mac experience than a bunch of pretty icons or customized toolbars. That's why they're considered basics!

Set the Time and Date

The time and date for your Mac are pretty important items. For instance, if you use iCal to remind yourself of upcoming appointments, you would be wise to make sure your Mac's time and date are accurate, lest you upset clients by being late or not showing up. Got an anniversary coming up? It would be nice to be reminded *before* as opposed to after, I guarantee!

To make sure the time and date don't become the reason for any litigation between you and your spouse, you'd better check their settings. Open System Preferences and click the Date & Time icon. On the Date & Time tab, be sure to accurately set the date in the small calendar on the left and set the time using the clock on the right. Alternatively, let your Mac set the time automatically, by checking the box next to "Set date and time automatically," then choosing the nearest time server in the pop-up menu.

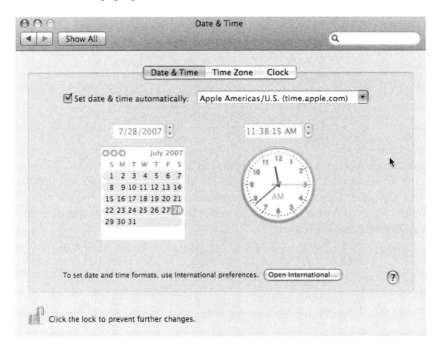

To make sure your time stays accurate, click the Time Zone tab and select your location on the map.

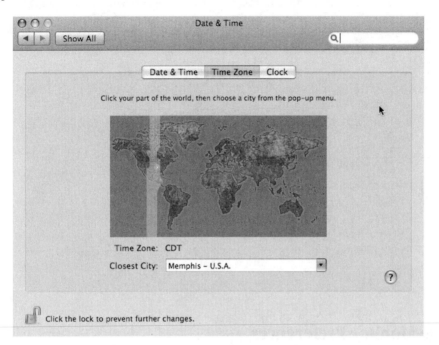

You can change the way your clock is displayed in the menu bar by going to the Clock tab and choosing one of the many options. The neatest option on the Clock tab is not a display option but rather is the "Announce the time" option. For those of us who are too enthralled with our work to glance at the upper-right corner of our screen to check the time, the Mac will actually announce what time it is at the intervals specified. To further maximize the coolness factor, click the Customize Voice button and try out all the available settings.

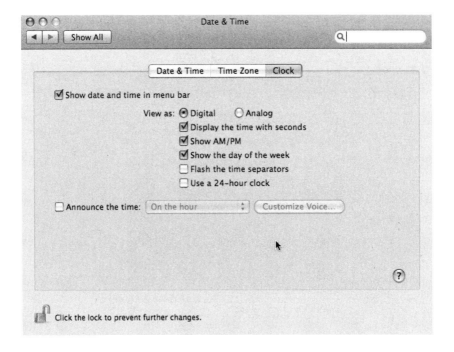

Change Monitor Preferences

Changing monitor settings can make a huge difference in how you work with your Mac. Looking at the screen is the main way you interact with a computer, so if the resolution or color isn't optimized, it can make using your Mac an uncomfortable experience.

Open System Preferences and click the Displays icon in the Hardware section, and then click the Display tab; set the resolution, brightness, and number of colors to your liking. The resolution you choose determines how large or small the items on your screen appear. A rule of thumb for selecting a resolution is to understand that the lower the number the larger the icons are going to be. For example, icons at 800×600 are much larger than those at 1280×800.

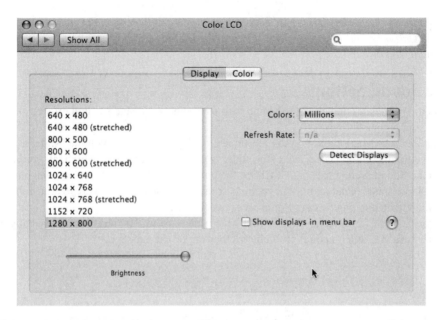

Click the Color tab to change the way colors are represented on your screen. Select one of the available display profiles from the list on the left and use the one that makes your eyes' rods and cones the happiest. Bear in mind that for most users the default color profile works just fine; changing profiles is mainly a tool used by graphics professionals.

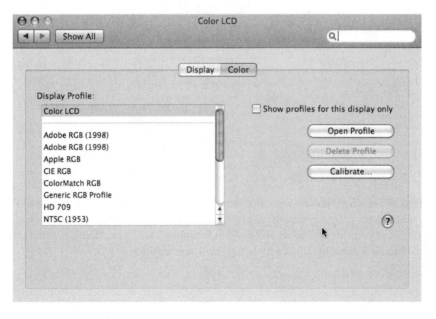

If none of the preset color profiles please your palette, you can make your own! Click the Calibrate button on the Color tab, and the Display Calibrator Assistant will merrily guide you through the process.

Change Sound Settings

Open System Preferences and click the Sound icon to change your Mac's sound effects, as well as the input and output settings.

You can set your Mac's default system volume by using the "Output volume" slider at the bottom of the Sound preferences pane. (This slider is present regardless of which tab you are viewing in the Sound preferences pane.) Check the box next to "Show volume in menu bar" to place the volume status menu icon in the menu bar; this is a much simpler way to adjust the main system volume than opening System Preferences every time.

Click the Sound Effects tab to change your Mac's alert sound. The alert sound is what your Mac uses to warn you of a potential problem or other important message.

The Output tab is where you choose what device to use for your Mac's sound output. Your Mac comes with a built-in speaker, or speakers, that is selected by default. If you attach a set of external speakers to your Mac, you can select them from this list as your default output devices. You can also change the output balance by using the Balance slider.

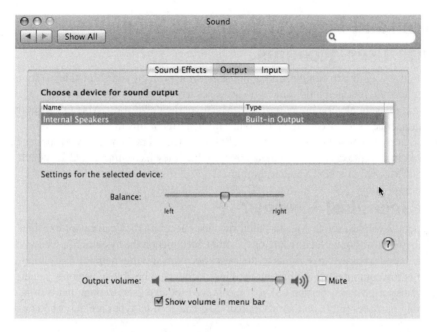

Use the Input tab to choose what device your Mac uses to receive input. Newer Macs have a microphone built right in, and this is the default input device. To use a headset or an external microphone, connect it to your Mac and choose Line In from the list of available devices.

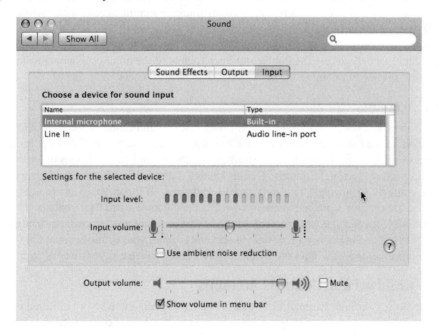

Personalize (and Protect) Your Mac Even Further with User Accounts

There is no better way to personalize, and at the same time protect, your Mac than to set up a separate user account for each individual who accesses it.

User accounts were never a big part of the "Mac experience" prior to Mac OS X, but with its introduction, Mac users discovered the wonderful benefits of this methodology. While user accounts were a part of Mac OS 9 (though I doubt most Mac users were aware of them), they never received the attention or reached their potential like they have in Mac OS X, which is a direct result of Mac OS X's UNIX underpinnings.

Why Use Individual Accounts?

When each person who uses your Mac has their own user account, they can customize their account in any way they like without affecting any of the other accounts on the system. For example, moms and dads can assign administrative rights to their user accounts, giving them (almost) unfettered access to the entire computer, while limiting the kids' accounts to be able to use only select applications and perform only certain tasks. You can even set up a user account that is used only for troubleshooting purposes (more on that in Chapter 20). The account types are described next.

Administrator Accounts

When you first logged onto your Mac, you created a user account for yourself. This account was automatically given administrative rights, which allows the owner of that account to make system-wide changes and to install software. Administrator, or admin, accounts can also add new accounts or remove current ones.

Admin accounts are able to do almost anything they want, but there are some limitations. Admin accounts can only access the Public and Sites folders of the other user accounts; all other user folders are off limits, retaining the privacy of the individual users.

Standard Accounts

Standard accounts are unable to make any system-wide changes and cannot administer other accounts; however, they still retain control of their own account and can install software for their use only. These accounts can be limited even further with the use of Parental Controls, as discussed in detail in the section "Parental Controls Need-to-Knows" later in this chapter. Standard accounts are great for children, for anyone completely new to computers, or for an office environment in which the IT administrator wants to maintain control of the computers and their content. If you aren't quite confident enough in your mastery of the Mac, you might want to create a standard account for yourself and use it to do your daily work, and log into your admin account only when necessary to install an application for use by all accounts or to change a system-wide setting.

Managed with Parental Controls Accounts

You have the power, through Parental Controls, to control the content that your children can access on the Internet and the applications they can use on your Mac. See the section "Parental Controls Need-to-Knows" later in this chapter for much more information.

Sharing Only Accounts

This account type only allows someone to remotely connect to your Mac so that they can view shared files and folders. Sharing Only accounts cannot be used to log in to the Mac through the login window, and they cannot change any settings for the computer.

Add a New User Account

Open System Preferences and click the Accounts icon in the System area; this opens the Accounts preferences pane, as shown in Figure 4-5. Check to see whether the lock icon at the bottom left of the window is closed or open. If it is closed, click the lock and type in your account password when prompted; this allows you to make changes to the system, as described in the following sections.

 Remember, as an administrator you rule this Mac with an iron fist. This not only means you are in control, but you are also able to break the entire system rather easily if you aren't careful.

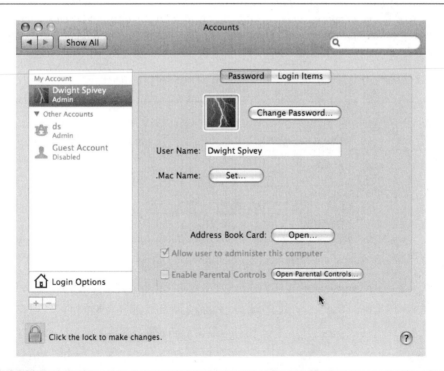

FIGURE 4-5   Accounts are in the system administrator's control.

Set Account Types, Usernames, and Passwords

On the Password tab of the Accounts preferences pane, click the + button in the lower-left corner to add a new account. This opens a new dialog box (see Figure 4-6) in which you choose the account type and enter the name of the new account, the short name for the account, and the account's password. Mac OS X automatically assigns the short name, but you can change it if you prefer.

CAUTION *This doesn't happen often, but I must take issue with Apple on something here. The Password Hint field allows you to enter a statement or question that may jog your memory if you forget the password for your account. In spite of Apple's affinity for this option (notice the words "Recommended"), I have to warn you that using a password hint not only helps you remember the password, but also helps someone else to figure it out! Be wary of this recommendation.*

If you would like to encrypt the contents of this account's home folder, check the box next to "Turn on FileVault protection" (more on FileVault in Chapter 14). Click the Create Account button to add the new account.

TIP *If you are having a hard time coming up with a password for your account, click the small key icon to the right of the Password field to have your Mac generate a password for you. You can choose from many different types of passwords, and even see the quality rating of the password. The quality is determined by how difficult the password may be for someone else to figure out.*

FIGURE 4-6 Adding a new account

The new account now shows up under the list of Other Accounts on the left side of the Accounts preferences pane (see Figure 4-5). Let's make a few changes to it, shall we? Click the new account to see its settings.

"Allow user to administer this computer"

Checking this box will give a standard account or a managed account new life as an administrator account, with all the rights and privileges (and responsibilities) such status entails.

Choose User Pictures

The picture you choose to represent your user account is a bigger deal than you may think. When a friend or colleague watches you log onto your Mac, which user account picture would you rather have them see: something cool like a lightning bolt shooting through the sky, or a picture of the donkey from the old television variety show, *Hee Haw*? That one's a no-brainer.

To make this "all-important" decision, click the tiny picture preview at the top of the Password tab. Apple has been kind enough to supply us with a few nifty pictures; feel free to choose whichever one you like.

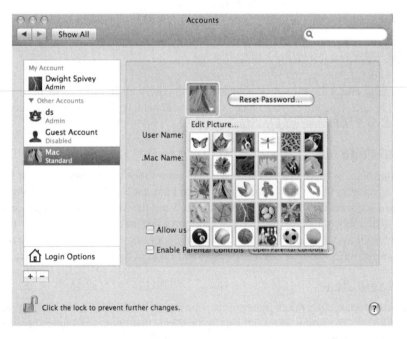

However, if you are the adventurous type, why not use your own unique picture? To do so, click the "Edit picture" button to open the image-editing window (see Figure 4-7). From here, you can either drag your desired picture into the picture window or click the Choose button to browse your Mac for the file you want. You can resize your picture, if you like, by using the slider.

FIGURE 4-7   Make your own login picture here.

Another option is to click "Take a video snapshot" to use your built-in iSight camera (if your Mac is so equipped) to take a picture of you. Once you've decide which picture to use and have edited it to your liking, click Set to use it for your account.

Use Parental Controls

Parental Controls helps you protect the little ones, and sometimes the big ones, in your life from seeing or participating in things they ought not to. With Parental Controls, you can police what users of standard accounts can do on the Internet when using the Mac, giving you peace of mind and security usually only gained by purchasing third-party Internet filter software. For those of you who have children, Parental Controls is such an important part of your Mac life that it warrants its own section, "Parental Controls Need-to-Knows," a bit later in this chapter.

Configure Login Items

The Login Items tab of the Accounts preferences pane can only be accessed by the account that is currently logged in. The Login Items tab lists applications that open, sometimes behind the scenes, when you first log in to your account.

You may not even realize that some of these applications are running. For instance, if you have an appointment in iCal and set iCal to remind you of that appointment, the iCalAlarmScheduler is an application you will see on the Login Items tab.

Some people like to have frequently used applications open up automatically when they first log in. You can add any application on your Mac to the Login Items list by clicking the + button in the bottom left of your screen and browsing your Mac for the application. To remove an item from the list, simply select it and then click the – button to remove it. Don't worry; you haven't deleted the actual application, just an alias of it.

Parental Controls Need-to-Knows

The use of Parental Controls allows an admin account to allocate permissions for a standard account. The Enable Parental Controls check box is available at the bottom of each account's settings window. Check this box to turn on Parental Controls for a standard account. If you check the box for an admin account, you are warned that turning on Parental Controls automatically changes the account type to managed. Be sure to click No if you don't want to change the account type.

If you enabled Parental Controls, click the Open Parental Controls button to open the Parental Controls preferences pane (see Figure 4-8). Parental Controls can also be accessed by clicking its icon in System Preferences.

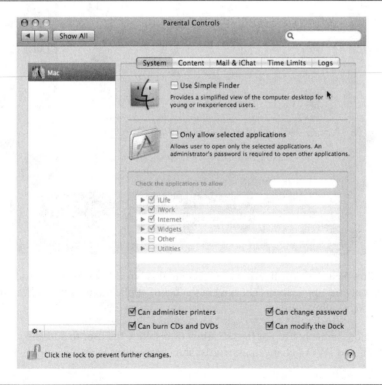

FIGURE 4-8   Don't let all this power go to your head!

The left side of the Parental Controls window lists all the standard and managed accounts for your Mac. Select the account you want to alter from this list.

The Parental Controls preferences pane has five tabs: System, Content, Mail & iChat, Time Limits, and Logs. Each tab contains different elements for securing access to your Mac and the Internet. The following sections describe each of the tabs in turn.

System

Figure 4-8 shows the following options available on the System tab:

■ **Use Simple Finder**   Checking this box provides a much more basic user interface that is perfectly suited to the less-experienced user. As shown here, the icons are larger (and can be activated with just a single click) and the Dock has only a limited choice of folders:

■ **Only Allow Selected Applications**   Checking this box allows the user to access on the Mac only the applications checked in the list of applications in the "Check the applications to allow" area.

The other options at the bottom of the tab allow or disallow the user to add and remove printers, burn CDs and DVDs, change passwords, and change the Dock.

Content

Figure 4-9 shows the Content tab, which has the following settings:

- **Hide Profanity in Dictionary**   Yes, Virginia, there are some dirty words in Mac OS X's Dictionary program. Checking this option prevents small eyes from discovering them.

- **Website Restrictions**   Use these options to allow the user of the account to surf the Web unhindered or to access only sites that you give the "thumbs up."

Mail & iChat

The Mail & iChat tab, shown in Figure 4-10, has the following options:

- **Limit Mail and Limit iChat**   Check these boxes if you want to limit the managed account's ability to send and receive email and chat. The great thing about this feature, should you choose to enable it, is that you can select whom the users of the account

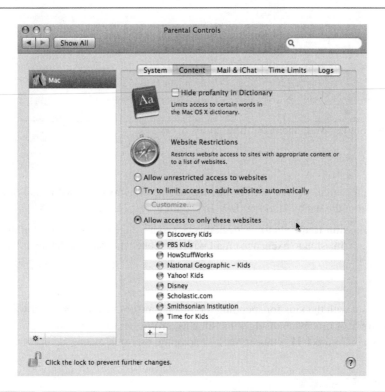

FIGURE 4-9   Use the Content tab to allow or disallow access to specific content.

FIGURE 4-10   Setting Mail and iChat limitations

can exchange email with or hold instant messaging conversations with. Add or remove contacts from the list by clicking the + or – button, respectively.

■ **Send Permission Requests to**   Check this box to have the user send an email to an admin requesting permission to exchange email with someone who isn't on the default list.

Time Limits

It's easy to get upset with the kids for spending too much time on the computer, but we also know it's easy to lose track of time when using something as effortlessly cool as a Mac. On the Time Limits tab, shown in Figure 4-11, you can set how long the user of a managed account can use the

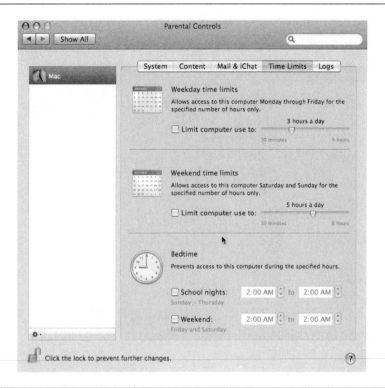

FIGURE 4-11   Time is up when time's up.

Mac before it locks them out. You can specify separate time limits for weekday and weekend use, and even use the Bedtime settings to set times of day the user can't log in to the Mac at all.

Logs

Monitor the activity of the account with the Logs tab (see Figure 4-12). You can see all the websites the user has visited (or was blocked from visiting), the applications they used, and their iChats. See everything that happened today, last month, or go all the way to last year.

FIGURE 4-12   I know what you did last summer! (And yesterday afternoon, too.)

Summary

When you begin customizing your Mac, your familiarity with it grows exponentially. When you first buy a car, you don't leave everything as you found it; you adjust the seats and steering wheel, set the temperature, program your favorite radio stations, hang fuzzy dice from the mirror, and so on. These customizations make the car *your own*, just as your customizations to the Mac make the Mac *your own*.

Chapter 5

Getting Started on the Internet

How to...

- Understand the difference between dial-up and broadband
- Choose between DSL and cable for your broadband access
- Open and use the Mail application
- Browse the Internet
- Chat with friends using instant messaging

Are you ready for some real fun? You're about to use your Mac to reach out to the rest of the entire world, right from within the safety and convenience of your own home or office. Today, emailing and surfing the Web are as commonplace as using the telephone or driving a car. What once seemed like something out of a science fiction movie is now reality, and it's waiting for you to join in.

This chapter serves as a springboard to get you up and running on the Internet as quickly as possible and with minimal hassle. It covers the bare-bones basics of getting email, surfing the World Wide Web, and chatting with a friend using instant messages. Chapters 16 and 17, respectively, are dedicated to the intricacies of web browsing and using email.

Get Connected

Before you can merge onto the "information superhighway," you need a way to access it. To access the Internet, you need to sign up with an Internet service provider (ISP). There are more ISPs to choose from than you can imagine, and you can quickly become overwhelmed with all the options available. This section briefly covers the main connection types used for accessing the Internet and answers some basic questions about their services. Hopefully this will give you a leg up when it comes to choosing an ISP, if you haven't done so already.

Dial-up or Broadband?

I'm sure you've probably seen advertisements on television by ISPs who tout the many features you can use if you sign up with them. They boast about having technologies that separate them from the rest of the pack, but in reality the most important feature you need to consider is this: speed. It's all about the speed, bubba. Well, it's not *all* about the speed; price should be considered, but that isn't as large a factor as it once was because competition has driven down prices. Let's check out the pros and cons of the two primary methods of accessing the Internet: dial-up and broadband.

Dial-up Modem Connections

In the "pioneer days" of the Internet, there was only one option for the average user when it came to Internet access: dial-up. Unfortunately, to further carry the "pioneer days" analogy, using a dial-up modem in the 21st century is akin to driving a covered wagon down the interstate.

Dial-up modems use your phone connection to access the Internet, but at very slow speeds. The theoretical maximum speed of a typical dial-up modem is 56 kilobits per second (56 Kbps), which may sound like something extra special, but it's not. In most cases, you won't get very close to the full theoretical speed because of phone line noise and other factors. At this speed, tasks that are typical for today's Internet users, such as video conferencing and watching movie trailers, won't be a pleasant experience at all. Some services, like using a Voice over Internet Protocol (VoIP) phone carrier such as Vonage, are impossible at dial-up speeds. Another mark against dial-up is that the connection isn't always on, and when you are connected, your phone line is tied up by the modem; to make or receive a call, you must suspend the Internet connection.

The positive side to this kind of connection is the price, which is lower than any broadband service, but the difference in cost between dial-up and broadband is fairly negligible these days. Some dial-up ISPs offer free Internet access, but the time allotted is limited and you have to contend with advertisements, which is what the ISP uses to support this free service.

Another positive point to ponder is that when you travel, broadband may not be available, but there's a phone line almost anywhere you go. Having dial-up as a fallback plan is a great idea. If you will be using dial-up only in such instances, an ISP that offers free Internet access is the way to go.

The Need for Speed!

Broadband is the general term for broadband Internet access, and is capable of handling much more data at much faster speeds than dial-up. Broadband is also always on; there's no need to connect and reconnect over and over again. Broadband access takes many forms, such as

My Mac Doesn't Have a Modem!

You may have discovered by now that your Mac, assuming it's fairly new (less than two years old), doesn't have a built-in modem. Take this as an indicator of the direction in which Internet access is going. However, if my less-than-compelling description of dial-up still hasn't swayed you from your interest in it, or if you need a dial-up modem for sending and receiving faxes with your Mac, have no fear, Apple is here!

Apple does offer an optional dial-up modem that you can purchase and attach to one of your available USB ports. You buy the modem from Apple's online store or from your local brick-and-mortar Apple Store.

digital subscriber line (DSL), coaxial cable, fiber optic cable, and satellite. Since the advent of broadband, the Internet has taken off in terms of services afforded the common household. Consider these scenarios:

- A grandfather in Spokane, Washington can video chat with his granddaughter in Gulf Shores, Alabama with incredible ease and speed. Why wait until the next family reunion to see how she's sporting that new gap in her front teeth?

- A nephew can email a short movie clip of himself scoring a touchdown in tonight's game to his uncle on duty in Iraq.

- Companies can set up board meetings, and every executive can chime in from the comfort of their own home, car, or golf cart.

- A young woman in Ohio is about to earn her bachelor's degree from a university in Virginia, without having ever attended a class outside of her home state. She hasn't taken a class outside of her own home, for that matter, because she attends classes via the Internet with her broadband connection.

The communication possibilities are mind-boggling! These are just a few examples of what broadband Internet access has meant to the growth of the Internet, and is but a glimpse of what it can accomplish in the future.

You're probably saying, "Okay, okay, you've sold me on the speed, but what about the cost?" Well, it may come as a surprise to some that the cost of some broadband connections is about the same as many dial-up services. The difference between crawling and flying on the Internet may be only a few dollars, if that. The benefits gained by broadband far outweigh the slight cost differences between it and dial-up.

DSL or Cable?

Now the question remains, what type of broadband connection to use? As DSL and coaxial cable (or simply "cable," as I'll refer to it from here on) are the two most prevalent services for consumers, these are the two I will compare.

A big plus for DSL is that it works with your existing phone lines, so there is no need for someone to come in and wire your home for Internet access. Also, even though it uses your phone line to connect to the Internet, you can still continue to use your phone for calls without having to suspend Internet access. The download (loading items from the Internet to your Mac) speeds for DSL are significantly faster than those for dial-up, but the upload (loading items to a server on the Internet from your Mac) speeds are not very fast at all, although still speedier than dial-up.

Cable uses the same wiring provided by your cable company, and is also always connected. Cable is currently the fastest of the three connection types I've discussed, but is usually a little costlier, too. A major advantage of cable over DSL is that it is more widely available. The distance of the home or office from the telephone company's main exchange limits the availability of DSL in some areas. The general consensus is that cable tends to be a more reliable connection than DSL as well. A possible downside to cable is that your speed could be hindered if a large number of cable customers are using the same connections, such as in an apartment complex or condominium.

Use the Network Setup Assistant

True to form, Apple has provided a simple way for you to configure your network settings: let the Mac do it for you with the Network Setup Assistant. Here's how:

1. Open System Preferences and click the Network icon to open the Network preferences pane, and then click the "Assist me" button at the bottom.

2. Click the Assistant button when prompted with this dialog box:

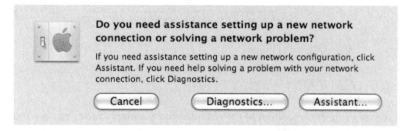

The Network Setup Assistant window opens.

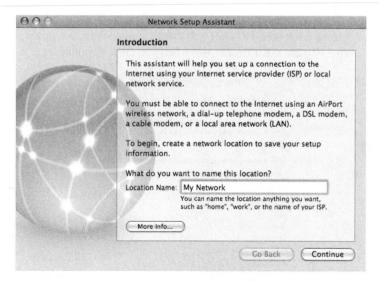

3. Read the introduction, give your location a descriptive name, and then click Continue.

4. Specify the method you intend to use to connect to the Internet, read the note below the options, and then click Continue.

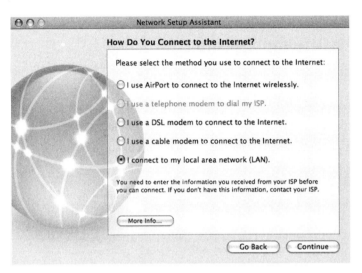

Heed the message at the bottom of the How Do You Connect to the Internet? page. Otherwise, the Network Setup Assistant won't be any help to you at all. Make sure you have (or get) all the pertinent connection information from your ISP before continuing.

5. The Network Setup Assistant now wants to know if you are ready to connect. Some ISPs and networks allow computers to connect to them automatically, and that's just what the Network Setup Assistant will attempt to do when you click Continue.

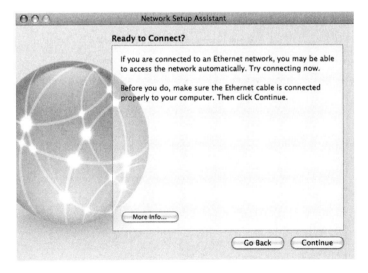

If the Network Setup Assistant was able to configure everything without need of any further input from you, congratulations and happy Internet surfing! Otherwise, the next page will tell you that you can't connect automatically and that you need to enter your ISPs information before you can connect to the Internet. After you enter the appropriate information for your connection type (the information will vary based on how you are attempting to connect, such as with a DSL modem or a cable modem), the Network Setup Assistant should be able to get you up and running.

TIP   *Contact your ISP or network administrator if you have any difficulty connecting to the Internet at this point.*

Communicate with the World

Now that you're (hopefully) up and running on the Internet, it's time to play with your newfound powers. Again, for now we're just going over the basics of email, web browsing, and chat (a.k.a. instant messaging), and we'll delve more deeply into the subjects of web browsing and using email in Chapters 16 and 17, respectively.

Understand Email Basics

Email is such a common part of our lives that it's now hard to imagine being without it. Did you know that email has actually been around since 1965? It wasn't until the Internet became available for the average computer user that email reached its true potential, though. To depict email's influence on our daily comings and goings, let's do a little comparison. The United States Postal Service estimates that it processes and delivers 213 billion pieces of mail a year. That is an incredible number, and you need to give your postal carrier a hug the next time you see him or her. Now, how many emails were sent in 2006? Only 171 billion—per day!

Mac OS X comes with its own email application, called, appropriately enough, Mail. As is standard practice for Apple, Mail is a very intuitive and easy-to-use application that takes no time to get used to. We'll get to particulars later, in Chapter 17, but for now let's explore the very basics of Mail.

To get started, open the Mail application by clicking its icon in the Dock, or by opening a new Finder window, opening the Applications folder, and double-clicking the Mail icon.

CAUTION   *The ISP you have chosen will provide most of the information that Mail requires to create a new email account. Make sure you have this information available before you get started or you may not be able to properly set up your account, and you won't be able to send or receive email.*

Create an Email Account

If you have never created an email account for this user account, Mail greets you with the "Welcome to Mail" window. Proceed as follows:

1. Enter your name, email address, and the password for your email account, and then click Create or Continue here; clicking Cancel just closes Mail.

NOTE   *Whether you see Create or Continue on the "Welcome to Mail" page is determined after you type in your email address. If Mail recognizes the ISP, the "Automatically set up account" check box appears under the Password field. Checking the box changes the Continue button to Create, and when you click it, Mail handles the upcoming configuration settings automatically. If Mail doesn't recognize the ISP, you have to click Continue and enter your information manually.*

2. All account types, except .Mac, next see the Incoming Mail Server window. Choose the account type, describe the account (for example, "Work Email" or "Dwight's Home Account"), and enter the address of your ISP's mail server, your username, and your password.

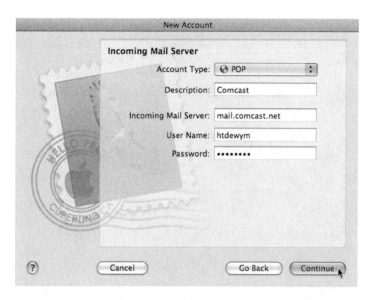

The account types you can select from are your .Mac account, a POP account, IMAP, or an Exchange account (typically used for corporate networks); I'll use POP for illustration purposes. Your ISP or network administrator provides the account type and email address. Click Continue to advance to the Incoming Mail Security window.

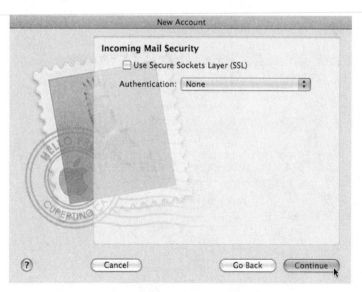

3. The email account information provided by your ISP should tell you if you're required to use Secure Sockets Layer (SSL) and whether to use authentication. Enter this information if required; if not, simply click Continue.

4. Enter your information for the Outgoing Mail Server. If your outgoing server requires a username and password, be sure to check the Use Authentication box and input them. Click Continue.

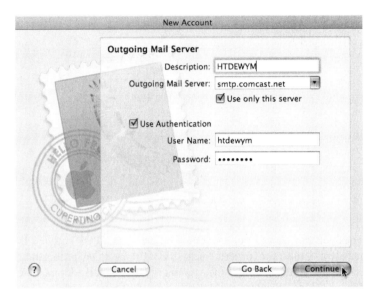

5. The Account Summary window shows you all the information you have entered for your account. Click Create if everything is correct.

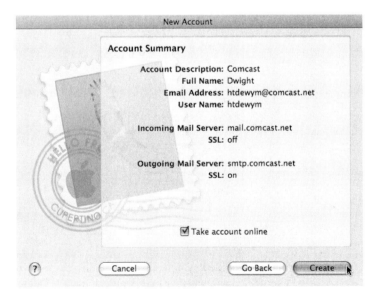

Create a New Email Message

Before you attempt to create a new email message, take a look at the basic interface of Mail, shown in Figure 5-1, so that you can get your bearings.

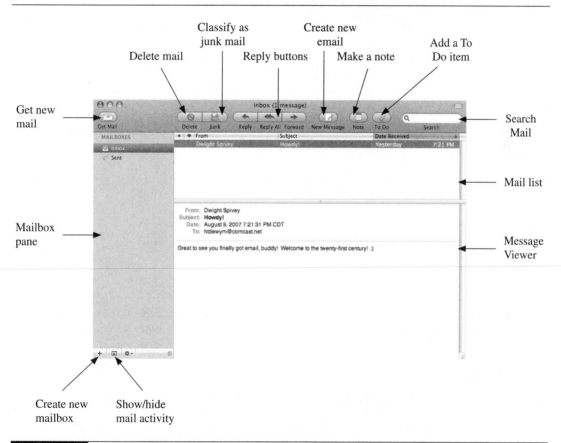

FIGURE 5-1   Mail has an elegant, uncluttered interface.

Now you are ready to get creative and send your own unique e-mail message. Click the New Message button in the toolbar of the main Mail window.

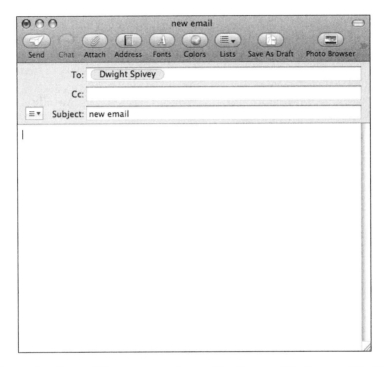

Enter the email address of the person you're sending the email to, type a subject line for your message, type the message, and click Send. Boom! You're officially a member of the emailing masses.

Read an Email Message

Your next mission: read an email. Tell a friend who has email to send a message to your new account. Click your Inbox in the Mailbox pane; your mail appears to the right, in the mail list. Click the email in the mail list to display its contents below in the Message Viewer, as shown in Figure 5-1.

You may find that you prefer reading messages by "opening" them in a separate window. To do so, double-click the email in the mail list, which causes it to open in its own window.

Reply to an Email Message

To reply to an email you have received, just open the email and click the Reply button in the toolbar (or choose Message | Reply). If there were other people included on the original email and you would like for them to see your reply, click the Reply All button instead.

Add your response to the email window and click the Send button in the toolbar.

Delete an Email Message

Deleting an email message has it pros and cons. On the pro side, deleting emails frees up space on your computer, gets rid of old or spam emails, and cleans up the clutter that can quickly jam your Inbox. The only real con to deleting emails is either accidentally deleting an email you wanted to keep or intentionally deleting an email you later realize you needed. Fortunately, Mail has a Trash mailbox that contains the emails you have deleted, so they aren't really completely gone until they are removed from there (more on this in Chapter 17).

To delete an email, click the email to highlight it, and choose Edit | Delete. You can also right-click or CTRL-click the email and choose Delete from the pop-up menu.

Again, there is much more information on Mail in Chapter 17.

Surfin' Safari!

Email and instant messaging are great communications tools, but surfing the Web is essentially the holy grail of Internet functions. With the combination of Mac OS X, a great web browser, and an Internet connection, you can get your news, shop for anything you can possibly imagine, download movies and music, attend online classes at a major university, keep track of the day's sports scores, play chess with someone on an entirely different continent, accomplish an endless array of chores and tasks, and engage in a wide variety of activities and amusements.

A web browser is an application that acts as your window into the Internet world. Mac OS X already comes loaded with one of the best web browsers available: Safari.

Browsing Fundamentals

Browsing the Internet may sound really daunting, but it only gets as complicated as you let it. By this I mean that every web browser out there has basic functions that are common to all web browsers, and simply sticking to the bare basics will be fine for most Internet activities. Browsing gets complicated only when you begin to use specialized functions of individual browsers, which is beyond the scope of this discussion.

Get started on the Web by opening Safari, either by double-clicking the Safari icon in the Applications folder or by clicking the Safari icon in the Dock. Let's get acquainted with Safari's browser window, shown in Figure 5-2.

When you first open Safari, you are taken to your default home page, which is Apple's own Internet start page. This is a good page from which to learn how to interact with web sites in general.

Previous/Next page   Refresh   Address field   Google search   Bookmarks bar

Toolbar

Viewing
window

FIGURE 5-2   The basic features of the Safari interface

There's lots to see when the start page first loads, but there's lots more to see further down the page. A web site works like other windows on your Mac, so you can use the scroll arrows and scroll bar on the right side of Safari window to move up and down the page.

Move your mouse pointer over the entire web page and you will notice that as the pointer passes over certain items (pictures and some text), its icon changes to look like a small hand (is that Michael Jackson's missing glove?).

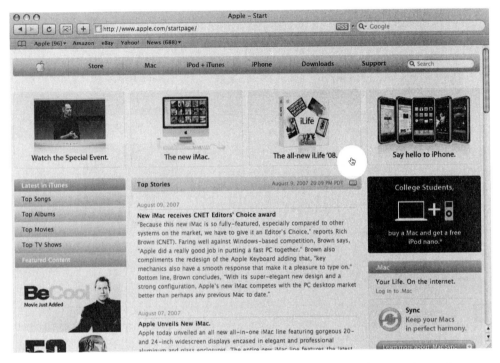

The hand is giving you an indication that this picture or text is a link to another web page. Click one of the items to see where the page leads you; typically the picture or text is clearly indicative of what the destination page's contents are. To get back to the previous web page, click the left arrow button in the upper-left corner of Safari's window.

You've just dipped your toes into the Internet; now you're going to take the plunge. Check out Apple's .Mac home page, by typing its address, www.mac.com, into Safari's address field and pressing the RETURN key. You are transported to your new destination.

That's all there is to it. You've now become a semiprofessional Internet surf-hound! This little bit of information should whet your appetite for more Safari fun in Chapter 16.

Chat It Up with iChat

Instant messaging lets you communicate in real time with other computer users over the Internet by typing messages back and forth. Instant messaging has been around quite a while, but it's never been as easy to use as it is now, using Apple's iChat. iChat can do much more than just send text back and forth, but you'll just have to be patient regarding the really awesome stuff, which comes a bit later in the chapter.

Instant Messaging Basics

Open iChat by clicking its icon in the Dock or by double-clicking it in the Applications folder. The first time you crank up iChat, you see the welcome screen.

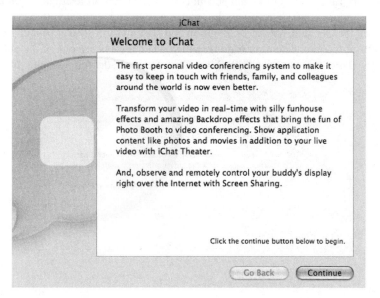

The welcome screen gives you a bit of a teaser regarding the "really awesome stuff" I mentioned in the previous paragraph. Click Continue to go the Account Setup screen.

You must have an instant messaging account to use iChat. Your first and best bet is to use a .Mac account, but if you don't have one, you're still in good shape. iChat supports three of the other most popular instant messaging applications: AIM (AOL Instant Messenger), Jabber (open source), and Google Talk (uses your Gmail account). You can use your username and password from these other services with iChat. If you don't have an existing account with AIM, Jabber, or Google Talk, click the Get an iChat Account button and sign up for a 60-day trial of .Mac. This will get you kick-started into instant messaging, and you can always use one of the other account types later on if you prefer not to stick with .Mac. Click Done to add your account to iChat.

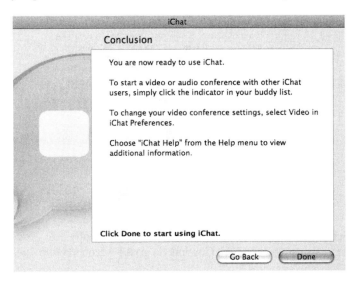

Once your account info is squared away, you're almost ready to begin chatting. I say "almost" because it's hard to chat...with no one! When you start up iChat, you see your buddy list and everyone that you've added to it, but since this is your first time logging in, none of your buddies have been added yet. Go ahead and add a buddy by clicking the + button in the lower left of the buddy list, shown here, and then select Add Buddy. Enter your buddy's account information into the appropriate fields to add him or her.

Now that you've got someone added to your buddy list, it's time to begin chatting with him or her. Double-click your newly added buddy in the buddy list and a chat window will open. Type in your message and press RETURN to send it. Your message will show next to your user account login picture. When your buddy replies, you will see a picture representing them on the left side of the chat window, followed by the text of their message back to you. You are now chatting away!

Now, Let's Get to the Cool Stuff!

I promised the cool stuff, and Apple has delivered. Text chatting is still good, but how about audio chatting? "That's what my phone is for," you might be saying. Okay, good point. Let's see if this sounds better—video chatting! That's right, I'm talking about *2001: A Space Odyssey*–style video phone conversations, right there on your Mac.

The iMac and MacBook have video cameras built right in, but the Mac mini requires an external FireWire camera. You can video chat with any of your buddies who have video chat capabilities on their Mac or PC. There is no better and more intimate way for families to stay in touch across the miles, and the benefits to businesses with executives in multiple offices around the country or the world are obvious. Being able to see the person you are speaking with adds a more personal touch to long distance conversations. And you can video chat with up to three people at once.

Open your Buddy List, select the name of the person you want to video chat with (if they can video chat, there will be a camera icon next to their name), and then click the green camera button in the upper-right corner of the Buddy List window to start the video chat.

As fun as video chatting is, Apple, being the creative folks that they are, thought it would be a great idea to add a little fun to the video by adding special effects. These effects range from funny distortions to placing pictures of exotic locations in the background. Here are a few of the neat effects included with iChat:

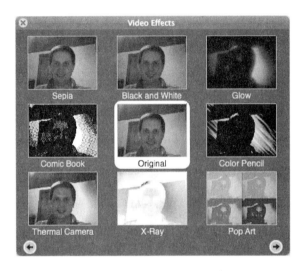

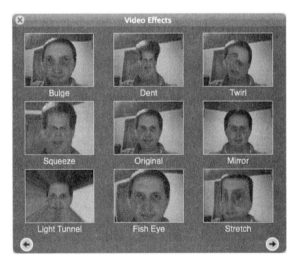

Summary

You are now a full-fledged member of Internet society. You've learned the minimum basics of sending and receiving email, surfing the Web, and chatting with friends, so you've got a good grasp of just how great the Internet can be. As we move further along, you'll find even more great things to enjoy on the Internet, and this chapter has given you the tools to begin making those discoveries.

Part II

Making Your Mac Earn Its Keep

Chapter 6

How to Use Your Mac's Applications

How to...

- ▓ Discover what the applications that come with your Mac actually do
- ▓ Know the basic functions and commands that are common to most Mac applications

Certainly you've already noticed the abundance of applications available in your Mac's Applications folder. While the titles of some of them give a good indication of the functions they perform, not all of them are that easy to decipher. There's also no doubt that you would like to know how to perform at least the basic tasks that all Mac applications have in common. Thus, the two purposes of this chapter are to introduce the preinstalled applications that are available to you so that you can get the most out of your Mac, and to show you how to perform the basic tasks that are common to these applications.

TIP *From now on, when you need to know what application to use for a specific task, this chapter will be a good resource.*

Realize What Applications and Utilities Come with Your Mac

Apple has loaded your Mac with tons of useful applications already. Everything you need for basic daily computer usage is ready and waiting for you to discover. Let's get down to brass tacks with a tour of the Applications and Utilities folders and a very brief description of what each application and utility can be used for.

Applications

The following list identifies and describes the applications that come preinstalled on your Mac:

- ▓ **Address Book** This is one of those self-explanatory titles I mentioned. Obviously, you can keep all the important contact information you need for friends, family, and associates, but the neat thing about Address Book is that all of those contacts can be accessed by many other applications, such as email and calendar programs. Chapter 9 covers Address Book in more detail.

- ▓ **Automator** Automator does what it says: it automates things for you. Using scripts, called Workflows, that you can easily create, Automator performs repetitive tasks automatically for you, which can be a huge timesaver. For example, you could create a Workflow that tells Automator to rename a big batch of files all at once, create a Workflow to copy particular types of files to a central location, and so forth. Whatever repetitive tasks you find yourself constantly performing, now's the time to stop and let Automator do the work for you.

Calculator   Betcha can't guess what this does! Calculator crunches your numbers for you, either in Basic, Scientific, or Programmer mode. You can even use the Paper Tape feature that functions similarly to an old-fashioned adding machine tape, without the little curled up pieces of paper, of course.

 Chess   This is Apple's take on the game of all classic games. You can compete against another player or your Mac, and can even change the level of your Mac's playing skill. Chess also lets you speak your moves using your Mac's built-in microphone.

 Dashboard   Use Dashboard's Widgets to perform all kinds of tasks quickly and easily. Chapter 3 covered Dashboard in much detail.

 Dictionary   Can't quite come up with that certain word that says it all? Dictionary is for you, but this one doesn't weigh a ton or take up half your desktop when you open it, unlike its hardback cousin. Dictionary also includes a thesaurus.

 DVD Player   Watch your favorite movies from the comfort and safety of your trusty Mac's beautiful screen. Don't forget the popcorn!

 Exposé   Organize, hide, or show your open windows with ease. Chapter 3 discussed Exposé.

 Font Book   Some of you may be saying, "I know what a book is, but what the heck is a font?" Well, according to the aforementioned Dictionary program, a font is "a set of type of one particular face and size." See how handy these applications are? Anyway, Font Book allows you to easily manage the fonts that reside on your Mac.

 iCal   Keep all your appointments and never forget an important date by using iCal to organize your daily tasks. iCal can even publish calendars to a website so that you can share your calendars with others. There's much more on iCal in Chapter 9.

 iChat   Communicate with other computer users throughout the world with instant messaging, audio, or video chats. See Chapter 5 for details on how to use this neat application.

 iDVD   Create your own custom DVDs with iDVD. You can create menus and add titles and music, making your home movies look like you just rented them from your favorite movie store. iDVD is part of Apple's iLife suite of applications, which may or may not have been included with your Mac.

 Image Capture   Image Capture is the application you use to get images from scanners, and can be used to get individual pictures from your camera.

 iMovie   If you have a digital video camera and love to make your own home movies, iMovie will soon take the place of your dog as your best friend! iMovie allows you to easily make and edit your own home movies, even adding special effects, music, and credits if you like. iMovie is another member of Apple's iLife applications suite. More on iMovie in Chapter 13.

iPhoto   Keep all your photos organized and even edit them if you need, using iPhoto. You can also order bound books of your pictures within this great program. iPhoto is another of the great applications included with the iLife suite created by Apple. Chapter 11 will give you the complete skinny on iPhoto.

 iSync   Your list of contacts may vary between different devices such as your Mac and your cell phone. iSync will synchronize those devices so that you can keep current and accurate information. See Chapter 9 for more on iSync.

 iTunes   iTunes is your Mac's music hub. You can buy music, play music, share music, and burn your music to CDs with iTunes. But wait, that's not all! iTunes is fast becoming an all-encompassing entertainment application, because you can also use it to buy movies and television shows to view on your iPod, as well as watch movie trailers, music videos, and much more. We'll cover iTunes in much more detail in Chapter 12.

 iWeb   You can create your own webpages with incredible ease with iWeb. iWeb is one of the applications included in Apple's iLife suite, and you must have a .Mac account to publish your webpages.

 Mail   Mac OS X's default email application is Mail. Much more information on Mail is provided in Chapters 5 and 17.

 Photo Booth   Use Photo Booth to take funky pictures of yourself, using your Mac's built-in camera.

 Preview   Preview is a really nifty application that can open all sorts of files, including PDFs and picture files of all sorts (JPEG, TIFF, GIF, and so on), and can take screenshots (pictures of your computer's screen).

 QuickTime Player   Use QuickTime to watch movies and listen to music. Chapter 10 will render more information about QuickTime.

 Safari   The web browser of choice for your Mac, Safari makes surfing the Web a breeze. See Chapter 5 for more details.

 Spaces   Organize your work into separate spaces. Spaces was covered in more detail in Chapter 3.

 Stickies   Most of us have used sticky notes at some point or another. The Stickies application is just a digital version of the tried and true sticky note. Use it to quickly jot down to-do lists, phone numbers, or anything else you need to quickly take note of.

 System Preferences   This is what you use to make your Mac behave the way you want it to. See how in Chapter 14.

 TextEdit   TextEdit is a very basic text editing application (much like WordPad, for you newly converted Windows users).

 Time Machine   Back up and restore your Mac's files and folders with incredible ease. Chapter 24 will give you all the details of using this revolutionary program.

Utilities

The following are the utilities that come preinstalled on your Mac:

 ■ **Activity Monitor**   Fittingly, Activity Monitor monitors your Mac's activity. When it's running, Activity Monitor shows you what functions are running on your Mac and how much of the computer's performance power is being used by those functions.

 ■ **AirPort Disk Utility**   You can connect hard disks to your AirPort base station so that all Macs on your network can access them. AirPort Disk Utility discovers those disks and helps connect to them.

 ■ **AirPort Utility**   Use AirPort Utility to set up your AirPort Extreme base station with amazing simplicity. If you've ever used any other wireless routers in the past, you will truly appreciate the ease with which you can set up your connections with AirPort Utility. More details on AirPort Utility are offered in Chapter 15.

 ■ **Audio MIDI Setup**   Configure the audio input and output devices you use with your Mac by using Audio MIDI Setup. These devices may be speakers, keyboards, or even an electric guitar, using an array of different connection types, including FireWire and USB.

 ■ **Bluetooth File Exchange**   This handy utility lets you use your Mac's built-in Bluetooth adapter to wirelessly communicate with other Bluetooth-enabled devices, such as cell phones, printers, and PDAs.

 ■ **Boot Camp Assistant**   This little beauty helps you to effortlessly set up a Microsoft Windows partition on your Mac. Boot Camp only works with Intel-based Macs. Chapter 18 covers all the gory details.

 ■ **ColorSync Utility**   ColorSync is the technology Apple created that delivers the beautiful colors you see on your screen. ColorSync Utility manages color profiles for your Mac and any other device you may use with it, such as a printer or scanner. If accurate color matching is important to you, get to know ColorSync.

 ■ **Console**   Your Mac keeps a log, or journal, of all its applications' comings and goings. Console allows you to access and read these logs, which can prove quite helpful when troubleshooting system or application problems.

 ■ **DigitalColor Meter**   This one's fun to play with for the average user, but clearly has the graphics professional in mind. Use DigitalColor Meter to measure colors on your Mac's screen, and then use the data to match the colors in graphics applications.

 ■ **Directory**   If you work in an office environment, chances are good that you have a directory server that you use to access contacts and other group services. Directory allows Mac users to access that information on those servers. You must use Directory Utility to set up your access servers before using Directory.

 ■ **Directory Utility**   Use this utility to set up your Mac so that it can access your company's or organization's directory servers with Directory.

Disk Utility   Disk Utility is a toolbox for your Mac's internal and external drives. You use it to repair damaged files on your disks, to erase disks, to burn files to CDs or DVDs, and to create disk images. Disk Utility is covered in depth in Chapter 23.

 Grab   Grab is used to take captures, or screenshots, of anything displayed on your screen. You can take a screenshot of the entire desktop or a single window, take a timed shot of the screen, or draw a box around a particular area on the screen you want to capture. Many of the figures and illustrations throughout this book were taken with Grab.

 Grapher   Create two-dimensional and three-dimensional graphs with this utility. Grapher has the seriously math-oriented Mac user in mind.

Java   The Java folder contains three utilities for getting the most of Java-based applications. Java is a cross-platform programming language, meaning that any computer running the Java Runtime Environment can use any program written in Java. Java is available as a download for all computer platforms, but Mac OS X incorporates Java as a native, or built-in, part of the operating system.

 Keychain Access   Store your passwords and other sensitive information in a central location with Keychain Access.

 Migration Assistant   This is one fantastic utility for transferring all the important information, such as user accounts, files, and computer settings, from another Mac to this one. If you are using an older Mac and want to move all your stuff from it to your new one, Migration Assistant will be your hero for the day. This is the simplest way to set up a new computer for established Mac users.

 Network Utility   Network Utility gives you a graphical user interface to lots of tools used to monitor your network's activity that normally would have to be typed in from a command line. This is a great tool for the lazy geek who likes to pass his or her down time by observing the traffic on their network.

 ODBC Administrator   ODBC stands for Open Database Connectivity, which is a standard protocol for accessing databases. If you regularly use your company's databases, ask your IT administrator for help configuring this utility.

 Podcast Capture   This is a utility for recording and distributing podcasts from your Mac. Podcasts are audio files that iPod users can download and listen to. To use Podcast Capture, you must have another Mac that has Mac OS X Server installed and running a program called Podcast Producer.

 RAID Utility   RAID stands for "Redundant Array of Inexpensive Disks," which is a fancy way of saying you can group together two or more disks so that they act as one single disk. RAID Utility makes the process of creating a RAID easy, but it only works on Macs that have a RAID card installed; the RAID card is an option only on Mac Pro models and Apple's Xserve, which is an enterprise server solution. In other words, if you aren't a geekazoid, you shouldn't pay this utility any mind.

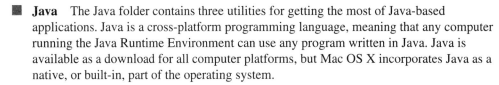

■ **System Profiler**   This is "information central" for your Mac. System Profiler will tell you everything there is to know about your Mac's hardware and peripherals, in one handy location.

 ■ **Terminal**   Terminal is a command-line application that will make UNIX nerds immediately feel at home in Mac OS X. Windows converts are probably somewhat familiar with DOS, which is also utilized via a command line, so Terminal won't be an entirely foreign environment to you. However, if you are an old-school Mac OS 7 aficionado, you might slowly, but surely, lose your mind, because no matter how many times you click that blasted blinking cursor, nothing happens! Look at the cursor, just sitting there, blinking incessantly and mocking you! You may actually be forced to use your keyboard to type in a command.

 ■ **VoiceOver Utility**   VoiceOver is another way of navigating the Mac OS X interface, for those users with visual impairment or other reasons for needing to hear what's on the screen. VoiceOver describes for the user exactly what's on the screen, and can read aloud any text the user points the mouse cursor over. This utility sets the preferences for the VoiceOver technology.

 ■ **X11**   Your Mac can also run UNIX applications along with Mac OS X programs. There are GUI UNIX applications that use the X Window System to give the applications an interface similar to their equivalent Mac or Windows applications. Run X11 to use these X Window System applications.

Find Common Ground for Mac OS X's Applications

There are some common tasks shared by most applications that you would do well to familiarize yourself with. Learning these common tools of the trade can make it easier to adjust to any application. For consistency's sake, you may want to use TextEdit (you used it earlier, in Chapter 3) as your test application.

Launch an Application

Launching, or opening, an application is very simple: just double-click the application's icon. Applications are typically located in the Applications directory at the root of the hard drive (Hard Drive | Applications). An even easier way to get to the Applications folder is to choose Go | Applications while in the Finder. The Go menu can take you to lots of other places quickly, too; give it a look.

> **NOTE**   *Your Mac's hard drive can be named anything you like. For demonstration purposes, I will refer to your Mac's hard drive generically as "Hard Drive" throughout the book.*

If you keep an icon for the application you want to open in the Dock, simply click its icon once to open it. An application is already running if its Dock icon has a small arrow underneath it.

Find More Details about the Application

Sometimes you may need to know a bit more about the application you are using than just its name. Knowing the version of the application can be very beneficial when troubleshooting problems or when deciding on upgrade options at a future date. To see this information and more, click the application's menu next to the Apple logo in the top left of the screen, and choose About *Application Name*. The application's menu has the same name as the application; for instance, if you are using TextEdit, the application's menu will be called TextEdit. This also helps you easily see what application you are currently working in.

Set Your Application's Preferences

Every application is set by its developer to work a certain default way from the start, but developers are usually nice enough to give you, the end user, the power to change some of these behaviors and appearances. You can see what changes you can make by clicking the application's menu and choosing Preferences. As an example, Figure 6-1 shows the TextEdit Preferences pane; here, you can change the way TextEdit creates new documents, opens documents, or saves them by changing its preferences.

The preferences pane is different for each application. I cover making changes to the preferences of some of these applications in upcoming chapters; for those I don't cover, you need to consult the application's documentation for help if you don't know what the various options are for.

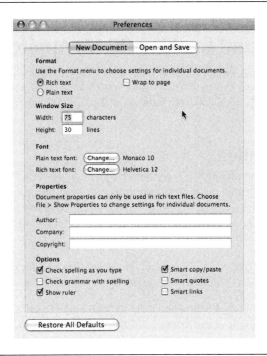

FIGURE 6-1   Preferences for TextEdit

Create a New Document

Most applications such as word processors (Pages, TextEdit, Microsoft Word, OpenOffice.org Writer), spreadsheet programs (Microsoft Excel, OpenOffice.org Calc), page layout applications (Quark QuarkXPress, Adobe InDesign), and others enable you to create new documents. Some applications prompt you to open a new document when they first launch, but if not, follow these easy instructions.

The typical method for opening a new document is to open the File menu and choose New or New Document (⌘-N is the usual keyboard shortcut). Some applications may be slightly different, so you need to consult the documentation that came with the application for specific instructions.

Select, Cut, Copy, and Paste Items

Moving items such as text and pictures from one document to another is an extremely common task. An example would be if someone emailed you a webpage address, also known as a link, to an interesting article, but you just don't know what to do with it. You could manually type the address in your web browser's address field, but if it's a long address you might be there all day, switching back and forth between your email application and your web browser to see what the next few letters or numbers in the address are. (Just reading that last sentence was tedious enough, never mind actually performing such a mind-numbing task!) The easiest way to access that link is to simply click the link itself, if you're using Mac OS X's default email program, Mail; this action will automatically open Safari, Mac OS X's web browser, to the webpage the link is pointing to.

However, sometimes a link may not be clickable, possibly due to the email being formatted as plain text. For such cases, there's an amazing technique (heavy sarcasm intended) called "copy and paste" that has made human coexistence with computers go pretty smoothly for a couple of decades now. Before teaching you the power of copy and paste, you must first learn to select the items you want to subject to your newly discovered talents.

For this example, we'll use TextEdit again. Open a new document and type **www.apple.com** on the new page. Follow these steps to select that text, copy it, and then paste it into Safari's address field, ultimately accessing Apple's outstanding website:

1. To select the text, click the space immediately in front of the first letter being copied, continue to hold down the mouse button and drag over the entire line of text, and then release the mouse button. You've now highlighted the text, as indicated by the light-blue color surrounding the text.

2. Right-click (or CTRL-click) the highlighted text and choose Copy or Cut from the list of options. The Copy command copies the text to the clipboard yet leaves the text in the original document; Cut moves the text to the clipboard and deletes it from the original document. While you can't see the contents of the clipboard, rest assured that your Mac knows what's there, and it's waiting for you to do something with the clipboard contents.

3. Open Safari and triple-click (three rapid clicks) the address field to highlight all the text it contains, and then press the DELETE key to remove it.

4. Right-click (or CTRL-click) the address field and choose Paste, and then press ENTER to see Apple's website. Behold the wonder of Copy and Paste!

> *I'm going to beat the keyboard shortcuts drum again! You can perform the exact same tasks with a few simple keystrokes and save your mouse (and wrist) the mileage. To select all the text in a document, press ⌘-A. To copy the selected text, press ⌘-C; to cut the text, press ⌘-X; and to paste the text, press ⌘-V (the more intuitive ⌘-P couldn't be used for Paste because it was already taken by Print).*

Save Documents

After expending hours of blood, sweat, and tears pouring over a sales plan or your monthly budget, you certainly don't want to accidentally lose all that precious work. Saving your documents is one of your Mac's most important functions.

To save documents, click the File menu of the application you're working in and select Save or Save As (see Figure 6-2). Use the Save command to save changes you make to your documents. The Save As option can be used to create a new document from the one you are currently using. If you have not saved this particular document before, the Save command functions like Save As, and prompts you to specify where to save the file on your hard drive and what to name the file; of course, the choice of name and choice of where to save the document are entirely up to you. As shown in Figure 6-2, the keyboard shortcut for Save is ⌘-S; there usually isn't a shortcut for the Save As command.

> *Save early and save often! Don't wait until you've finished a document to save it; save your files often while working on them so that you won't lose all of your information in one fell swoop if the power goes out or you get abducted by aliens. The last thing you want to do after an intergalactic space flight is retype this week's entire grocery list.*

Open Documents

What good is saving your documents if you don't know how to open them? Thankfully, opening a document is one of the easiest things to do on your Mac. To open a file, just double-click it. That's it! When you save a file, part of the information contained in that file is the name of the

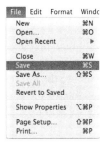

FIGURE 6-2   Saving a document

application that created it. Double-clicking the file causes the Mac to match the file with its parent application and open it up.

If you already have the application open in which you are going to open the file, instead of browsing your Mac's hard drive for the file in question, you can open it directly from within the application. Choose File | Open (or press ⌘-O), browse your hard drive for the file you need, and then double-click to open it.

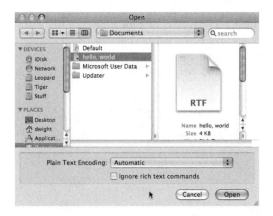

Occasionally, you may have a file you created in one application, but need to open it within a different application for whatever reason. For example, perhaps you don't have the particular application that your colleague created a file in, but you still need to open that file and edit its contents. Many applications use proprietary file types, meaning that files created in those applications can be opened only by those applications, but some applications use file types that are more universal in nature and can be used by several different applications. For example, let's say the aforementioned file sent to you by your colleague was created in Microsoft Word, but you don't have Microsoft Word installed on your Mac. Luckily you have the formidable TextEdit on your trusty Mac, which can open, edit, and create Word-compatible files. To open this Word file in TextEdit, right-click (or CTRL-click) the file and hold your mouse over the Open With menu; your Mac will present you with a list of applications that can open this type of file. Click TextEdit and the Word document will open in TextEdit.

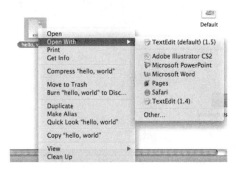

Print Documents

While the world of digital documents is certainly cool and beneficial, still nothing beats the printed word. Putting ink (or toner) to paper is still the way to go for most people, businesses, and organizations. Macs are known far and wide for their printing capabilities, but we won't get our hands too dirty with printing until Chapter 8. For now, simply knowing how to quickly print a file will suffice.

1. Open a document, email, webpage, picture, or whatever you would like to print. It's always wise to check the size of the paper your Mac is about to print on first, so choose File | Page Setup. Make sure to choose the correct paper size for your job (typically Letter, or 8.5 × 11 inches), and then click OK.

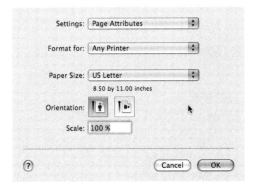

2. Choose File | Print (or press ⌘-P), and then click the Print button in the bottom right of the dialog box.

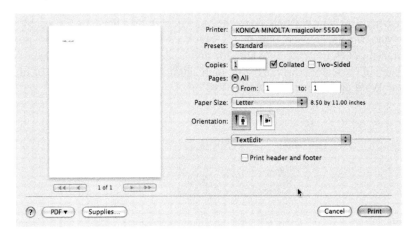

Assuming everything goes smoothly, you will soon be rewarded with a hard copy of your file. Happy printing!

Quit Applications

It's the end of the day and time to wrap things up before heading to the homestead, so you start quitting the applications you've been working with. But what's this? The application's icon is still in the Dock and the glowing dot beneath it tips you off that it's still running. Most likely, you only clicked the red dot in the upper-left corner of the document's window you were using, which only closes that particular window and doesn't shut down the application (there are rare exceptions to this rule).

To properly close the application, choose File | Quit (or press ⌘-Q). If you have any documents open at the time, you may be prompted to save them before the application completely shuts itself down. You can also quit an application by clicking its icon in the Dock, continue holding down the mouse button until a menu pops up, and then select Quit.

> TIP
>
> *It's not necessary that you quit applications every time you finish using them, but it does keep down the clutter in your Dock. Also, some applications, such as Photoshop, may take up a large portion of your Mac's memory when they are running; if you don't have much memory on your Mac to begin with, quit the application to free up that memory. However, keeping a frequently used application open prevents waiting through its entire startup process every time you need to use it, which, for some applications, may take quite a while.*

Identify Basic Application Commands

On the following page is a handy list of the most common basic commands used in applications. Not all applications support each of these commands, or they may not use the same keyboard shortcuts.

Key Combination	Function
⌘-H	Hide the application
OPTION-⌘-H	Hide all other applications
⌘-N	Create a new document
⌘-O	Open a document or file
⌘-S	Save
⌘-SHIFT-S	Save As
⌘-P	Print
⌘-SHIFT-P	Page Setup
⌘-W	Close document
⌘-F	Find
⌘-G	Find Next
⌘-SHIFT-G	Find Previous
⌘-C	Copy
⌘-V	Paste
⌘-A	Select All
⌘-Z	Undo last action
⌘-M	Minimize window
OPTION-⌘-M	Minimize all windows
⌘-TAB	Switch between open applications
PAGE UP or CTRL-UP ARROW	Move up one page
PAGE DOWN or CTRL-DOWN ARROW	Move down one page
⌘-Q	Quit
⌘-COMMA	Preferences
⌘-OPTION-ESCAPE	Force Quit

Summary

Now that you understand the basics of working with most applications, there's not much you can't do on your Mac. These fundamentals are fairly universal and will help you use almost any application out there, if only for the bare minimum of the tasks it may be capable of. You've just taken some small steps into a much larger world of computing.

Chapter 7

I Work, You Work, We All Work with iWork

How to...

- Discover what iWork can do for you
- Learn the basics of word processing
- Create great presentations easily
- Use Numbers to build beautiful spreadsheets, graphs, and charts

You've probably heard that you should play at least as hard as you work. Well, with a Mac, that saying gets turned around a bit: your work should be at least as fun as your play!

Macs are just as capable crunching numbers in an office environment, in the research field, in a science lab, or in a classroom as they are for downloading music, playing games, or editing movies in your home. Macs are every bit the workhorses their PC counterparts are, but with a twist: they're actually enjoyable to work with.

Apple has created a suite of applications designed to put your Mac to work, and together they are rightly called iWork. Three applications are currently included in this suite:

- **Pages**   A word processing program that combines ease of use with advanced graphics and layout features.
- **Keynote**   Helps you create some of the most stunning presentations you will ever see.
- **Numbers**   Presents a new way of building spreadsheets, Apple's way, which automatically means its gotta be pretty good.

iWork is included with every Mac on a trial basis, and can be purchased from Apple for only $79 as of this writing. Find and open the iWork folder in your Applications folder (Hard Drive | Applications) and you will find the icons for each of the apps in the suite.

> **NOTE**   *As a reminder, because you can name your Mac's hard drive anything you like, I refer to it generically as "Hard Drive" throughout the book.*

This is by no means an exhaustive tutorial on every function incorporated into iWork; that would be a different book entirely. This chapter is intended to give you the basics of each application in the suite so that you can get a taste of how well they function. iWork comes with a *Getting Started* manual (PDF) that covers a good bit more information than I cover here, and the iWork Help system is crammed with information. There are even tutorial videos available at www.apple.com/iwork/tutorials/. However, the best information can be found in the *User's Guides* for the applications, which are PDFs included on the iWork DVD.

Identify Common Tools

The applications in the iWork suite are designed to enable you to jump from one application to another without seeming to land in a foreign world each time. The toolbars of each application look almost identical to those of their siblings for this very reason. The following are four tools that are common to all three applications, the icons for which are located on the right side of the toolbar in each application:

■ **Inspector**   Open the Inspector by clicking its icon (a blue circle with an *i* in the middle of it). The top row of the Inspector window lists inspectors for different tasks, giving you most of the formatting tools for your document in one place. You can open multiple Inspector windows by holding down the OPTION key while clicking the Inspector icon in the top row for a particular task. This technique allows you to have multiple windows open, such as one for text and one for graphics, to gain quick and easy access to their tools.

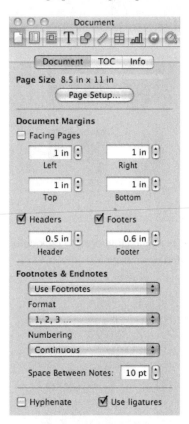

■ **Media**   Clicking the Media icon opens the Media Browser, allowing you to peruse the contents of your Mac for items such as photos, audio, and movies. You can add these elements to your documents by dragging-and-dropping them from the Media Browser window to where you want them to reside in your document.

■ **Colors** Clicking the Colors icon enables you to pick colors for your documents using the color wheel, sliders, palettes, or crayons.

■ **Fonts** Clicking the Fonts icon enables you to choose the fonts you want to use for your document.

Get to Know Pages

Pages is much more than just a word processor: it's a gift from above! Pages' expertise isn't limited to just being a word processor: it's also a page layout program. You can create a full-color travel brochure as easily as you can create a double-spaced book report. If you've ever used Microsoft Word, you will be blown away by how Pages does essentially the same job but with so much less effort. Pages is actually a pleasure to use due to its intuitive interface and the huge array of predesigned templates that make laying out a project nearly effortless.

Pages has two modes: word processing and page layout. Open Pages by double-clicking its icon in Hard Drive | Applications | iWork:

You are presented with a huge range of templates to choose from (see Figure 7-1). These templates are divided into the two modes just mentioned, and you should choose which mode best suits your needs.

Figure 7-2 gives a quick peek at a word processing window, and Figure 7-3 shows what a page layout window looks like.

As with every other application, knowing the functions of all the buttons and menus in Pages is a huge help. Figure 7-4 spells them all out for you.

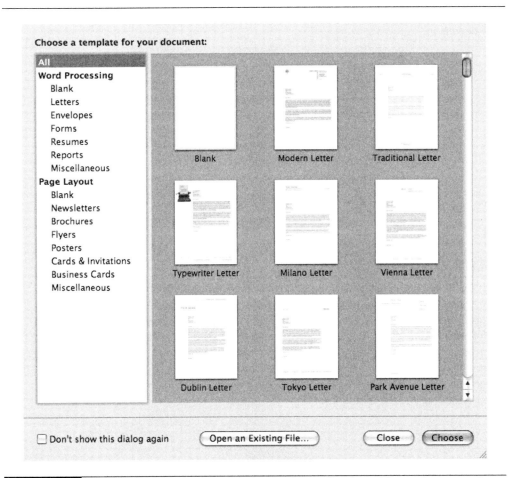

Choose a template for your document:

All
Word Processing
  Blank
  Letters
  Envelopes
  Forms
  Resumes
  Reports
  Miscellaneous
Page Layout
  Blank
  Newsletters
  Brochures
  Flyers
  Posters
  Cards & Invitations
  Business Cards
  Miscellaneous

Blank   Modern Letter   Traditional Letter

Typewriter Letter   Milano Letter   Vienna Letter

Dublin Letter   Tokyo Letter   Park Avenue Letter

☐ Don't show this dialog again   (Open an Existing File...)   (Close) (Choose)

FIGURE 7-1   Pages, like the rest of the iWork suite, is overflowing with templates to make your document-building experience the very best that it can be.

Use Templates

Templates are just another way that Apple makes your life so much easier. Why build a document from scratch when Apple has already done all the heavy lifting? Apple has already put text and pictures into the templates; these items are called *placeholders*. When you select a template, all you have to do is enter your own text and pictures where the placeholders are, and—voilà!—you have an instant document.

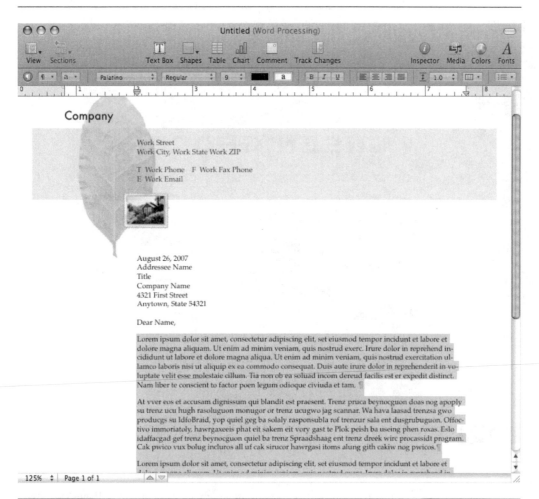

FIGURE 7-2   The Woodland Letter template

To replace placeholder text in a template, click the text you want to change and it will highlight. Type the text you want to insert and it will replace the highlighted text. Figure 7-2 in the previous section is a good example of a letter template; the highlighted text is about to be replaced by my own remarks.

To replace the images in a template, such as the picture of the vegetables in Figure 7-3, simply drag the image you want to use from the Media Browser on top of the placeholder image. The new image takes on the size and settings of the placeholder.

FIGURE 7-3   The Green Grocery Newsletter template is a great example of Pages' layout capabilities.

Templates are great to use, and you could choose to never create a document in Pages without using a template to do it, but you wouldn't learn much about the application because most of the work is already done for you. To get to know Pages a little better, you should open a blank document and enter the information using your own unique design, as described next.

Start from Scratch: Use a Blank Document

Let's build a basic document in Pages. To do so, choose File | New or press ⌘-N, select Blank from the template list, and click the Choose button; this opens a blank document, waiting for you to add something to it.

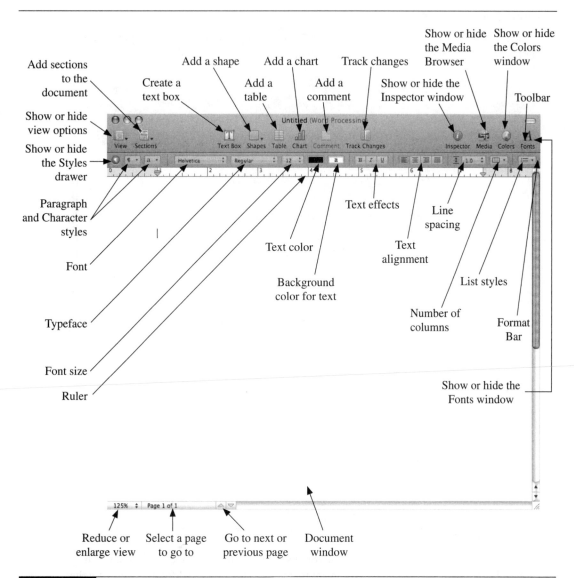

Add sections to the document

Create a text box

Add a shape

Add a table

Add a chart

Add a comment

Track changes

Show or hide the Inspector window

Show or hide the Media Browser

Show or hide the Colors window

Toolbar

Show or hide view options

Show or hide the Styles drawer

Paragraph and Character styles

Font

Typeface

Font size

Ruler

Text color

Background color for text

Text effects

Text alignment

Line spacing

Number of columns

List styles

Format Bar

Show or hide the Fonts window

Reduce or enlarge view

Select a page to go to

Go to next or previous page

Document window

FIGURE 7-4   The default Pages window is so deceptively simple it masks the surprising power of the application.

Enter and Format Text

The first item you need to add is a little text, which is oh so simple to do: just start typing. Enter whatever text you want, but keep it clean; this is a family book.

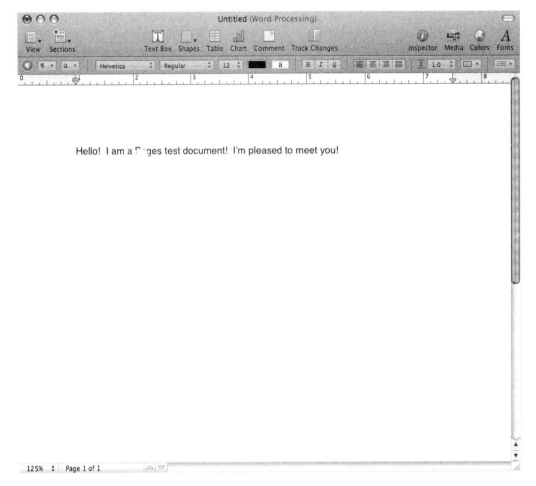

What's the matter? Not happy with the font you just used for the text? Well, then change it. To perform this great feat, select the text you want to change and choose a different font from the huge list in the Format Bar, or click the Fonts icon in the toolbar to browse through Mac OS X's font list.

Don't like the changes you just made? No need to worry; you can undo any changes by choosing Edit | Undo Change or by pressing ⌘-Z. If you then decide that you liked your change after all, just redo the change by choosing Edit | Redo Change or by clicking ⌘-SHIFT-Z.

To make your text really stand out, you should add a little color to it. Select the text you want to work with, click the text color button in the Format Bar (refer to Figure 7-4), and then choose the color you like from the palette provided, as shown here.

Use Styles

Styles are formats that have been preconfigured for different types of text entries, such as paragraphs or individual characters. Paragraph styles can modify only entire paragraphs, while character styles can only change individual words or letters.

The Styles drawer button is located on the far left of the Format Bar (refer to Figure 7-4). Click the Styles drawer button and the Styles drawer will "pop out" on the right side of the Pages window. This drawer shows the available styles for paragraphs, character, and lists.

To use a Style, select the text you want to apply the style to, and then choose a style from the list in the Style drawer. You can also apply Styles to text by clicking the paragraph style button or character style button in the Format Bar and choosing a paragraph or character style.

Place Graphics and Pictures in Your Document

Nothing jazzes up a document like adding photos, audio, movies, and graphics, such as color charts and boxes. They give a document instant "pop," and up the reader's interest quotient exponentially. Pages refers to these kinds of files as *objects*.

Adding these objects to a Pages document is ridiculously simple. Drag-and-drop an object from your Mac's folders or Desktop directly onto the area of the document that you want it placed. That's all you need to do, unless you want to format the object.

Notice the small boxes around the border of the picture I've inserted into my document in Figure 7-5. These boxes are called selection handles, and they allow you to resize the picture by clicking-and-dragging any one of them.

To move the picture to a different location in the document, click-and-drag the center of the picture to move the picture to its new location.

Use Floating and Inline Objects

See how the text "flows" around the two pictures in Figure 7-5? The text flows around them because they are both floating objects, as opposed to inline objects.

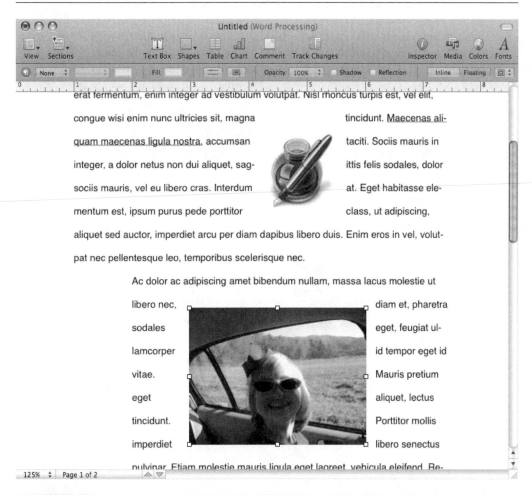

Placing and resizing objects in a Pages document is a snap!

An inline object is embedded in a sentence or paragraph and will move along with the text when characters are removed or added. Floating objects can be positioned anywhere at anytime, and remain stationery on the page regardless of what manipulations you make to the text around them.

To change an object from one type to the other, click the object to highlight it and then click either the Inline or Floating button in the Format Bar.

Add Shapes to Your Document

Shapes also add pizzazz to your document, especially because you can just type in them to add text. Click the Shapes button in the toolbar to see all the different shapes, shown here, that Pages provides.

Select a shape from the list and Pages automatically places it in your document. You can move shapes in the document just like an object, so click-and-drag the center of the shape to move the shape to where you need it. Also notice the selection handles; they work just like the selection handles for objects, allowing you to resize the shape.

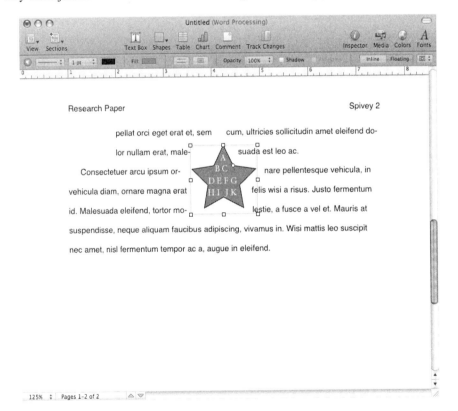

To put text into the shape, just click inside the shape and begin typing. Nothin' to it!

Save and Export Files

Save your documents by choosing File | Save (⌘-s) or File | Save As. The Save dialog box should look very similar to this one:

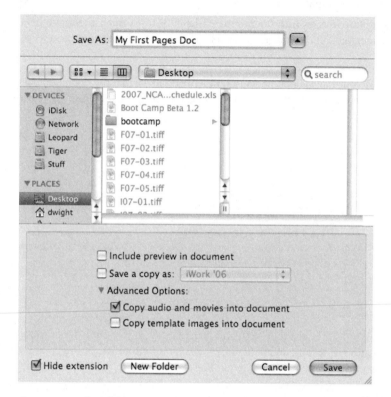

Give your document a descriptive name in the Save As field, choose where on your Mac to save the document, and then click Save. The are four options you can select at the bottom of the Save dialog box:

- ■ **Include preview in document**   Check this box to have a preview of your document saved with the file. This allows Quick Look to show you the contents of the entire document instead of just the first page of the file. This will increase your file's size but saves you time later when you want to preview the document.

- ■ **Save a copy as**   Check this box to save your document in such a way that it is backward compatible with older versions of iWork. This is helpful for sharing your documents with other users who may not have the version of iWork that you do.

- ■ **Copy audio and movies into document**   Check this box to add a full copy of audio and movie files to your Pages document. This is helpful for sharing the document with others, but it increases its file size. If you do not include these files in the document, part of its meaning and impact may be lost.

- ■ **Copy template images into document**   Check this box to ensure that others who open this document get all the images if you chose to use a template and keep its original images.

You can export your Pages documents into other formats so that the document can be opened by people who may not have iWork installed. Choose File | Export and you will be prompted to select from these options:

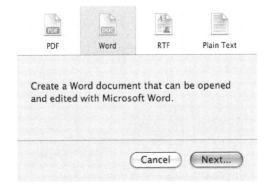

Choose PDF, Word, RTF, or Plain Text, and then click Next. Give the document a descriptive name, select a location to save it, and then click the Export button. Exporting creates a new document in the specified format; your original Pages document remains unchanged.

iWork Is Compatible with Microsoft Office

Documents you create in any iWork application can be exported to the corresponding Microsoft Office formats. Pages documents can be exported to Word files, Keynote to PowerPoint, and Numbers to Excel. What's even better is that iWork applications can also open Microsoft Office documents. iWork is backward compatible with all Office versions starting with Microsoft Office 2007.

To import these files into an iWork application, click File | Open or press ⌘-O, browse the Mac for the file you need, click to highlight it, and then click the Open button.

Get to Know Keynote

Keynote is, in my opinion, the best presentation software going. Creating presentations with Keynote is a breeze, and they are absolutely stunning! I've used the rest, but now I only use the best, and that's Keynote.

Use Keynote to make presentations for work, whether you are employed by a Fortune 500 megacorporation or are a one-person consulting firm trying to impress a new potential client. Teachers can grab their kids' attention with a media-rich presentation on the solar system. Students can add new dimensions to their school project reports with a snazzy slideshow created with Keynote. The software is rich enough for the staunchest professional and simple enough for a seventh-grader. Now that's versatility!

To open Keynote, double-click its icon in Hard Drive | Applications | iWork.

Figure 7-6 shows Keynote's default window, and the following list explains several of the toolbar options labeled in Figure 7-6:

- **New slide button**   Adds a new slide to the slideshow.
- **Slideshow Play button**   Plays the slideshow, beginning with the first slide selected in the Slide Organizer.

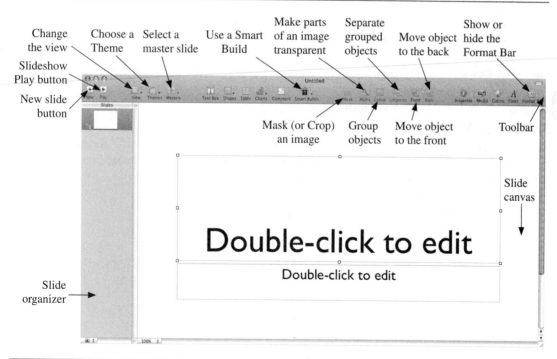

FIGURE 7-6   A new Keynote slideshow window, which shares many of the same options as Pages and Numbers

- **Change the view**   Pick which view to use when creating your slideshow, as well as what tools are visible in the window, such as Rulers and Comments.
- **Choose a theme**   You can change the theme of your slideshow instantly with the Themes button.
- **Select a master slide**   Choose which master to use for the slide you are currently working with. A master slide is a template, a preformatted slide complete with fonts, background colors, layouts, and so forth.
- **Use a Smart Build**   Smart Builds are preconfigured animations you can select to add a little "bada-bing" to your slideshow.
- **Mask an image**   "Masking" an image is the same as cropping it: trimming the image so that only the part you need is visible.
- **Make parts of an image transparent**   This tool lets you change elements of a photo to a transparency, making it invisible. For instance, you could use this tool to eliminate your spouse's old boyfriend or girlfriend from their high school dance picture.
- **Group objects**   This tool lets you choose several objects to manipulate as a single object, such as a group of photos that you want to move from one area of the slide to another.
- **Separate grouped objects**   Stating the obvious, this is exactly the opposite of "Group objects." This option ungroups grouped objects so that they can be manipulated apart from one another.
- **Slide Organizer**   This pane enables you to select a slide to edit, or rearrange the order of slides in the slideshow by clicking-and-dragging them into place.

Create a New Slideshow

If you are just opening Keynote, you are prompted to choose a template from the list. If Keynote is already open, choose File | New or press ⌘-N to open a new blank template, or choose File | "New from Theme Chooser" to see the list of templates again.

Select the theme you'd like to use, choose the size of the slides, and then click Choose. Your new slideshow window appears, displaying the first slide in your slideshow (see Figure 7-7).

TIP *The size of your slides should match the resolution of the device on which the slideshow will be presented.*

Edit your slides by entering your information in the text and image placeholders, exactly as you would in Pages. For text, double-click the placeholder and type the text you want to appear there, and for images, drag-and-drop the picture or graphic that you want into an image placeholder.

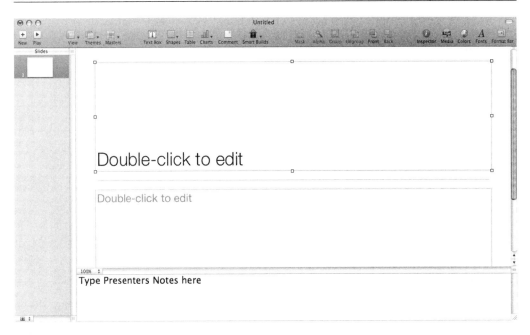

FIGURE 7-7   A new slideshow ready to be edited, shown with the Presenter Notes field

How to ...   Use Presenter Notes in Your Slideshow

Presenter Notes are items you want to mention to your audience during your presentation. When you show your presentation to others by using an external device, such as a projector, the Presenter Notes are only visible to you on your Mac, and not to them.

If the Presenter Notes field doesn't open automatically when you create a new slideshow, you can open it by choosing View | Show Presenter Notes. Of course, feel free to enter into the field whatever information you need to impart to your audience.

Add New Slides

No slideshow worth its salt is only one slide in length, so add a few to spice things up. To add new slides to the slideshow, click the New (+) button on the far left of the toolbar.

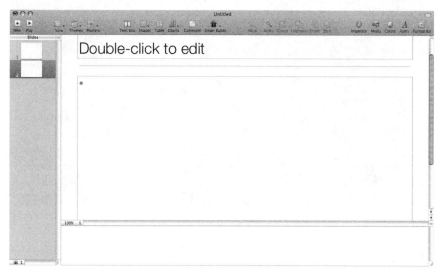

Keynote adds slides according to which master slide you have selected in the toolbar. Click the Masters button to see the wide range of preconfigured slides, some of which contain only text or images, and others that contain a combination, each with its own design layout. Each theme in keynote contains a family of master slides for you to choose from.

Select a different master slide for the new slide you just created to add some "oomph!" to the slideshow.

Edit Text and Objects

As mentioned before, manipulating text and objects in Keynote is as easy as it is in Pages. Type your own text into the text placeholders and format it using the Format Bar or the Text Inspector.

You can add audio, photos, and movies to any slide in Keynote, but if the slide already has an image placeholder, you can drag-and-drop the media onto the placeholder from the Finder or the Media Browser. Remember, when you add an item to a placeholder, the item automatically conforms to the settings of the placeholder, such as its size and shape.

Slides can also contain tables and charts that you've created in Keynote, Pages, or Numbers. To add a chart or table from within Keynote, simply click the Charts or Table button in the toolbar, choose the style you wish to use, and then edit it as needed using the Chart or Table Inspector, respectively.

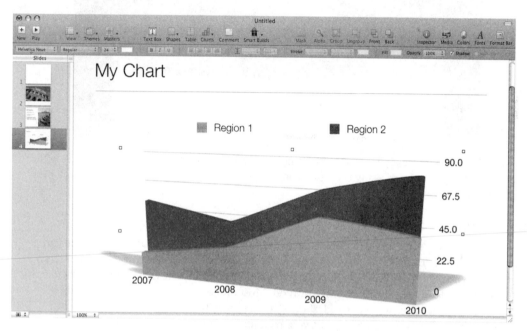

Play, Save, and Share Your Slideshow

Save your slideshow by pressing ⌘-s or choosing File | Save. Give the slideshow a descriptive name, browse your Mac for the location you wish to save the file to, and then click Save.

Play Your Slideshow

Before showing your slideshow to the world you want to make sure that everything is just right. To preview your slideshow, or to present it to your audience, click the Play button on the left side of the toolbar. By default, your slideshow opens in full-screen mode.

To advance to the next slide, click the mouse button or the button on your trackpad. Stop the slideshow at any time by pressing Q or ESC. You can go back to a previous slide by pressing the LEFT ARROW key.

Export Your Slideshow

Keynote is nothing if not flexible. For instance, the number of other formats in which you can export your slideshow borders on overkill. Export your slideshows into one of these formats so that others who don't have Keynote or other presentation software can view them: QuickTime, PowerPoint, PDF, Images, Flash, HTML, or iPod. Most of the format options have several settings to configure to ensure your slideshow's smooth transition.

Choose File | Export to save a copy of your slideshow in one of the aforementioned formats. Select the format you need to export to, make any configuration settings you want, and click Next.

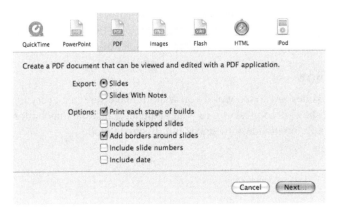

Assign the file a name, select an export location, and then click Export. You now can share the slideshow with others who have the application to which you exported the slideshow.

Get to Know Numbers

Numbers is the newest sibling in the iWork family, and has also been one of the most anticipated. Numbers makes iWork a fully functional suite of applications that is suitable for implementation in any office environment.

Numbers has one task in this life, and that is to create impressive spreadsheets using the data you give it. It carries out its mission in the same manner as Pages and Keynote: with cold, calculated ease and efficiency, with a splash of "Wow!"

NOTE *A spreadsheet helps you to arrange data in an organized fashion through the use of columns, rows, cells that contain the data, and formulas that calculate the numbers in the cells. You can present the information in a spreadsheet via tables or charts that easily arrange the data into a visual presentation.*

To open Numbers, double-click its icon in Hard Drive | Applications | iWork.

The layout of Numbers main window, shown in Figure 7-8, is intuitive enough for even a "first-time spreadsheeter" to handle. The following list describes the Numbers elements identified in Figure 7-8:

- **Add a sheet** Organize a Numbers spreadsheet by using multiple sheets to group information, such as creating new sheets for each day of the month so that the data can be viewed on a daily basis.

- **Select view options** Show or hide items that you choose in the main window, such as rulers.

- **Choose a Formula** Select a precompiled formula, or create and edit your own formulas by using the Formula Editor.

- **Format Bar** The Format Bar differs a good bit from those in Pages and Keynote. The tools are specifically geared to the building of great spreadsheets and let you quickly change commonly used formats, such as currency and percentage.

- **Formula Bar** Create and change formulas for the cell you are currently working in.

- **Sheets pane** Navigate the sheets in your spreadsheet easily by clicking the one you need.

- **Styles pane** Select one of the preconfigured styles for your spreadsheet from this pane.

- **Tables** Choose the kind of table you want to use from the list.

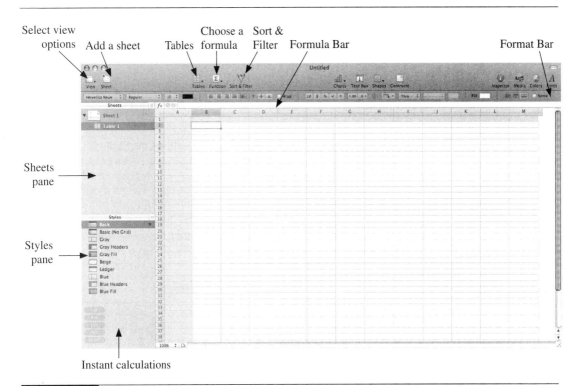

Select view options
Add a sheet
Tables
Choose a formula
Sort & Filter
Formula Bar
Format Bar

Sheets pane

Styles pane

Instant calculations

FIGURE 7-8   The Numbers interface is surprisingly simple for a spreadsheet application, but is extremely powerful.

■ **Sort & Filter**   Use to sort data in cells you've selected. Click this icon in the toolbar to set the sorting and filtering options. Click the + and – buttons, respectively, to add and remove sorting and filtering criteria.

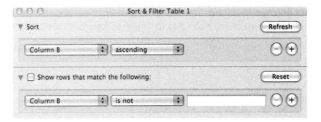

■ **Instant calculations**   Select a group of cells and Numbers will automatically calculate several formulas using their data. For instance, the Sum calculation shows the results of adding the numbers in the selected cells.

Create a Sample Spreadsheet

There are business professionals who have used spreadsheets for years and still don't command a total mastery of them, so I certainly won't make you a spreadsheet guru in the next few paragraphs. But I can give you a feel for how a basic spreadsheet is created and help demystify what may seem to some to be a daunting task at best.

Select a Template

As is the case for the other two iWork applications, Numbers presents you with a slew of preconfigured spreadsheet templates to choose from. Select a template from the Template Chooser window, which opens when you first start Numbers, or can be opened later by pressing ⌘-N or choosing File | New.

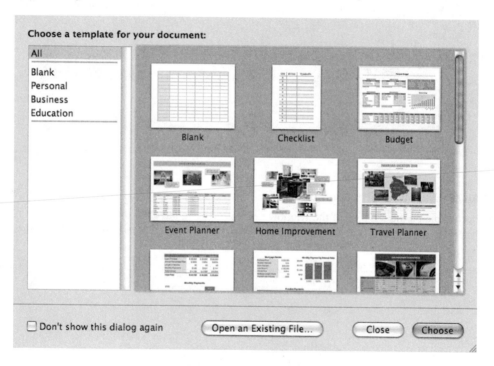

To follow along with the descriptions in the following sections, select the Budget template and click Choose. This opens the Budget template, which is already set up and ready to go.

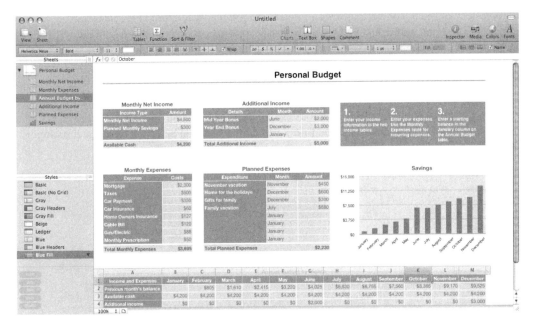

Organize Data with the Sheets Pane

The Sheets pane on the left side of the window helps you to organize the information in your spreadsheet. It also lists all tables and charts that are part of a sheet, which Figure 7-9 illustrates.

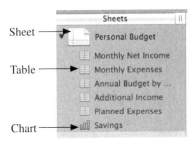

Elements of the Sheets pane

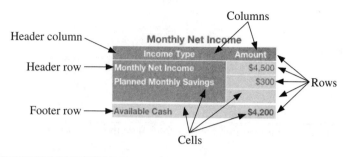

FIGURE 7-10   The anatomy of a table

Arrange Data with Tables

Tables neatly arrange data into categories separated by rows and columns, as shown in Figure 7-10, the upper-left table from the Budget template.

- **Header column**   Comprises the cell farthest to the left in each row. Header columns are used to label sets of data in their columns.

- **Header row**   Comprises the topmost cell in each column. Header rows are also used for naming sets of data in their respective rows.

- **Footer row**   Always the very bottom row, typically used for showing calculated values from the rest of the table.

- **Cells**   Any of the individual blocks in your spreadsheet. Enter data for your table into these cells and apply formulas to the cells if the cell's function will be to calculate values of other cells.

Work with Tables

Click the Monthly Net Income table name in the Sheets pane to highlight the table in the main window. You can also select the table directly within the main window by moving your mouse pointer around the outside edges of the table until the mouse pointer changes to a black arrow and a set of black directional arrows, and then clicking the mouse button to highlight the table. Resize and/or move the table by clicking-and-dragging the selection handles around it (see Figure 7-11).

Move your mouse pointer over the cells in the table and your pointer will change to a white plus sign (+) to indicate you are in cell-selection mode. Clicking any cell in the table puts you into edit mode (see Figure 7-12). Click a cell to highlight it, and then change any values necessary by using the keyboard to enter alphanumeric characters. Notice the table handle in each corner of the table; drag these handles to add rows and columns with super ease.

Selection handles

Drag any of the selection handles to change the size of the table.

Understand Formulas

Tables use formulas to calculate the values of other cells. To see the formula used by a cell, click the cell in the very bottom right of the Monthly Net Income table. The Formula Bar shows the formula that has been assigned to that cell, and even color-codes the values of other cells according to which part of the formula they affect (see Figure 7-13). I know the pictures in this book are black and white, but you can still tell by the shades of gray that there is a difference between the colors of cells B2 and B3. The color of Amount Monthly Net Income in the formula corresponds to the color of cell B2, and the color of Amount Planned Monthly Savings corresponds to the color of cell B3. This makes it even easier to tell which cell goes with which value in the formula.

The formula used to calculate the value of cell B5 is written as "=Amount Monthly Net Income —Amount Planned Monthly Savings," which means the same thing as the value in cell B2 minus the value in cell B3 equals the value in cell B5. Formulas can get much more complicated than this, of course, but this is a good example of how cells and formulas work with one another in a spreadsheet.

Table handles

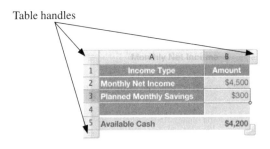

Edit cells by clicking them and entering new values, or add cells and columns by clicking-and-dragging the appropriate table handle.

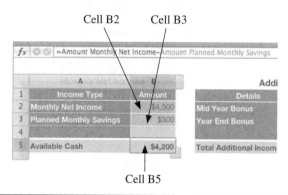

FIGURE 7-13 The Formula Bar displays the formula used to calculate the value of cell B5.

Use Charts

Charts are used to represent data in a table graphically. They are used to make more effective comparisons of data than can be achieved sometimes with just mere numerals.

The Budget template we are using has one chart already built into it: the Savings chart. The Savings chart is representative of the data in the Savings footer row of the Annual Budget by Month table, as Figure 7-14 shows.

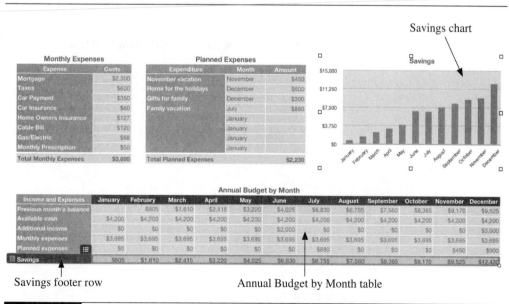

FIGURE 7-14 The data in the Savings chart graphically reflects data from the Annual Budget by Month table.

Make a Simple Spreadsheet from Scratch

You've learned the bare-bones basics of using a spreadsheet template, so now it's time to create a new spreadsheet from scratch. We'll make a small weekly expenses table to get you going. This is meant to be a very basic tutorial for making a simple spreadsheet, and not every function of Numbers is discussed.

Choose File | New and choose Blank for the template. Click the Tables button in the toolbar and select Plain from the list of options. Numbers inserts a new table at the bottom of the sheet.

Add Rows and Columns

Make the number of columns in our table eight and the number of rows five. Dragging the table handles is the simplest way to add rows and columns to your new table, as illustrated previously in Figure 7-12. However, you can add rows and columns using another method as well:

1. Run your mouse pointer over the rows in the table and click the arrow next to any of their numbers.

2. Choose Add Row Above or Add Row Below to add a row to the table, or choose Delete Row to remove it.

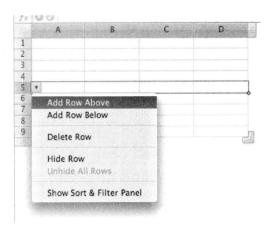

The same concept applies to adding and removing columns. Hold your mouse over one of the column headings, click the arrow that appears next to it, and then choose Add Column Before, Add Column After, or Delete Column.

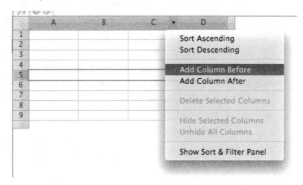

You can select multiple rows and columns by holding down the ⌘ key while clicking the desired items. An alternative to that method is to click the first row or column you want to edit or delete, hold down the SHIFT key, and then click the last row or column you want to manipulate; right-click or CTRL-click the selected items and choose the desired action from the list.

Next, add header columns, header rows, and footer rows by highlighting the table and then using the buttons on the right side of the Format Bar to add these items to the table.

Assign names to the header columns and rows and to the footer rows. To add text to the cells, double-click the cell and start typing. Mine looks like this:

	A	B	C	D	E	F	G	H	I
1	Expense	Monday	Tuesday	Wednesday	Thursday	Friday	Saturday	Sunday	Weekly Totals
2	Gas								
3	Groceries								
4	Doctor								
5	School								
6									
7	Totals								

Finally, give your table a name. Select the table, double-click Table 1 in the Sheets pane, and then enter the desired name for your table. To see the name appear above your table, check the Name box on the right side of the Format Bar.

Weekly Expenses

Expense	Monday	Tuesday	Wednesday	Thursday	Friday	Saturday	Sunday	Weekly Totals
Gas								
Groceries								
Doctor								
School								
Totals								

Add Data to Your Table

Your table won't be very useful until you enter data into it. For this example, the data you enter will be the dollar amounts spent for each expense item (gas, groceries, and so on) for every day of the week. Double-click the cells and enter each item's respective dollar amounts. Your table should look something like this:

	A	B	C	D	E	F	G	H	I
	Expense	Monday	Tuesday	Wednesday	Thursday	Friday	Saturday	Sunday	Weekly Totals
1	Gas	0	0	35	0	0	22	0	
2	Groceries	15	0	110	0	7	45	105	
3	Doctor	0	15	0	0	0	0	0	
4	School	3	0	0	12	0	0	0	
5									
6									
7	Totals								

Work with Your Data

You've got data now, but what do you do with it? The whole point of a spreadsheet is to compile the data into clear and meaningful information. Of course, you know what you spent for each item on each day, but what were the totals for each day and for the week as a whole? For this kind of calculation, you need to use formulas. There are three formulas you need so that the table can shape your data into something coherent:

- A formula that gives you the sum of each individual expense for the week
- A formula that calculates the total amount of money you have spent for each individual day
- A formula that gives you the total amount of money you have spent over the course of the entire week

Apple has done a great deal of the work for you by creating preconfigured functions. To create your first formula, click cell B7, which is where you want the total of Monday's expenditures to appear. Next, click the Function button in the toolbar and choose Sum.

Sum
Average
Minimum
Maximum
Count
Product
More Functions...

Formula Editor

This automatically creates a formula in cell B7 that adds the data in all other rows of the B column and displays the results in B7.

Weekly Expenses

Expense	Monday	Tuesday	Wednesday	Thursday	Friday	Saturday	Sunday	Weekly Totals
Gas	0	0	35	0	0	22	0	
Groceries	15	0	110	0	7	45	105	
Doctor	0	15	0	0	0	0	0	
School	3	0	0	12	0	0	0	
Totals	18							

For your second formula, you need to show the total amount that you spent for each item during the week. Click cell I2 to work with it, and then click the Function toolbar button and choose Sum again. This formula adds all data for row 2 under each column and displays the total in I2.

	A	B	C	D	E	F	G	H	I
1	Expense	Monday	Tuesday	Wednesday	Thursday	Friday	Saturday	Sunday	Weekly Totals
2	Gas	0	0	35	0	0	22	0	57
3	Groceries	15	0	110	0	7	45	105	
4	Doctor	0	15	0	0	0	0	0	
5	School	3	0	0	12	0	0	0	
6									
7	Totals	18							

The last formula gives the total money you paid for the week. Click the I7 cell, click the Function button, and choose Sum. This adds all the totals for each individual day in row 7 and displays the results in cell I7.

Create a Chart Using the Table's Data

Charts always liven up a spreadsheet, and our example spreadsheet certainly needs a little life pumped into it. To create a quick chart from your table, select the Weekly Expenses table in the Sheets pane, and then click the Charts button and click the first chart in the upper-left corner.

This action automatically creates a chart that shows all the data you entered for the week, and even color-codes it for you.

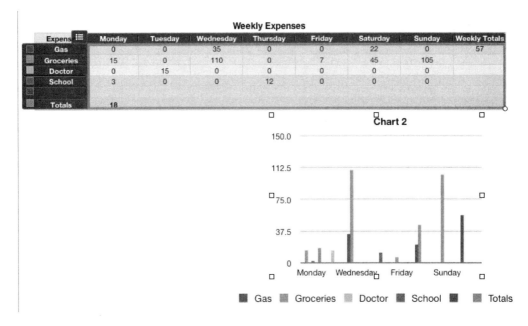

This is simply as easy as anyone can expect it to get. But let's not just leave it at easy, let's go for cool! Delete that chart and create another one using the Charts list. I selected this chart…

…and got this really neat result:

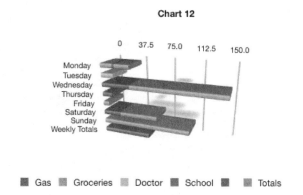

Chart 12

Continue to play with the chart options to see what neat creations you can come up with.

You now have a basic spreadsheet created from scratch. While this isn't the most detailed tutorial you will find (Apple has many more in their documentation and on the Web), this gives you an idea of how simple it is to use Numbers to create spreadsheets to organize all the data in your life.

Summary

This chapter barely scratched the surface of what the applications in iWork can do for you. Covering all the abilities of these three great apps is beyond the scope of this book, so you should certainly explore them further.

I believe there's not a better office suite available in terms of price and functionality. You may find the occasional Excel spreadsheet whose formatting doesn't quite translate perfectly in Numbers, or text may not be centered correctly after importing a Pages document into Word 2003, but those instances will not be commonplace. Give Apple some time and those kinds of issues will become almost extinct.

Happy iWorking, people!

Chapter 8

Start the Presses! Printing and Faxing Your Documents

How to...

- Decide what type of printer is best for your needs
- Know what cables you need for your printer
- Understand what a printer driver is used for
- Connect your printer to your Mac or your network
- Install printer drivers and set up your printer for use
- Select options for and manage your print jobs
- Make PDF files from your documents
- Fax from your Mac

You just used your Mac to create a shopping list for next week's vacation, but you can't lug your Mac with you from store to store (bummer, isn't it?). What to do? Well, if you have a printer, you can print that list and take it along. A sheet of paper is much lighter than your Mac, and it doesn't require a power cord or battery.

There was once, a very long time ago, a dream of the paperless office. The advent of computers was supposed to *decrease* our daily dependence on paper documents and shift the emphasis to digital documentation. Paper manufacturers everywhere rejoice that indeed the opposite occurred: paper consumption has gone through the roof! Of course, this doesn't bode well for environmentalists, but that's another subject for a different book and author.

Determine What You Need to Get Started

There are a few preliminary topics that we need to cover before you jump into printing files. Obviously, the first thing you need is a printer. Let's start there.

Inkjet or Laser Printer?

There are two major types of printers available for consumers: inkjet and laser printers. Which type of printer will best suit your needs? This section looks at each type individually, listing their pros and cons, so that you can make up your own mind.

Inkjet printers are more prevalent in homes and small businesses due to their very low initial cost point and wider availability. Inkjet printers are capable of producing beautiful, photo-quality output because they use ink, which produces richer color than the solid toner used in laser printers. However, the cost of ink is much higher than the cost of toner. While the initial purchase cost of an inkjet printer is very low, the cost of replacing the ink cartridges can be quite high, particularly if printing photographs is your forte. Potential problems with inkjet printers could include clogged heads on the cartridges and the potential to easily damage output with moisture.

Laser printers are great for printing documentation, but typically cannot produce the glossy color quality one might expect when printing photographs. Output from laser printers is of archival quality, and is, therefore, much more durable than output from inkjet printers. If you have an important contract for a client to sign, print it with a laser printer as opposed to an inkjet printer, or you risk the contract being damaged or destroyed if someone sneezes on it or spills coffee on it. The initial purchase cost of a laser printer, particularly a color model, is a good bit higher than that of an inkjet printer, but the cost of consumables (toner, drums, and so forth) will be less over the life of the device.

The bottom line is that if you absolutely need to print photographs that look like you just got them developed at a photo developer, stick with inkjet printer, but if you need to print manuals and business documents, a laser printer is your best bet. And don't forget: you can have more than one printer connected to your Mac at once, so you could have the best of both worlds by using a laser printer and an inkjet printer together.

If you need a printer to be used by multiple Macs, the best thing you can do is buy a printer with a network connection (a.k.a. Ethernet or RJ-45).

The Type of Cables You Need

The kind of cable you use to connect your printer depends first on what kind of cable the printer supports, and second on whether you are connecting the printer to a network or directly to your Mac. Most modern printers, inkjet and laser, support USB connections, but they typically don't ship with a USB cable, so you need to purchase one with your printer.

If you plan to connect your printer to a network, you most likely need to purchase an Ethernet (RJ-45) cable. Ethernet cables and their connectors look very much like oversized telephone cables. Some network routers, such as an Apple Airport, have USB ports, but most do not. If you have the option, always go with the Ethernet cable because it has better connection reliability.

Choose Print Media

You will certainly be up the creek without a paddle if you try to print without paper. Printers support various types of paper and paper sizes. Be sure that the media you purchase is compatible with your printer.

One major warning I would offer is to not run inkjet media in a laser printer unless the media specifies that it is laser-safe. Inkjet media may have a coating on it that will come off when subjected to the very high temperatures used in laser printers, which can ruin the printer.

Install Printer Drivers

Every device you connect to your Mac needs a driver. A printer driver is software that lets your Mac know how to talk to your printer, what kind of printer it is, and what features it supports. Without the proper drivers installed, your Mac may not print correctly to your printer, if it can print at all.

Mac OS X comes with a variety of preinstalled printer drivers from several major printer manufacturers. If drivers for your particular printer are already installed, you will have very little difficulty installing your printer. If drivers for your printer aren't already installed, check whether your printer included installation CDs or DVDs in the box; if so, they will handle the installation of the driver files for you automatically. If you still have problems, consult your printer manufacturer for instructions on finding and installing the driver files; you likely can download the drivers from the Web.

Be sure to install your printer's driver files before you connect the printer to your Mac or network. This greatly increases your chances for a successful installation on the first try. Installing the driver files does not complete the installation of your actual printer, though. That procedure is covered in the following section.

The Print & Fax Preferences Pane

Open System Preferences by choosing Apple | System Preferences. Click the Print & Fax icon to open the Print & Fax preferences pane (see Figure 8-1).

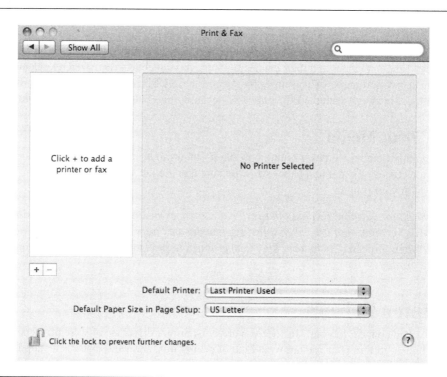

FIGURE 8-1   Print & Fax preferences pane

The Print & Fax preferences pane is printer central for your Mac, where all printer installations and communications are handled. From here you can add new printers, delete printers, check the status of print jobs, and change settings. Some printer drivers even allow you to communicate with the printer to view the consumables' levels, change the printer's internal settings, and order supplies.

Notice the + and – buttons in the lower left of the Print & Fax preferences pane. Clicking + opens the printer browser window, whose menu bar offers many different methods for installing printers. The methods we are concerned with in this section are the two most relevant and oft used: USB and network. To find out more about using the other installation methods, click the Help sign (the circled question mark) in the bottom-right corner of the Print & Fax preferences pane.

Install Your Printer

Have you decided how you are going to connect your printer yet, USB or network? If your printer only supports one connection type, your decision is a pretty simple one, but if you have the option, the decision can be tricky. Here are two questions and answers to help make your decision easier:

- Do you have only one Mac? If yes, USB is the simplest method.
- Do you have a network router? If yes, a network connection is your best bet, even if you have only one Mac.

Now that you've decided on your connection, let's start installing.

How to ...   Use USB Hubs

Some computer users like to utilize a USB hub, which provides extra external USB ports that a Mac otherwise doesn't have. Using a USB hub is similar to using an electrical extension cord in your home to gain several sockets from a single wall outlet. USB hubs are well and fine, until they don't work. Don't get me wrong, most USB hubs function perfectly for their entire lifespan. However, when the typical computer user begins having connection problems with devices on their USB hub, the hub is usually the last suspect when it should actually be the first. If you experience problems with your printer, or any other device, when connected to a USB hub, try connecting the printer directly to your Mac and see if the problem goes away. If it does go away when directly connected, the problem is the USB hub, not the printer or your Mac.

Connect Your Printer via USB

To connect your printer with USB, you need to have your USB cable handy, and you need to decide which USB port on your Mac to connect your printer to. Which port to use is a decision you will have to make on your own. Once you've decided on a port, go ahead and connect the printer to your Mac.

To install the printer on your Mac—that is, to make it available to all of your applications and users for their printing needs—click the + button in the lower left of the Print & Fax preferences pane (see Figure 8-1); this action opens the printer browser window, shown in Figure 8-2.

Click the Default tab in the upper-left corner, and you should see the name of your printer in the Printer Name column and USB in the Kind column. Click the printer's name to highlight it, and your Mac will "talk" to the printer to find out what information it can from it, such as what driver it should be using, whether it is a color or black-and-white device, and so forth. Notice the Print Using pop-up menu near the bottom of the printer browser window; it should reflect the manufacturer and model of your printer. If it does, click the Add button in the bottom-right

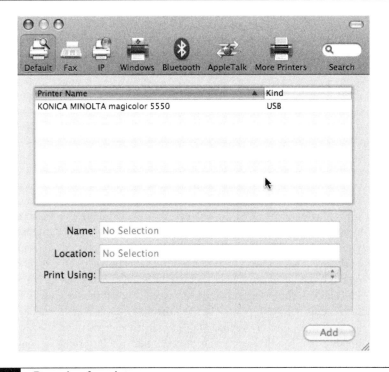

FIGURE 8-2   Browsing for printers

corner to complete your printer installation; if it does not, click the Print Using pop-up menu and manually choose the manufacturer and model, as shown next, and then click Add.

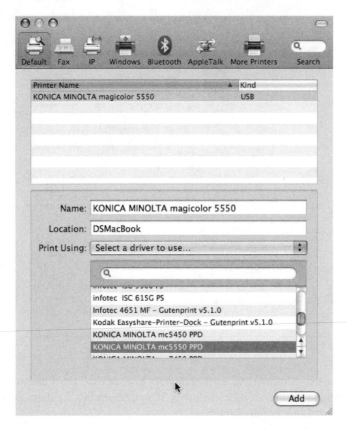

The name of your printer now appears in the list on the left side of the Print & Fax preferences pane and is ready to accept print jobs (see Figure 8-3).

Connect Your Printer via a Network

Macs play equally as nice with network printers. Connect your printer to the network by inserting one end of your Ethernet cable into the printer's Ethernet port and the other end into an available port on your router. The printer will begin conversing with your router.

Most network printers can use one of three methods to converse with your Mac:

■ **Bonjour** Bonjour is a network protocol that was first known throughout geekdom as Zero Configuration Networking, which is a derivative of TCP/IP that needs no configuration to operate. This means that a device running the protocol automatically discovers and talks to other devices running the protocol, without any settings being

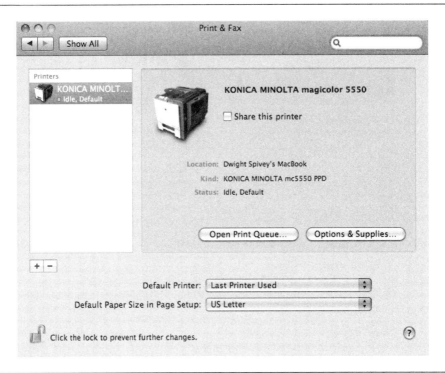

FIGURE 8-3 The USB printer is installed and ready to print.

made by the users of those devices. The devices just see each other and start talking, instantly opening communications with few, if any, headaches for users. Most new printers support Bonjour out of the box.

■ **AppleTalk** Apple developed this protocol during the Stone Age of desktop PCs, way back in the 1980s. The concept of AppleTalk is the same as Bonjour: to allow devices to simply talk to one another with very little, if any, configuration by the end user. Although the protocol is old and just the tiniest bit slower than Bonjour and TCP/IP, it is still more than adequate unless you have heavy-duty printing requirements. Apple is actually trying to wean Mac users from AppleTalk, as evidenced by AppleTalk being disabled by default in Mac OS X. However, if you own an older-model printer that doesn't support Bonjour, AppleTalk is a great choice and well worth enabling. To enable AppleTalk, see Chapter 16.

■ **TCP/IP** Transfer Control Protocol/Internet Protocol is the standard communications protocol of the Internet. When a device is connected to your router, whether wired or wireless, the router automatically assigns an IP address to it. TCP/IP uses these addresses to route network traffic to and from devices. When you connect your printer to a router, it should be assigned an IP address. Consult your printer's documentation on how to find out what its IP address is. You need the IP address if you're using TCP/IP for your installation method.

Why Use TCP/IP Instead of Bonjour or AppleTalk?

This question is a fair one. Why use TCP/IP, going through the process of assigning addresses to devices, instead of a protocol that requires no configuration?

Bonjour is great for small office networks, but wasn't designed for larger networks. AppleTalk was designed for large networks, but some configuration is involved once a certain number of devices are on the network. AppleTalk also still suffers from the stigma of being known by IT administrators as a "chatty" protocol. The first implementations of AppleTalk were constantly broadcasting large packets over the network, causing unnecessary slowness and bottlenecks. While this problem was later resolved in AppleTalk II, the reputation stuck and AppleTalk has been on the slow path to extinction ever since.

TCP/IP is a reliable protocol, is speedy, and is universal across any network that accesses the Internet. In some cases there is no alternative.

Back to the installation. Click the + button in the lower left of the Print & Fax preferences pane to open the printer browser window. If you're installing with Bonjour or AppleTalk, click the Default tab in the upper-left corner of the printer browser window, and the printer should simply show up in the Printer Name column. The Kind column will display whether it is running Bonjour or AppleTalk (you may even see it listed twice, as some printers may be using both protocols).

As with USB, your Mac should begin talking to the printer to gain some information from it, and the Print Using field should match the manufacturer and model of your printer (if it does not, click the Print Using pop-up menu and manually choose the manufacturer and model). Click the Add button in the bottom-right corner, and your printer will show up in the list on the left side of the Print & Fax preferences pane. Your Bonjour or AppleTalk printer is ready to roll!

Using TCP/IP? Click the IP tab in the printer browser window. Consult your printer's documentation for information on the correct protocol to use (IPP, LPD, or Socket), and then enter the Address and Queue information (if needed).

The Name and Location fields should automatically populate, but feel free to change them if you like (see your printer's documentation for more information if necessary). You may need to manually select the manufacturer and model of your printer in the Print Using pop-up menu when using TCP/IP. Once the selection is made (whether automatically or manually), click the Add button to finish installing your printer. It is now available for use and is shown in the list on the left side of the Print & Fax preferences pane.

Print a Job

This is the fun part of the chapter, where we actually get to put the printer through a little workout. Since we're striving for simplicity, let's open our tried and true friend TextEdit. Type whatever you like on the blank page, and then choose File | Page Setup to open the Page Setup window. Page Setup is where you select the printer you will be printing to, the paper size you want to print your job on, the orientation of the job on the page, and to what size to scale the job.

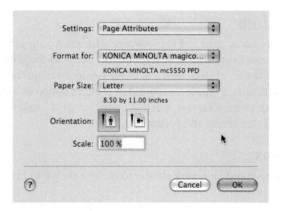

Once you've set the options to your liking, click OK.

TIP   *The "Format For" option should always be set to the name of the printer you are using, not to "Any Printer." This avoids any possible problems your printer may have with the generic paper size information it will receive from your Mac. Different printers may have different page size constraints that they must adhere to, and if they are receiving conflicting messages from the generic constraints used with the "Any Printer" selection, your job may not print correctly.*

Choose File | Print (or press ⌘-P) to open the Print dialog box. Figure 8-4 shows the default Print dialog box, which is simplicity itself, with only six options: you can choose the printer to send the job to, choose a preset if you have created any, create a PDF of the job, see a preview of the job, cancel the job, and print the job. In the interest of getting that first job out, click Print, and your printer will print your designated output.

TIP   *A preset is a group of saved printer driver selections that you change often, such as media type and color model, for printing certain documents. For instance, if you print a lot of photos, make the necessary changes in your driver settings for the type of paper you will be using and whatever color-matching selections you like. Click the Presets menu near the top of the Print dialog box and choose Save As. Give the preset a descriptive name, such as Glossy Stock Photo Paper, and click OK. Now, instead of having to go through all the driver settings to find the right selections every time you want to print photos, just choose the preset you created. Much easier!*

FIGURE 8-4   A typical Print dialog box

Choose Print Options

The "bare necessities" approach is great and suffices nicely for most print jobs, but occasionally you may need to get a bit more fancy with your settings. To access all the printing options, click the downward-pointing arrow that's just to the right of the printer name in the Print dialog box. The dialog box expands to display a whole new world of printing options, as shown in Figure 8-5. Let's see what the basic options are all about. Keep in mind that we are using TextEdit, and not all options will be exactly the same across all applications.

Main Print Dialog Box

Your main Print dialog box should look very similar to the one shown in Figure 8-5, with the following options:

- **Copies**   Specify the number of copies you wish to print of your document.
- **Collated**   If you're printing a document containing several pages, check the Collated box (it is checked by default) to have the printer print one full copy of the document at a time instead of printing several copies of each individual page at a time. In other words, if you print three copies of your four-page document with the Collated box checked, your printer prints the pages in this order: 1234, 1234, and 1234. If you print the document without collation, the pages print like this: 111, 222, 333, and 444.
- **Two-Sided**   If your printer has a duplexer, this option will be available. A duplexer allows your printer to print on both sides of a single page.

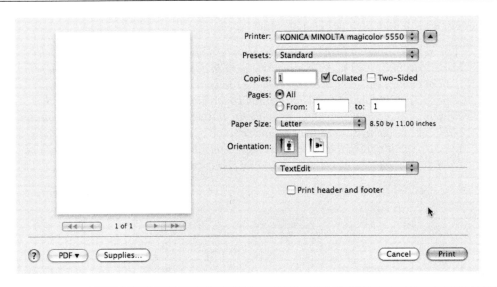

FIGURE 8-5   Several more options are available in the main, or expanded, Print dialog box.

- **Pages**   Choose whether to print an entire document or just a specific range of pages in the document.
- **Paper Size**   Choose your paper size from the pop-up menu; the size, in inches, for your choice is displayed to the right.
- **Orientation**   Select portrait (tall) or landscape (wide) mode.

Layout and Color Matching

Click the TextEdit menu and you will see the options for the other panes of the Print dialog box in the pop-up list. Select Layout to see that pane's options.

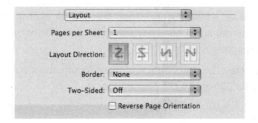

- **Pages per Sheet**   Click this pop-up menu to choose how many pages of your document will print on one side of a single sheet of paper.
- **Layout Direction**   Select which direction to print the pages of your document. This option is meant for use when printing multiple pages of a document on a single sheet of paper.
- **Border**   Use this menu to apply a border around the individual pages when printing multiple pages per sheet.
- **Two-Sided**   This menu allows you to duplex with long-edge or short-edge binding.

Click the Layout menu and choose Color Matching. This option allows you to let the Mac handle the color for your document (ColorSync) or leave that up to the printer (In Printer).

TIP   *ColorSync is the tool your Mac uses to compare and match color from one device to another. If you are having trouble getting the color in your onscreen documents to match the color on your printed pages, ColorSync may be of help to you. To learn much more about this very broad subject, in the Finder, choose Help | Mac Help, and then search for ColorSync.*

Paper Handling and Paper Feed

To see the Paper Handling pane, click the Color Matching pop-up menu and choose it from the list. The following options are available:

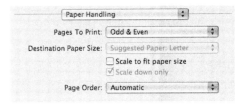

- **Pages To Print**   Choose whether to print just the odd- or even-numbered pages in a document. This feature comes in handy when you want to print on both sides of a sheet of paper (manual duplexing).
- **Destination Paper Size**   Use this option if your document size is larger or smaller than the physical size of the paper you are printing on.
- **Page Order**   Use this option to print your job in reverse page order.

Click the Paper Handling pop-up menu and choose Paper Feed. On the Paper Feed pane, you can choose which tray the printer pulls paper from, assuming your printer has more than one tray. You can also specify whether the first page of the job prints from a separate tray than the rest of the pages.

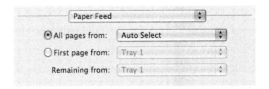

Cover Page

Click the Paper Feed pop-up menu and choose Cover Page. A cover page is used to separate print jobs in an environment where many people use the same printer. You can use the Print Cover Page options to specify whether you want to use a cover page and, if so, whether it should be printed before or after your document.

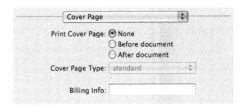

Scheduler

To see the Scheduler pane, click the Cover Page pop-up menu and choose Scheduler. Scheduler allows you to choose when your Mac will send a document to be printed. You can even specify an exact time for it to print.

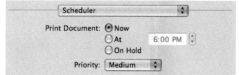

- ■ **Print Document**   Choose to print the job now, print it at a specific time of day, or hold the job in the print queue so that you can print it at your leisure.

- ■ **Priority**   Set the level of importance for scheduled jobs.

Manage Print Jobs

As "Master of Your Mac" you have the final say over the tasks it performs, including printing documents. Even after you've clicked the Print button and sent the job, you are still in control of what happens to that print job.

After you click the Print button, a new icon appears in your Dock with a picture of your printer on it. The Mac is opening your printer's queue window, which appears on your screen a second or two later (see Figure 8-6).

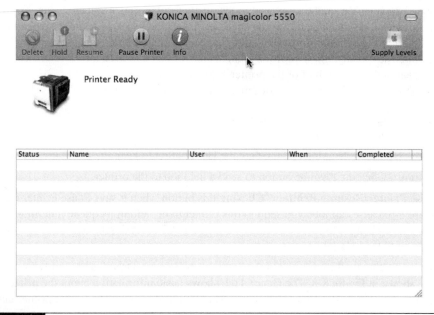

FIGURE 8-6   The printer's queue window

This queue can also be opened at any time by opening the Print & Fax preferences pane, clicking the name of the printer in the list on the left, and clicking the Open Print Queue button.

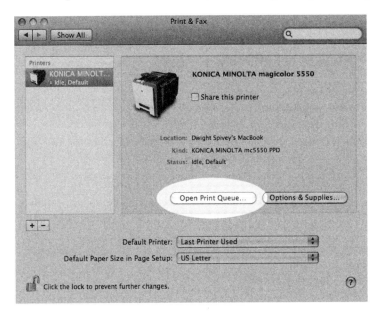

When you first click the Print button, the job does not immediately go to the printer—it has to be processed by your Mac and then placed in the queue for the printer you are using. From there, the printer receives the data, builds the page, and prints the job. If you simply typed the word "hello" and printed it, you probably wouldn't even see the job in the queue because it would go through so quickly, but if your job contains lots of text and even a picture or two, you will see it appear in the bottom half of the printer's queue window.

Here's a short explanation of the buttons in the queue window's menu bar:

- **Delete**   Highlight the job in the queue by clicking its name, and then click the Delete button to completely cancel the job.

- **Hold**   Highlight the job and then click the Hold button to keep the job in the queue.

- **Resume**   Click the Resume button to send a held job to the printer.

- **Pause Printer/Resume Printer**   Clicking this button when it says Pause Printer (see Figure 8-6) causes all jobs you send to this printer to be held in its queue indefinitely. This button changes to Resume Printer (see Figure 8-7); clicking the button in this state sends all of the held jobs to the printer.

- **Info**   Clicking the Info button opens a pane with General, Driver, and Supply Levels tabs, shown in Figure 8-8. The General tab shows basic information about the printer's name and location. The Driver tab shows what driver is associated with the printer and

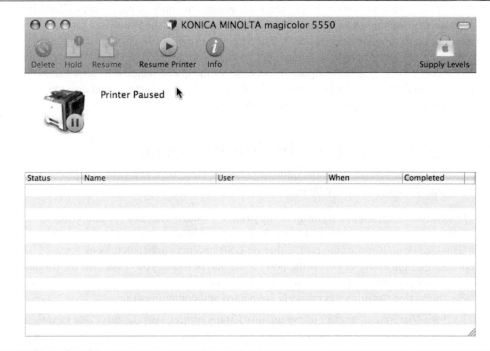

FIGURE 8-7   A paused printer queue

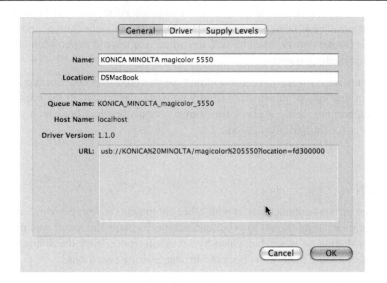

FIGURE 8-8   Information about your printer

what options are installed on the printer, such as extra memory or paper trays. The driver can also be manually changed from this location by clicking the Print Using pop-up menu and choosing the desired driver. The Supply Levels tab shows you the amounts remaining for your printer's consumables. You can also get this information by clicking the Supply Levels icon in the upper-right corner of the queue window. Whether this information displays or not is controlled by the printer's manufacturer and also may be limited by the way the printer is connected to the Mac.

Troubleshoot Printer Installation Problems

Did your printer installation not work out quite as planned? Here are a few common problems and what you can do to try to resolve them:

- *My printer's name doesn't show up in the printer browser.* This is a communications problem. The cable might be bad or might be connected to the incorrect port or to a damaged or nonfunctioning port, either on USB or a network router. Look for a connection light above or below the port on the hub or router you connected the printer to. Consult your hub's or router's documentation to make sure the state of the connection light shows that the printer is properly connected and communicating.

- *The Print Using menu doesn't automatically list my printer manufacturer and model.* Your driver is probably not installed correctly or the Mac can't communicate with the printer to discover the manufacturer and model information. Try reinstalling the driver, and then follow the connection advice mentioned in the preceding bullet point.

- *I can send jobs but they never print.* The print queue may be paused. Open the Print & Fax preferences pane and see if there is an exclamation point next to the printer name. If there is, the printer has been paused. Click the Open Print Queue button, and then click the Resume Printer button. Also, be sure the printer isn't out of paper. Many times the problem is something obvious.

- *I can't see my supply levels.* The connection type you are using may not support the gathering of that kind of information from your particular printer, or the printer driver may not support the ability to check the printer's supply levels. Check with your printer manufacturer for further information.

Share Printers

Your Mac can share printers connected to it with other computers on your network, and it can also send jobs to printers being shared by other computers. To share and use shared printers, you must enable printer sharing on your Mac. Open System Preferences, click the Sharing icon to open the Sharing preferences pane, and check the Printer Sharing check box.

To share a printer that's installed on your Mac, open the Print & Fax preferences pane, select the printer name in the Printers list, and then check the "Share this printer" box.

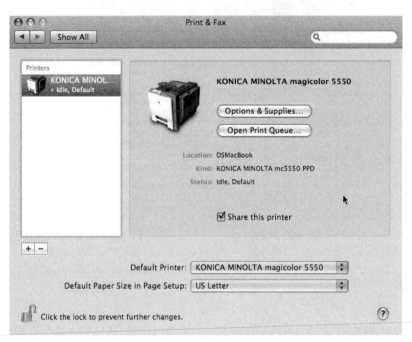

To use a printer that is being shared by other computers, open the Print & Fax preferences pane, click the + button, and then do either of the following depending on whether the printer you need is being shared by a Mac or a Windows-based PC:

- **Mac**   Click the Default tab of the printer browser window and select the shared printer in the Printer Name column. Your Mac should automatically discover the correct driver to use for it, assuming the driver has been installed on your Mac (see Figure 8-9). Click the Add button to use this printer.

FIGURE 8-9   Installing a printer shared from a Mac

■ **Windows-based PC**   Click the Windows tab of the printer browser window, browse your network to find the shared printer, and then click Add to use it.

What Is PDF?

Portable Document Format (PDF) is a standard for sharing documents with colleagues and over the Internet. PDF is a cross-platform standard, meaning that anyone with a computer can read the document as long as they have a PDF reader application installed. You can read PDF files (often called PDFs) on your Mac using the Preview application.

PDF technology is a major part of Mac OS X. PDF isn't just for creating documents, but the underlying technology can be used to render graphics for many different types of devices. Much of what you see on your screen when you look at your Mac is PDF-based. Apple has taken advantage of PDF's wide array of abilities to add wonderful functionality that isn't available on any other operating system.

One example of this functionality is the ability to create a PDF file from any document using any application on your Mac. There was a time when the only way to make a PDF was to purchase very expensive software from Adobe, create a PostScript file of your document, and then "distill" (convert) the PostScript file into a PDF using Adobe Distiller. Those days are long gone for users of Mac OS X.

Make Your Own PDF Files

Open a Print dialog box from within any application and notice the PDF button in the lower-left corner.

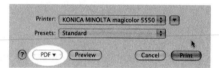

When you click the PDF button, you are given the following options (see Figure 8-10):

- **Open PDF in Preview**   Select this option to create a PDF of your document and open it automatically in the Preview application.
- **Save as PDF**   Choose this option to save any document on your Mac to a PDF file.

FIGURE 8-10   PDF options at your disposal

- **Save as PostScript**   A PostScript file is not something the average user will have to ever worry about. PostScript files are typically used in graphics and print houses.

- **Fax PDF**   This is a PDF workflow that saves your file as a PDF and then begins the process of faxing it (more on faxing in the next section).

- **Mail PDF**   Another PDF workflow that automatically saves your document as a PDF and opens your default email application so that you can send it to someone else.

- **Save as PDF-X**   This option is also aimed at the professional graphics crowd. A PDF-X file is still a PDF, but one that has been stripped of unnecessary information and certain types of images. Most readers of this book won't ever use this option.

- **Save PDF to iPhoto**   Choose this option to save a document as a PDF and store it in iPhoto.

- **Save PDF to Web Receipts Folder**   Another example PDF workflow. This workflow saves PDF files to the Documents | Web Receipts folder in your home folder. This is useful when you make an online purchase or bill payment, because you can save the online receipt as a PDF file.

- **Edit Menu**   You can use this option to edit the PDF buttons menu, adding custom workflows that suit your needs. One example would be to create a workflow that allows you to save PDF files directly to a specific location on your hard drive.

Just the Fax, Ma'am!

Please forgive the title for this section of the chapter, but anytime I get the chance to pay homage to Barney Fife I jump all over it!

You must have an optional modem connected to a phone line in order for your Mac to send and receive faxes. If you do have this modem, your Mac will automatically be able to send faxes. If you are using a dial-up ISP, you will have to disconnect from the Internet before you can send your fax.

Open the Print & Fax preferences pane to see if your fax has been automatically added to the Printers list. If not, click the + button, click the Fax tab in the printer browser window, select your fax machine from the list, and click Add, as shown here.

Send a Fax

To send a fax, follow these steps:

1. Open the document you want to fax.

2. Open a Print dialog box (File | Print or ⌘-P) and make sure the correct fax device is selected in the Printer pop-up menu.

3. Click the PDF button and choose Fax PDF to see the fax options in the Print dialog box (see Figure 8-11).

4. Type the recipient's fax number in the To text field.

5. If your phone system requires a dialing prefix to get an outside line (for example, dialing 9 or another number), enter it in the Dialing Prefix field.

6. To include a cover page, check the Use Cover Page box and type the subsequent information.

7. When you're ready to send, click the Fax button. You can check the progress of your fax by clicking the fax modem's icon in the Dock, just like when checking the status of print jobs.

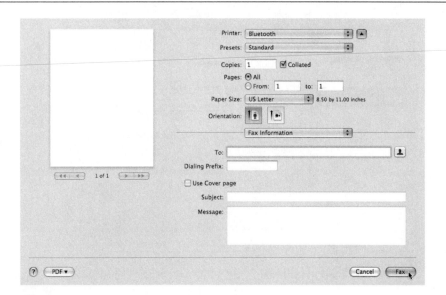

FIGURE 8-11 Print dialog box fax options

Receive Faxes

To receive faxes, follow these steps:

1. Open the Print & Fax preferences pane and click the fax modem to highlight it in the Printers list.

2. Enter your fax number in the Fax Number text field and then click the Receive Options button above it (see Figure 8-12).

3. In the options dialog box, shown in Figure 8-13, check the "Receive faxes on this computer" box and then set the other options to your liking. These options help you save the faxes to a specific location on your hard drive (in PDF format), automatically print your fax to a particular printer, or email the fax to any address you choose.

4. Click OK to return to the Print & Fax preferences pane. If you would like to share this fax or show the status of your faxes in the main menu bar, check the appropriate boxes. Faxing has never been so easy!

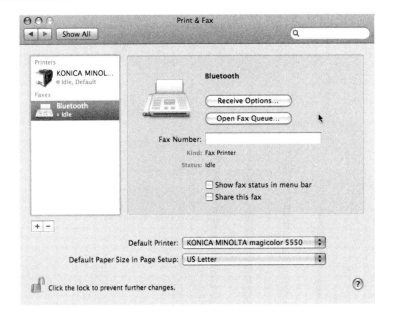

FIGURE 8-12   Fax preferences options

FIGURE 8-13   Setting up your Mac to receive faxes

Summary

Mac OS X has some pretty advanced printing options, but don't let them overwhelm you. If you follow the instructions in this chapter, you should be able to handle most of your printing needs without a hitch. Being able to print your documents at any time is a primary function of computers, and you now know how to successfully print anything you need from your trusty Mac.

Chapter 9

Connected and Organized: Two Things Most of Us Are Not!

How to...

- Add contacts to your Address Book
- Use iCal to create, publish, subscribe to, and print calendars
- Synchronize handheld devices such as cell phones and PDAs with your Mac

Are you one of the blessed folks in this world who are organized and have all their ducks in a row? Must be nice! I'll admit I'm envious, but thankfully Apple had people like me in mind when they came up with great tools such as Address Book, iSync, and iCal. These three tools are a powerful combination for maintaining contact information across multiple devices and for keeping up with your important dates and appointments. And true to form for Apple, these tools are remarkably easy to use.

Let Your Mouse Do the Walking: Using Address Book

Address Book is a really simple way to keep up with all your contacts and their pertinent info. You'll never have to hunt down Grandma's address again! Address Book is fully integrated into many of your Mac's applications, such as Mail, so entering a contact into Address Book makes it instantly available in those applications as well.

Address Book creates a card for each contact you create. This card contains areas for the contact's addresses, phone numbers, and email addresses. You can also import contact information from other sources, such as your cell phone.

To get started, open Address Book by opening it from the Applications folder (Hard Drive | Applications). Figure 9-1 shows the default Address Book GUI and affords you a quick look at its layout.

Add Contacts

To add a contact to Address Book, choose File | New Card, press ⌘-N, or click the + button under the Name column (see Figure 9-1). Enter the appropriate information for your friend, family member, or colleague, and your done. That's right, you're done!

Now, there is much more you can do, of course. You're not limited to just those few basic options that you see in a default card. To edit a card, click the card in the Name column and click the Edit button below the card, click Edit | Edit Card in the menu bar, or press ⌘-L.

You can add a little more spice to the card by adding a picture of the person to it, if you like. To do so, double-click the square to the left of the contact's name and browse your Mac for the picture.

Don't see a field you need, such as a place for the contact's birthday. When editing the card, click the Card menu in the menu bar and hold your mouse over the Add Field option to see all the additional fields you can add to your card. While you're there, don't miss all the other options in the Card menu. These are all very self-explanatory, so there's no real need for much detail here.

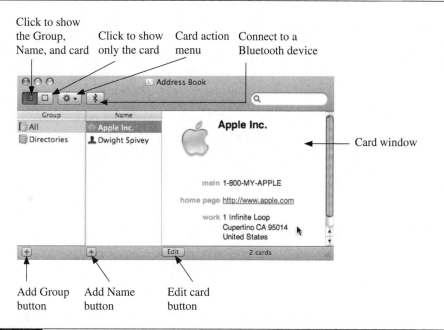

Click to show the Group, Name, and card

Click to show only the card

Card action menu

Connect to a Bluetooth device

Card window

Add Group button

Add Name button

Edit card button

Address Book default window

Create Groups of Contacts

Creating groups of cards is quite useful for categorizing contacts. For instance, to see all the cards associated with a company, you could just click the company's group to list them. Address Book is already preloaded with a group called All, which lists all of your Address Book contacts, regardless of their group affiliation.

You can create a group and then either add contacts within it or drag previously entered contacts from the All group and drop them into the new group. To create a group, choose File | New Group or click the + button under the Group column, and then enter the group's name in the text field.

Adding cards to groups is a snap, too. To add a card while in a group, simply click the + button under the Name column and enter the contact's information. As mentioned, another way to add cards to a group is to click the All group and then drag the card you want from that list and drop it in the group you want to add it to, as shown here.

A still more convenient way to add contacts to groups is to create Smart Groups. Smart Groups automatically add a new contact to their list if the card for the contact

contains information the Smart Group is to be on the lookout for. For example, you can create a Smart Group that looks for cards containing your family's last name, and then every time you add a card using that name, it will be added automatically to the Smart Group. Creating Smart Groups is as simple as clicking File | New Smart Group (or clicking the card action menu and choosing New Smart Group), and then entering the criteria for the group. There is a myriad of possibilities for Smart Groups, making your life even that much easier to organize! Thanks, Apple!

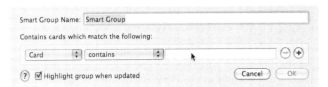

Print Your Contacts

Address Book does a bang-up job of printing your contacts by allowing you to easily format the contacts to fit different sizes and types of media. You can print your entire contact list, or just a certain group.

To print your contacts, click the group you want to print, and then choose File | Print. Notice the Style pop-up menu near the middle of the Print dialog box; this is where you can choose the formatting styles for your contact list (see Figure 9-2). There are four style options: Mailing Labels, Envelopes, Lists, and Pocket Address Book. Each of the options has several settings you

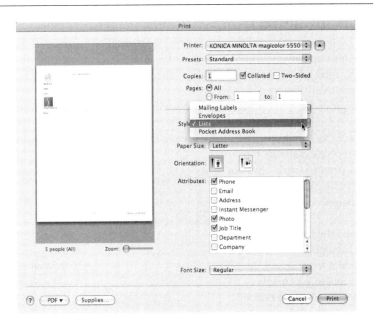

FIGURE 9-2   Printing contacts from Address Book

can configure to format to your needs. You can adjust the settings to your heart's utmost desire within these basic formats, which allow you to do such tasks as printing envelopes for all the contacts in a group, printing a properly formatted pocket address book, generating a sheet of mailing labels for the chosen contacts, or just printing a general list of all your contacts.

Your Scheduling iPal, iCal

iCal is a great piece of software. There, I said it, and I won't recant. It's such a simple application that performs such a simple task, but it does it so elegantly and easily that working with it soon becomes second nature.

iCal is a calendar application that helps you keep track of important dates. You can create multiple calendars for different areas of your life, share those calendars with your family or organization, and print your calendars so that you keep a hard copy wherever you go.

You can do more than just enter scheduled events or tasks in iCal. You can set alarms for events and set reminders that will tell you of an impending event; publish your calendars so that others can subscribe to them and subscribe to calendars that have already been published on the Internet; and synchronize your calendars with other devices such as your cell phone, iPhone, iPod, or PDA.

If your schedule is so jammed you can't remember everything, or if you're like me and can't remember an appointment to save your life, iCal is here to save the day (no pun intended). The default iCal interface is an exercise in simplicity, as you can see in Figure 9-3.

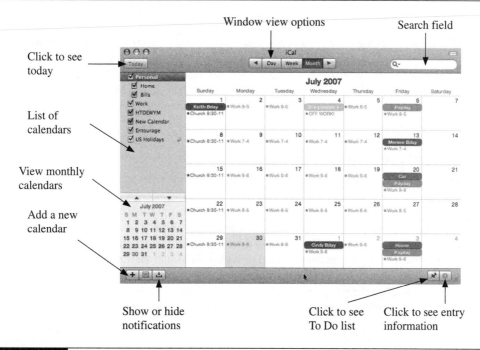

FIGURE 9-3 iCal's intuitive interface

Create Calendars

Create calendars for different areas of your life to help keep things organized. For example, create a calendar for entering payment due dates for your bills, another calendar to help you remember the football schedule for your favorite team, and yet another calendar for your garden club events.

To create a new calendar, choose File | New Calendar or click the + button in the bottom left of iCal's window. Type a descriptive name for the new calendar when it appears in the calendar list on the left side of the window. You may add as many calendars as you please.

TIP   *Notice that as you add multiple calendars to iCal, each has its own assigned color. This is to distinguish the events of one calendar from the events of another calendar. These colors are automatically assigned by iCal but you can change them by clicking the name of the calendar in the calendar list and choosing File | Get Info (or pressing ⌘-I). Choose the color you prefer from the pop-up menu to the right of the calendar name.*

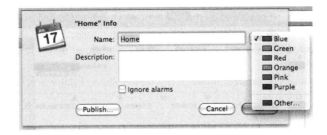

Grouping calendars is a good way to keep numerous calendars organized. Create a calendar group by choosing File | New Calendar Group, and then enter the group's name. To add previously created calendars to the group, just drag-and-drop them onto the group name. To add a new calendar to the group, click the group name to highlight it and then choose File | New Calendar.

To view a calendar's or group's events, click the check box next to the name of the calendar or group.

Create Events for Your Calendars

You can add as many events as necessary to your calendars. Events can be anything you like, from doctors' appointments to movie openings.

First, click the name of the calendar you want to create an event for. The view you use in iCal determines how you can add an event. If you're in Day or Week view, simply click-and-hold on the start time for your event and drag down to the end time of your event, let go of the mouse button, and enter the event name in the text field provided. In Month view, double-click the day of the event and enter a name for it in the text field.

To edit the event, click the event name to highlight it and choose File | Get Info (or press ⌘-I) to see the event's properties (see Figure 9-4). Here's a brief description of your choices:

- ■ **Location**   Enter a location for the event.
- ■ **All-Day**   Checking this box will make the event a day-long occurrence.

| New Event |

FIGURE 9-4   Event information

- ■ **From and To**   Specify a starting and ending point for your event.
- ■ **Repeat**   Choose how often to repeat an event. For example, you would repeat a birthday every year, a reminder to schedule a dental checkup every six months, and so forth.
- ■ **Attendees**   Send an email to people to notify them of your event.
- ■ **Calendar**   Change which calendar the event is associated with.
- ■ **Alarm**   Create an alarm to remind you of the event.
- ■ **URL**   Add an Internet address that's related to the event.
- ■ **Attachment**   Attach a file to your event by dragging it from the Finder to this field.
- ■ **Note**   Enter a short note to yourself about the event.

Share Your Calendars

"Why would I want to share my calendars?" you may ask. The most obvious reason is so people won't think you're stingy! Of course, there are lots of other reasons, too, but basically you share your calendars so that others can coordinate their schedules with yours.

There are two ways to share your calendars with other people: publish the calendar on the Internet, or export the calendar.

Publish Your Calendar on the Internet

Publishing your calendar on the Internet allows others to subscribe to it—in other words, they can link to your calendar via the Web. You can publish your calendars using a .Mac account or with a private server, such as the server that hosts your personal webpage or a corporate server. To publish a calendar to the Web:

1. Right-click (or CTRL-click) the name of the calendar and choose Publish to see your publishing options (see Figure 9-5).

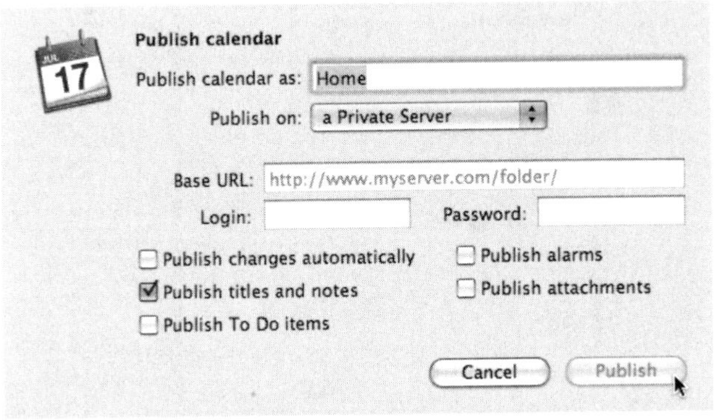

FIGURE 9-5   Publishing your calendar for all the world to see

2. In the Publish On pop-up menu, choose where to publish your calendar, .Mac or A Private Server.

3. If you are using a private server, you must enter the server information, including the login name and password, to publish your calendar.

> **TIP**   *You can discontinue the publishing of a calendar by right-clicking (or CTRL-clicking) its name and choosing Unpublish.*

Export and Email Your Calendar

You can export your calendar and email it to colleagues, who can then import the calendar into iCal or any other calendar application they may use. To export your calendar, click the name of the calendar to highlight it, and then choose File | Export. Attach the exported file to an email and send it to those you need to collaborate with.

Subscribe to Calendars

You can subscribe to calendars published by someone else by clicking the Calendar menu and choosing Subscribe. Enter the URL (web address) of the calendar and click Subscribe, and then choose whether to remove alarms, attachments, and To Do items (see Figure 9-6). Check the Refresh box and choose a time increment if you want to keep up to date with any changes made to the calendar. Click OK to add the calendar to your calendar list.

Apple provides lots of calendars you can subscribe to on their iCal website, located at www.apple.com/ical/library/. Use them to keep up with the schedule of your favorite professional sports team, add holidays to iCal automatically, and know when the next blockbuster movie is opening. There are several other sites on the Internet that host literally hundreds of other published calendars, so you can create a calendar list a mile long if that's your cup of tea.

FIGURE 9-6   Subscribing to a calendar

Print Calendars

Printing a hard copy of your calendars is a great way to keep up with your schedule without having to carry your Mac everywhere you go, which in turn may save several trips to your chiropractor.

iCal provides you with great print options so that you can customize your paper calendar in any number of ways, as you can see in Figure 9-7:

- **View**   Choose Day, Week, Month, or List.
- **Paper**   Choose the paper size.

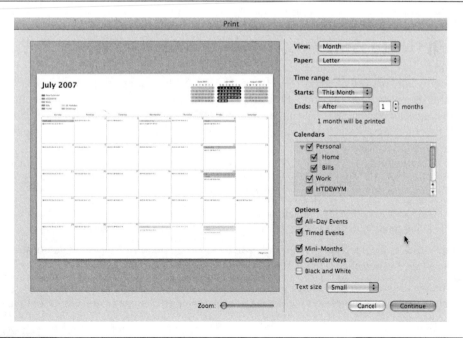

FIGURE 9-7   iCal's great printing options

■ **Time Range**   Set the starting and ending dates of the time period you would like to print.

■ **Calendars**   Choose which of your calendars you would like included in the printout.

■ **Options**   Choose which options you want to see.

■ **Text Size**   Choose a text size in the pop-up menu.

After you have made your choices, click Continue, make any changes necessary in the Print dialog box that opens, and then click Print.

iSync, Therefore I Am

Another of my past anti-organizational skills was to not have the right number or address handy when I needed it. For example, I would be at work but need a phone number in an address book in a desk drawer at home or on my cell phone that my wife had borrowed. Apple's answer to this dilemma is iSync. iSync compares your Mac's contacts and calendars to those of your cell phone or Palm-OS PDA, and then synchronizes them so that you have the same information on both devices. Any changes you make on one device will be automatically detected by iSync and synchronized on the other. For example, if you change your boss's phone number on your Mac, iSync will detect that the number has changed since the last time you ran iSync, and will automatically make the change to your boss's information on your PDA the next time you sync the two.

Your phone or PDA must use either USB or Bluetooth to connect to your Mac, and it must be compatible with iSync. To check your device's compatibility with iSync, open Safari and see the list of compatible devices at www.apple.com/isync/devices.html.

Add a Device to iSync

The first time you open iSync, you need to add a device for it to sync with. Choose Devices | Add Device to add your cell phone or PDA to the device list. Unless you've been exploring your Mac on your own instead of following this book, you most likely haven't set up your cell phone or PDA to connect with your Mac. Assuming that's the case, when you click Add Device, iSync opens the Bluetooth Setup Assistant (see Figure 9-8), which walks you through connecting your device to your Mac, as follows:

Be sure that your Bluetooth device is discoverable. Consult your device's documentation to find out how to enable this setting.

1. Click Continue in the Introduction window of the Bluetooth Setup Assistant.

2. In the Select Device Type window, choose the appropriate device type (for demonstration purposes, I'm selecting Mobile Phone), and then click Continue.

3. The next window displays a list of devices the Mac has discovered, as shown in the following illustration. Select the device you are trying to connect to and click Continue.

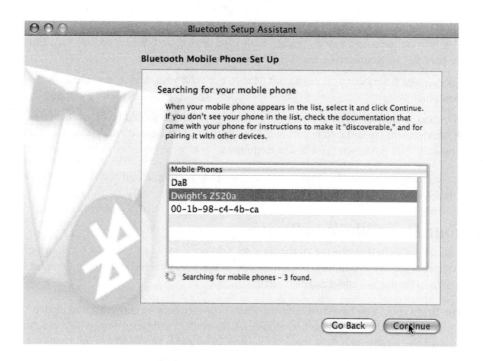

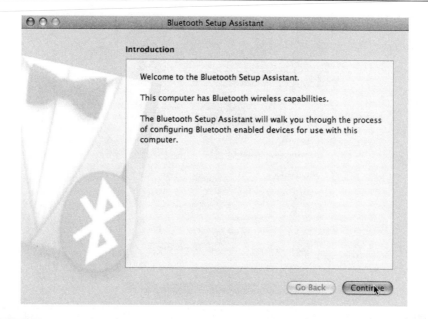

FIGURE 9-8   Bluetooth Setup Assistant is such a helpful chap!

4. Click Continue again after your Mac gathers some information about your device. Your Mac now attempts to connect, or pair, with your device, and displays a pass key. Enter the pass key on your device when it prompts you.

5. Choose which services you want your Mac to use with your device, and then click Continue.

6. iSync opens the Add Device window, in which your device should be listed. Double-click the device name to add it to iSync, and then close the Add Device window and quit the Bluetooth Setup Assistant if it is still running.

If your device shows up in the iSync window, the setup is complete; if it does not, you need to repeat the entire process from scratch.

Sync Your Mac with Your Device

Now that all the setup business is out of the way, let's do some syncing! An icon for your newly added device is in the iSync window; click that icon to see your synchronization options for the device, shown in Figure 9-9 and described next:

- **For first sync**   You have two options. Choose "Merge data on computer and device" to combine the information from both devices. Choose "Erase data on device then sync to" to remove any information from the cell phone or PDA and copy the Mac's information to it.

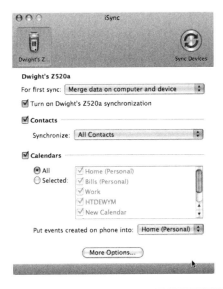

FIGURE 9-9   Your device's sync options

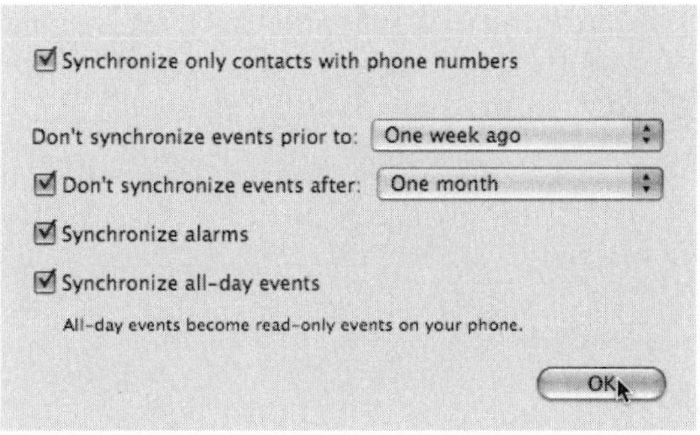

FIGURE 9-10   Even more sync options for your device!

■ **Turn on** *"Device Name"* **synchronization**   Check this box to enable synchronization of the device.

■ **Contacts**   Use this option to sync all of your contacts or only certain groups of contacts in your Address Book.

■ **Calendars**   Choose which iCal calendars you want to sync with your device.

■ **More Options**   Click this button if you need to utilize the extra iSync goodies shown in Figure 9-10.

After all the various options are set, click the Sync Devices button in the upper-right corner of the iSync window. At this point you will see the synchronization progress bar. The first time you sync, you are prompted that iSync will change more than five percent of your information on your Mac or the other device. To sync the items, click Allow. Once the sync is complete, your information should be the same across both devices. Done!

Summary

There's no reason to forget those "honey-do" lists now, guys! Your new Mac can keep track of your tasks and can sync them with your portable devices, so you will always be on top of things.

Part III

Pictures, Music, and Movies, Oh My!

Chapter 10

The Quick and the Time: QuickTime

How to…

- View or listen to many different types of media files in QuickTime
- Enhance the quality of your media files
- Use your web browser to view QuickTime videos
- Know if you should upgrade to QuickTime Pro

QuickTime. Funny name, huh? While the name may generate a head tilt, the technology behind it is serious stuff!

What the Heck Is QuickTime?

Glad you asked! QuickTime is Apple's multimedia platform that is easily the best available anywhere. QuickTime is able to facilitate the playback of most industry-standard file formats for audio and video, allows creation of audio and video content, and can jumpstart your car. Okay, that last one was a bit of a stretch, but QuickTime's list of capabilities is impressive. Content created using the QuickTime platform is the richest that you can find in terms of clarity and sound. The majority of the Web's best multimedia sites are built on QuickTime technology. QuickTime uses the latest video and audio codecs (coder/decoders, used to shrink, expand, and play multimedia files) to ensure that your multimedia experience is as up to date as it can be. QuickTime is the benchmark by which all other multimedia platforms are compared.

Is QuickTime really the best multimedia format? There are those who might argue that some other competing platform is better than QuickTime, but ask yourself what the majority of professionals use. Take motion picture studios, for example. Their entire existence is built around providing a great viewing experience for you, and to sell their products, they use the Internet to show trailers, or previews, of their movies to entice the movie-going public. Do you think these people, whose very careers are based on the video and audio quality of their work, are going to use a second-rate platform to share their products with the world? Of course not! They are going to use the very best product they can get their hands on. Can you guess what the majority of them use?

QuickTime is easily one of the most popular platforms in use today, and is built into Mac OS X (Windows versions must be downloaded from the Web). QuickTime 7 is the latest version of this groundbreaking software. The best thing about QuickTime? The basic version is free!

Cool Ways to Use QuickTime

The QuickTime Player is installed in your Applications folder automatically. Open the QuickTime Player to begin exploring your Mac's multimedia capabilities.

TIP   *Let me be honest with you, dear reader. While QuickTime can open all sorts of multimedia file types, video is the summit of QuickTime's abilities. Audio and picture files are much more suited to other applications that Apple provides with your Mac, as you'll see in the upcoming chapters. Can QuickTime open audio and picture files? Yes. Is it the best application for those tasks? No. Just giving you a "heads up."*

When you first open the QuickTime Player, it automatically opens the Content Guide, which gives you a glance at some of the newest QuickTime content available on the Web. Clicking the items in the Content Guide window will automatically open a webpage in Safari or open the iTunes Store, which I will discuss in much more detail in Chapter 12.

View Video Files

Grab your $8 box of M&M's and $12 soft drink, and settle down with your Mac for a night of motion picture viewing bliss! You can view several different video file formats natively with QuickTime. The most popular video formats supported by QuickTime are MOV, AVI, and MPEG (1–4), along with many others (see Apple's QuickTime website for a complete list of supported formats, which at the time of this writing is www.apple.com/quicktime/player/specs.html).

To open a movie in QuickTime Player, choose File | Open File, browse your Mac for the movie file, select it, and then click Open. You could also simply double-click the file from within the Finder. Your movie opens in a QuickTime Player window like the one shown in Figure 10-1. Notice the buttons at the bottom of the window; these buttons function exactly like those of your DVD player or VCR.

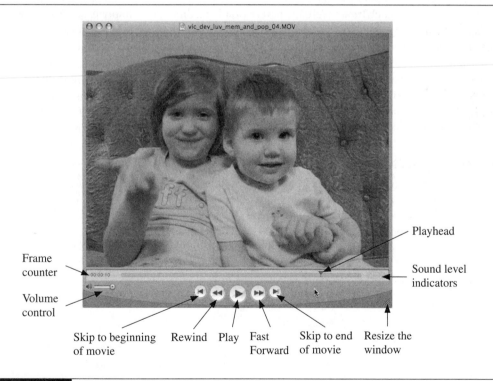

Frame counter

Volume control

Playhead

Sound level indicators

Skip to beginning of movie   Rewind   Play   Fast Forward   Skip to end of movie   Resize the window

FIGURE 10-1   QuickTime's virtual movie screen

Is full screen more your style? Choose View | Enter Full Screen (or press ⌘-F) to fill your Mac's display with glorious video. There are several other size options to choose from in the View menu as well. Keep in mind that if the resolution of your file is not very high, your video quality drops the larger you make the QuickTime Player window.

Listen to Audio Files

QuickTime is not intended to be a full-fledged music player like iTunes, so if that's what you're looking for, head on over to Chapter 12. However, QuickTime does play MP3 and many other audio formats. So, if iTunes is available, why ever use QuickTime to listen to audio? To listen to an audio file in iTunes, you have to import the file into your iTunes library, thereby creating another copy of the file on your Mac. Listen to the file first in QuickTime if you are unsure about adding it to your iTunes library. Choose File | Open File and browse for the file to hear the audio before you import it into iTunes.

View Picture Files

The merit of questioning the use of QuickTime doubles in the case of viewing picture files. Your Mac already has two programs that are more than capable of opening picture files, iPhoto and Preview, so why use QuickTime? Well, the best reason I can think of is simply because you can. That's the extent of my argument, because frankly the other two applications I mentioned are much more picture-friendly than QuickTime. If you simply want to open a picture file and give it a quick look, fine, use QuickTime (if you already have it open). But if you want to do anything else with it or you're already running iPhoto or Preview, don't bother. I don't believe even the most battle-hardened QuickTime-platform warrior would argue this point with me.

If you're still inclined, open your picture in QuickTime by choosing File | Open File and browsing your Mac for the picture file.

Enhance QuickTime Playback

While QuickTime is packed with all the latest and greatest technology for making your multimedia experience the best on any computing platform, it still can't compensate entirely for a bad recording. If your dad left the cover on the video camera's lens, QuickTime won't magically make video of your birthday party appear on your Mac. It's good, but it's not quite that good (yet!).

That caveat having being said, you can enhance the quality of your video and audio files using QuickTime's A/V Controls (see Figure 10-2). Open this tool by choosing Window | Show A/V Controls.

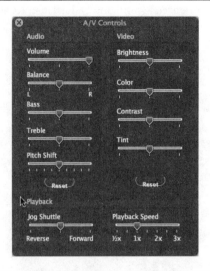

FIGURE 10-2   You can fine-tune your QuickTime experience with A/V Controls.

Adjust the following with A/V Controls:

- **Audio**   Adjust volume, balance, bass, treble, and pitch shift.
- **Video**   Adjust brightness, color, contrast, and tint.
- **Playback**   Use Jog Shuttle to rapidly scroll backward and forward in a file, and use Playback Speed to make your video play at half its normal speed or up to three times faster than normal. Quickly livens up any party!

Use QuickTime on the Web

There's not much you have to do as a Mac user to get QuickTime to work within your web browser, whether it be Safari or some third-party software, because Apple has already made all the necessary configurations in Mac OS X.

Thousands of websites use QuickTime for their multimedia needs, be they movies, music, picture slideshows, streaming video and audio, or any combination of file types. Website creators can deliver amazing Internet experiences by utilizing QuickTime. Apple has just the place for you to check out all of QuickTime's offerings: www.apple.com/quicktime/.

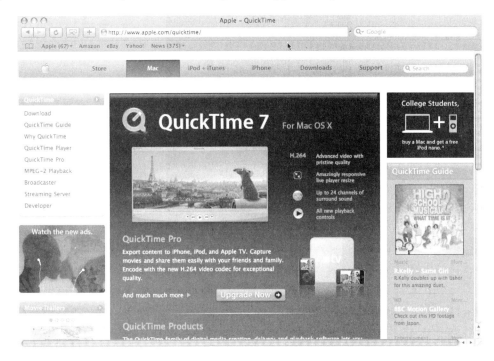

Apple's QuickTime site is *the* place on the Web for viewing the latest movie trailers. You can view the trailers in low, medium, or high resolution. The speed of your Internet connection determines which resolution is best for you, but know that the lower the resolution of the trailer, the smaller the QuickTime viewer window in the browser will be. If you really want to see how incredibly clear and colorful QuickTime media can be, download one of the high-definition trailers from Apple. These files are large and may take a bit of time to download, even on speedier connections, but their quality will blow you away!

The Internet is packed full of great QuickTime content. Besides Apple's QuickTime website, here are a few of the best sites on the Web for locating QuickTime content and putting QuickTime through its paces:

- **www.multimedialibrary.com/diana/qtvr_sites.asp**   This site is just a huge list of other sites on the Internet that utilize QuickTime content.

- **www.virtualguidebooks.com**   See beautiful 360-degree panoramas of locations all along western North America. This site does a great job of demonstrating QuickTime's panoramic abilities.

Decide Whether to Upgrade to QuickTime Pro

When you were browsing through QuickTime's menus, I know there's no way you missed all the grayed-out options listed as "Pro."

The "Pro" designation means that these options aren't available for you to use until you upgrade to the professional version of QuickTime. Upgrading to QuickTime Pro costs $29.95, but is it worth it?

The answer to that question is totally up to you and your needs. If you are a graphics professional who has purchased your Mac for its multimedia capabilities, the answer is an unqualified "yes." After all, that's why you're using your Mac! For the rest of us, let's examine the abilities of QuickTime Pro so as to make an informed decision.

Export Files

QuickTime Pro allows you to export your video and audio in lots of different standard formats, allowing you to share your content with those less fortunate than us QuickTime users. The range of file types you can export to is great, plus you can even specify devices you will be using the exported file with, such as an iPod or AppleTV (see Figure 10-3).

Record Audio and Video

QuickTime Pro gives you the ability to record audio (see Figure 10-4) and video (see Figure 10-5) on the fly.

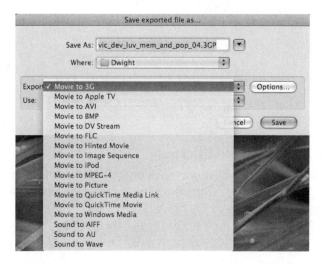

FIGURE 10-3   QuickTime Pro's export options are terrific!

FIGURE 10-4   Recording audio with QuickTime

In QuickTime Pro, you record audio by choosing File | New Audio Recording, which opens the Audio Recording window. Your Mac's audio input device, such as its built-in microphone, feeds the data to QuickTime, which records it as a MOV file.

Video is recorded using either your video camera (connected via a FireWire cable) or your Mac's built-in camera. Video files are also saved as MOV files, which you can convert to whatever format you need.

Share Your Files Easily

Sharing your creations is a snap with QuickTime Pro. Open the file you wish to share, and then choose File | Share. There are three options for sharing: via email, your personal webpage (requires a .Mac account), or Podcast Producer (you must have a Mac OS X Server with Podcast Producer installed).

Save QuickTime Files from the Internet

As you know, there's lots of great QuickTime content on the Web. Wouldn't it be great to be able to save your favorite files to your Mac? QuickTime Pro gives you that option, as the menu in Figure 10-6 shows.

FIGURE 10-5   QuickTime's video recorder

Adjust Movie Properties

The Movie Properties option in QuickTime Pro lets you modify your movies with ease. You can edit the sound and video tracks separately or together, change the way the file opens, delete or add tracks, and modify many other settings.

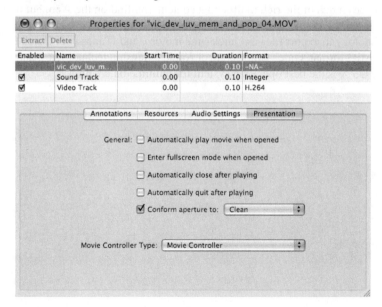

FIGURE 10-6   Saving QuickTime media to your Mac

Convinced Yet?

There are many more reasons to upgrade to QuickTime Pro, but most of them are beyond the scope of this book. The pros (there really are no cons, other than having to shell out $29.95) I've listed thus far should be more than enough to either entice the average Mac user to upgrade or not. If you do decide to upgrade, Apple will provide you with a registration code. Open the QuickTime preferences pane by choosing Apple | System Preferences | QuickTime, and then enter in the Registration Code field the code Apple provided to you. This key unlocks the professional features of QuickTime.

Summary

QuickTime provides much of the rich multimedia content you find on the Web, but it also performs many tasks behind the scenes. For example, other applications, such as iMovie, use QuickTime technology to export files as QuickTime movies, and iTunes uses QuickTime to export songs in MP3 format. QuickTime is one of Apple's flagship technologies, and is a major reason that Mac OS X is the best operating system for multimedia creation.

Chapter 11

Say Cheese! Managing Your Photos with iPhoto

How to...

- Understand the iPhoto interface
- Connect your digital camera to your Mac
- Import pictures from other sources
- Create and organize picture albums
- Edit your photographs
- Share your photos with others

Digital cameras have all but replaced traditional film cameras, and for many good reasons (although my wife and sister, who grudgingly use digital but remain firm believers in film, may argue the points). The cost of printing pictures from a digital camera is much cheaper than the cost of developing film. With a digital camera, you can take hundreds of pictures using a large (in terms of information, not size) memory module and can delete the pictures you don't want, thereby freeing up space on the camera's memory for more pictures and enabling you to avoid having to develop pictures you don't want. Also, with a digital camera, you can view a photo immediately after you take it, enabling you to decide whether you need to reshoot the scene, whereas with a film camera you might wind up with disappointing photos (and having to pay for them). You can even upload your digital photos via the Internet to your favorite photo-processing company, saving you a trip to the photo shop. Of course, if you buy a printer that is capable of printing photo-quality output, you can do everything yourself from within your own home or office. There's no need to carry around a big bag full of film rolls; you can carry a digital camera, extra batteries, and several memory modules in a small bag or tiny pouch.

This chapter shows you how to use iPhoto to get photos onto your Mac, and then organize, print, and share them.

iPhoto: A Darkroom on Your Desktop

iPhoto is Apple's gift to people who love their photographs. iPhoto imports pictures from your camera and from other resources, such as pictures e-mailed to you or scanned into your Mac with a scanner. You can then edit your pictures to your liking, making them brighter or darker, resizing them, and even removing the dreaded "red-eye" effect with incredible ease. Once done editing your picture, you can create an album for it, print it, e-mail it to friends and family, or create photo CDs. Apple has even included a great way for you to order bound photo albums online. Let's jump right into the coolness, shall we?

Understand the iPhoto Interface

iPhoto is designed to allow even the novice user to navigate without need of much help, as is customary for Apple applications. Launch iPhoto by choosing Go | Applications in the Finder and then double-clicking the iPhoto icon. When iPhoto opens, you are greeted with the main window, as shown in Figure 11-1, which identifies the following elements:

Sources list

Viewing window

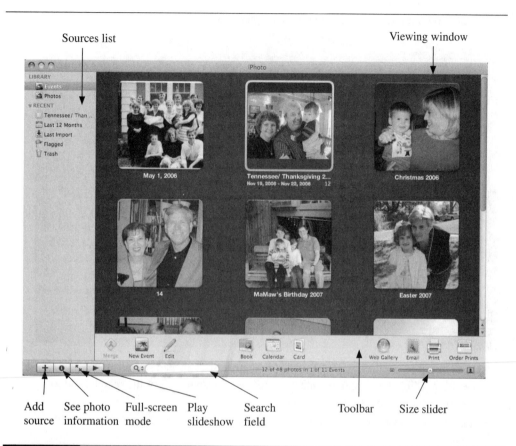

Add   See photo   Full-screen Play   Search   Toolbar   Size slider
source   information   mode   slideshow   field

FIGURE 11-1   Your first look at iPhoto (Events view)

- **Sources list**   Lists the sources of your photos, such as the main Library (holds all of your imported pictures), albums, slideshows, books, cards, calendars, and Smart Albums.

- **Toolbar**   Enables you to edit pictures, e-mail them, play a slideshow using the pictures in a particular source, order prints online, create a greeting card with the selected pictures, and so on.

- **Size slider**   Changes the size of the pictures in the viewing window.

- **Add source**   Enables you to create a new album, Smart Album, book, calendar, card, or slideshow.

- **See photo information**   Displays important information about the picture, such as its size (physical dimensions and memory), the date it was taken, the date it was edited, and so on.

- **Full-screen mode**   Displays the selected picture in full-screen mode.

- **Search field**   Enables you to search for pictures in a selected source by date, keyword, or rating. Click the up and down arrows to the immediate left of the search field to choose what type of criteria to search for.

- **Viewing window**   Shows a preview of all the pictures in the source selected in the Sources list.

- **Play slideshow**   Creates an instant slideshow using the pictures or album selected.

Use the Two Views: Events and Photos

iPhoto has two ways to view the pictures in your Library: Events view and Photos view. When you import photos into iPhoto, they are automatically organized into what Apple calls *Events*, according to the date they were taken.

Events view, shown in Figure 11-1, shows each Event with a caption underneath. By default, the caption is the date of the Event, but you can add a title to the Event to describe it, such as "Beach Vacation 2009." Simply click the caption to edit it.

When viewing all Events, you see only one photo for each Event; this photo is called the Key Photo. Hold your mouse pointer over the Key Photo in an Event and then slowly drag (or "scrub") the pointer across it. As you scrub the Event, you can see all the other photos it contains.

Photos view (see Figure 11-2) still sorts your photos by Events, but it lets you see all the individual pictures in the Event at one time.

FIGURE 11-2   Laying bare all the photos in an Event, using Photos view

Understand the Toolbar Options

The toolbar provides several items that extend the functionality of iPhoto and facilitates the use of common tasks. Some items are only available in certain views, as indicated in parentheses.

- **Merge** (available only in Events view)   You can merge, or combine, two or more Events. ⌘-click the Events you want to merge, and then click the Merge button. Click the Merge button in the dialog box that opens, and then rename the newly combined Event.

- **New Event** (available only in Events view)   Create your own Event by clicking the New Event button.

- **Split** (available only in Events view)   Events can be split into multiple Events. Open the Event you want to split, click the photo that will be the beginning of the new Event, and then click the Split button. Rename the new Event by clicking its caption, or subtitle.

- **Edit**   Open a selected picture in Edit mode by clicking this button. See the "Edit Photos" section for much more information.

- **Rotate** (available in Photos view and Edit mode)   Sometimes photos taken in portrait mode may appear sideways in iPhoto; use the Rotate tool to rotate the selected picture counter-clockwise so that it appears correctly.

■ **Hide/Unhide** (available in Photos view and open Events)   Sometimes you may not want to use a photo, but you may not be sure whether you want to delete it either. To facilitate this dilemma, iPhoto will hide the picture for you. Open an Event, click the photo you want to hide (select multiple photos by ⌘-clicking them), and then click the Hide button. "Show hidden photo" appears in the Event title bar, indicating that the Event contains a hidden picture. To see the hidden picture, click the "Show hidden photo" text. The photo appears with an "X" in its upper-right corner, indicating it is still considered a hidden photo. To take a photo out of hide mode, select the photo and then click the Unhide button in the toolbar.

■ **Flag/Unflag** (available in Photos view and open Events)   Let's say you are sorting through a stack of photos, and you set aside the photos you liked the best; this is essentially what you are doing in iPhoto when you flag a photo. Flagging photos lets you select a temporary group of photos that you will later create a new Event from or will add to an already existing Event. Select a photo that you want to flag and click the Flag button; a tiny flag icon appears in the photo's upper-left corner. If you decide you don't want to use the photo, select it and then click the Unflag button. To create a new Event from flagged photos, choose Events | "Create Event from Flagged Photos" and then click Create (this moves the flagged photos from their original Event to the new one).

■ **Book**   Click this button to get help laying out a picture book filled with pictures selected from your iPhoto Library. See how to do this in the "Share Your Memories" section of this chapter.

■ **Calendar**   Click this button to make a customized calendar using your very own photos. Detailed discussion is provided in the "Create Cards, Calendars, and Books" section later in this chapter.

■ **Card**   Clicking this button allows you to create a greeting or post card using the selected photo. This topic is also covered in more detail in the "Create Cards, Calendars, and Books" section.

■ **Web Gallery**   If you have a .Mac account, you can publish your pictures on the Internet for others to subscribe to. This is a great way to keep family and friends up to date.

■ **Email**   Clicking this button walks you through the necessary steps to email a selected picture or album to someone. More coverage follows later in this chapter in the "Email" section.

■ **Print**   To easily choose the best options for printing your photos, click this button for help. More details on printing are given later in the chapter in the "Print Your Pictures" section.

■ **Order Prints**   Click this button to place an order for individual prints of a selected picture or album. This is discussed in a bit more detail later in the "Order Prints" section.

Bring Your Memories into iPhoto

As we Southerners like to sometimes say, "there's more than one way to skin a cat." I have no idea where that saying comes from, but its meaning is perfectly clear: there's usually more than one way to get a job done. In our case, there is more than one way to get your uncle's mug into iPhoto: either connect your digital camera to your Mac and have the pictures automatically loaded into iPhoto, or bring them into iPhoto from another location on your Mac.

Connect Your Digital Camera

Mac OS X supports most digital cameras from the get-go, so chances are good that yours will work with iPhoto with little or no problem at all.

Connect your digital camera to your Mac with the USB cable that came with the camera. Once connected, Mac OS X automatically opens iPhoto and you are prompted when it is ready to import the photos from your camera; you'll see a screen closely resembling Figure 11-3.

You can choose to import everything in one fell swoop by clicking the Import All button, or import only specific photos by manually selecting the individual photos you want to import and then clicking the Import Selected button. iPhoto then asks whether you want to keep the original photos on the camera or delete them during the import. I recommend keeping the originals in case something goes wrong during the import process. You can always delete them directly from your camera later.

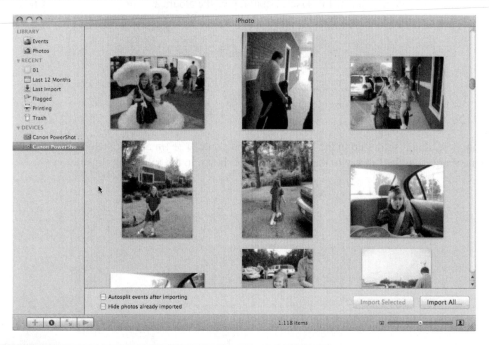

FIGURE 11-3   iPhoto is ready to import your pictures into its photo lab.

Import from Another Location

Perhaps you used a scanner to scan old pictures into your Mac in an effort to preserve them, or maybe your son just e-mailed you a picture of your new grandchild. You've saved these pictures in a folder on your Mac but now need to get them into iPhoto (just like you needed to get your photos from your camera into iPhoto). iPhoto makes this easy:

1. Choose File | Import to Library.

2. Browse your Mac for the individual picture, or a folder containing several pictures, you want to import.

3. Select the single picture or the folder and then click the Import button.

Your picture, or folder of pictures, is now added to your iPhoto Library. It doesn't get much easier than this, people.

Create Albums

Albums help you organize pictures in your iPhoto Library. Albums may be named for events such as birthdays or holidays, or you might have an album dedicated to pictures of your antique car. However you choose to organize your pictures, you'll be glad to learn about albums. Creating albums also helps you to avoid having to browse your entire iPhoto Library to find that one special photograph of Grandpa from Christmas two years ago.

To create a new album, choose File | New Album, give the album a name, and then click Create.

Your new album shows up in the Sources list, and you can begin adding pictures to it by dragging them from the Library to the new album, as shown in the following illustration.

Another way to easily make an album is to select the pictures you want to create an album from in the Library, and then click File | New Album From Selection. Once you give the new album a title and click Create, it shows up in your Sources list already populated with pictures.

> **TIP** *If you have several pictures to add to an album, dragging them all one by one can be a might tedious. To select multiple items, click the first item to highlight it, and then press ⌘ and continue holding it down while clicking each additional picture you want to select. Notice the thin yellow box that surrounds each picture you click; this indicates the picture has been selected. When your selections are complete, release the ⌘ key and then click one of the selected pictures and drag-and-drop it into the appropriate album; all of the selected items are added to the album.*

Smart Albums

iPhoto has another great way to organize your pictures called Smart Albums. Now, don't take this to mean your other albums are stupid, but they aren't quite as bright as a Smart Album. A Smart Album automatically adds items from your iPhoto Library when they meet the criteria you specified when creating the Smart Album.

Make a new Smart Album by choosing File | New Smart Album, give the album a title, and then add the criteria that must be met for a picture to be added to the album (click the + or – button to add or remove items, respectively, from the criteria list). Click OK to add the Smart Album to the Sources list.

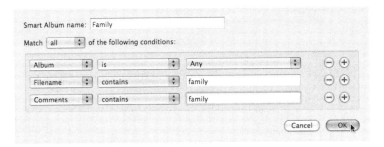

Put Together a Slideshow

One of iPhoto's slickest tricks is the ability to make a custom slideshow with your pictures, complete with music and even the Ken Burns Effect.

To begin building your slideshow extravaganza, follow these steps:

1. Select the album you want to create the slideshow from or manually choose the pictures you want to use from the Library.

2. Choose File | New Album and select Slideshow icon from the menu bar.

3. Type a name for your slideshow and click Create.

The slideshow appears in the Sources list and is populated with the pictures you selected. To add pictures to the slideshow, just drag them from your iPhoto Library onto the slideshow in the Sources list. Rearrange the order of photos in your slideshow by dragging and placing them from within the photo browser near the top of iPhoto's viewing area.

Once you've arranged the pictures in their correct order, you need to adjust the settings for the slideshow by using the toolbar (see Figure 11-4).

The options in the toolbar are as follows:

- **Play** Plays your slideshow in full-screen mode.

- **Preview** Shows a preview of the slideshow in iPhoto's viewing window.

- **Effect** Enables you to make your color slideshow appear in black and white or with sepia tones.

Play   Preview   Effect   Transition   Ken Burns   Adjust   Settings   Music
Effect

FIGURE 11-4   The Slideshow toolbar

- ■ **Transition**   Changes the effect used when your slideshow moves from one image to the next.

- ■ **Ken Burns Effect**   Causes the slideshow to slowly pan over images, while simultaneously zooming in or out during the transition, giving still images a sense of movement. This effect is very popular and definitely livens up any procession of still images.

- ■ **Adjust**   Enables you to change settings for an individual image in the slideshow, such as type and speed of the transition and the duration of time the image appears in the slideshow.

- ■ **Settings**   Enables you to choose the default behaviors for your slideshow. These settings are the default for each slide, but you can override some of them for individual slides by using the Adjust tool.

- ■ **Music**   Enables you to add any piece of music you like to your slideshow to really make it memorable. Music is a great touch and adds a huge punch to any slideshow.

Create Cards, Calendars, and Books

iPhoto has the very cool ability to create custom cards, calendars, and picture books using the pictures in your iPhoto Library. Create your item, set it up in any fashion you desire, and then place the order. In a few days, a beautiful custom-made card, calendar, or book appears on your doorstep. This is a fantastic way to create gifts that are unique, personal, surprisingly affordable, and unforgettable.

To make your own unique creation:

1. Select the picture(s) you want to use for your project.

2. Click either the Calendar, Card, or Book button in the toolbar.

3. Choose a theme from the list. Your choice of themes is determined by which project type you chose, as illustrated in Figures 11-5 (calendar), 11-6 (card), and 11-7 (book). If you're creating a book, the Book Type pop-up menu allows you to choose the size of your book. If your project is a card, the pop-up menu in the upper-left corner lets you choose whether it is a greeting card or postcard. To see what other options are available for your project, as well as a list of current prices, click the "Options + Prices" button in the lower-left corner.

4. Click the Choose button to proceed.

From this point, things get a bit more project-specific.

Calendars

After choosing the theme for your calendar project, you are asked to format your calendar.

Note that you can import your own iCal calendars to further personalize your calendar (that's pretty awesome). Click OK to move to the calendar-editing window, shown in Figure 11-8.

If you chose the pictures you wanted to use prior to clicking the Calendar button, those pictures are listed on the left of the iPhoto calendar-editing window. If you didn't select any photos before beginning your calendar, iPhoto prompts you to choose whether to add the photos

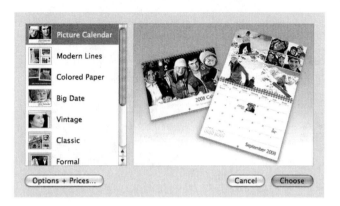

FIGURE 11-5   Calendar themes

now or later. If you specify "Ask Later" you are immediately taken to the calendar-editing window. To get pictures into your calendar later, open the Library or the album you want to get the pictures from and drag-and-drop the desired pictures on the calendar in the Sources list. If you specify "Add Now" all the photos from your Library or selected album are made available in your calendar.

FIGURE 11-6   Themes for a card project

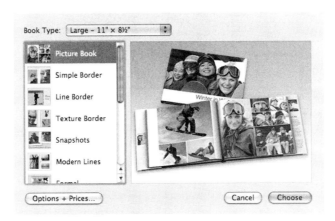

FIGURE 11-7   Book themes

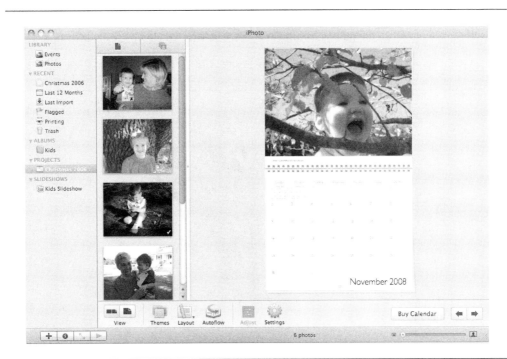

FIGURE 11-8   Customizing your calendar

Simply drag-and-drop the photos onto the calendar to place them where you want, or click Autoflow in the toolbar to have iPhoto place the pictures automatically.

To view the individual pages of the calendar, click the View Pages button (its icon looks like a piece of paper with the upper-right corner folded over) near the top of the iPhoto window. iPhoto automatically creates a layout pattern for your pictures, but you can change these patterns by clicking the Layout pop-up menu in the toolbar.

Add text to your pictures by clicking the Design tool and selecting the option with text under the photo area.

Should the look of the text not be to your liking, click the Settings tool and choose the Fonts tab to change the fonts used for your calendar.

Once you have completed the layout of your calendar, you can purchase your one-of-a-kind creation by clicking the Buy Calendar button.

Cards

Once you've chosen a theme for your card and clicked Choose (see Figure 11-6), you see the card-editing window, shown in Figure 11-9, in which you can personalize your card further by adding your own text. To change the fonts for your text, just click the Settings button in the toolbar; you can then change the headline, title, and body text separately.

FIGURE 11-9   Your personal in-home greeting card business

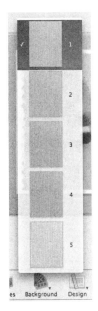

You can also change the background by clicking the Background tool and choosing a new one from the pop-up menu, shown at left. Most themes have this option.

You change the design, or layout, of the card as well by clicking the Design tool and choosing a different option from the pop-up menu, shown at right.

Click the Buy Card button when you are satisfied with your card's design. Believe me, these cards make a great impression on their recipients!

Books

The picture books offered by Apple are of very high quality and make perfect gifts that will be treasured and passed down. Giving someone a hardbound printed photo album filled with family photos and personalized titles is very unique and unexpected. Apple doesn't pay me to make these statements but the truth is the truth, compensated or not.

First, here's a glance at the book-editing window:

Now that you've picked a theme for your book, add photos to the book in the same manner as you would for a calendar. If you selected the pictures you wanted before clicking the Book button, those pictures are listed in the top of the book-editing window. If you didn't select any photos before beginning your calendar, iPhoto prompts you to choose whether to add the photos now or later. If you click "Ask Later" you are immediately taken to the book-editing window. To put pictures into your book at a later time, open the Library or the album that contains the pictures and drag-and-drop them on the book in the Sources list. If you specify "Add Now" all the photos from your Library or selected album are made available for the book.

Simply drag-and-drop the photos into the gray areas of the book to place them, or click Autoflow in the toolbar to have iPhoto arrange the pictures automatically.

To view the individual pages of the book, click the View Pages button (as with a calendar, its icon looks like a piece of paper with the upper-right corner folded over) near the top of the book-editing window. iPhoto automatically creates a layout pattern for your pictures, but you can change these patterns by using the Layout pop-up menu in the toolbar. If you don't have enough pages in your book for all of your pictures, click the Add Pages button in the toolbar. Keep in mind that extra pages will increase the standard cost of your book.

Should you decide to use fonts other than the default for your chosen theme, click the Settings tool, which gives you a variety of font options.

To preview how your book looks, click the Play button, which plays your book like a slideshow.

Purchase Your Masterpieces

Click the Buy Calendar, Buy Card, or Buy Book button and iPhoto will speak with servers at Apple to determine if you have an Apple account with 1-Click ordering enabled. If you do not have an account, click the Set Up Account button in the bottom right and follow the onscreen instructions. If you do have an account, you are asked to enter your quantity and shipping preferences. Click the Buy Now button to complete the transaction or click Cancel to not place the order.

If you're Bugs Bunny, a guy on a moped should zip up to your mailbox in just a few seconds with your newly minted calendar, card, or book, but otherwise it may be a couple of days before you receive it, depending on which shipping options you chose.

Edit Photos

Does the red-eye in that photo of your two-year-old boy make him look like the demon-seed of Davy Jones? Is there a big piece of spinach stuck in your teeth in an otherwise perfect wedding picture? Does Grandpa's hair (what's left, anyway) appear bluer than usual in the latest Christmas snapshots? It's frustrating when one tiny blemish ruins a perfectly good photograph. Fortunately, iPhoto has the tools you need to clean up those imperfections and make right what was once oh so wrong (yet another reason to go digital over film!).

To edit a photo, double-click it in the viewing window and iPhoto switches to Edit mode. You have several tools at your disposal for enhancing your pictures, identified in Figure 11-10 and described next.

- **Rotate** Each click of this button turns the picture 90 degrees counter-clockwise.

- **Crop** Click the Crop button to enter cropping mode. Uncheck the Constrain box and drag the handles in each corner of the photo to manually trim your picture.

- **Straighten** This option allows you to rotate a crooked photo by ten degrees or less in either direction. Select the photo, click the Edit button (or double-click the photo if in a slideshow, book, calendar, or card), and then click the Straighten button. Drag the Straighten slider to straighten the photo. If you don't like your results, click the Reset button.

- **Enhance** iPhoto automatically makes adjustments to brightness and/or contrast. You can enhance a photo as many times as needed. Choose Edit | Undo Enhance Photo to reset changes if you desire.

- **Red-Eye** Use this tool to instantly get rid of pesky "red-eye" effects in your picture. To use the tool, enlarge the image using the size slider, click the Red-Eye button, position the crosshair over the offending eye in the picture, and then click Red-Eye again. Works even faster than Visine!

- **Retouch** Smoothes, or blends, selected parts of the picture to reduce the appearance of damage or defects. Choose Edit | Undo Retouch to reset changes if you desire.

Rotate   Crop   Straighten   Enhance   Red-Eye   Retouch   Effects   Adjust   Done   Arrows

FIGURE 11-10   Editing your keepsakes has never been easier!

■ **Effects**   iPhoto shows you a window with eight versions of your photo with effects added to it. There is also a version of your original photo for comparison and so that you can instantly go back to it if you don't like the effects.

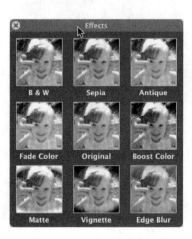

■ **Adjust**   Click this button to manually change various aspects of the picture, such as brightness, contrast, color, sharpness, and so forth, in the Adjust panel.

■ **Done**   Click this button after your editing is complete.

■ **Arrows**   Use these arrows to move from one picture to the next in your Library or album.

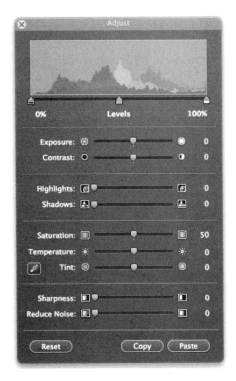

When you edit a photo, the changes are applied without confirmation, but iPhoto always keeps a copy of the original photo so that you can easily revert back to it. You can also edit your photos in full-screen mode, which gives you more room to work, as shown in the example below.

Share Your Memories

In Hollywood movies such as *Total Recall* and *Eternal Sunshine of the Spotless Mind*, the object was to erase your memories, but iPhoto lets you do just the opposite: share them!

I've already discussed some of the ways you can share your pictures—create custom calendars, cards, and picture books—but there are other ways as well. To see the options available, click the Share menu. Each menu option is described in turn in the following sections, as well as a sharing option that doesn't appear in the Share menu.

Email

iPhoto enables you to share your photos via e-mail by choosing Share | Email or by clicking the Email icon in the toolbar. Make your choices in the Mail Photo dialog box and click Compose.

iPhoto prepares your photo(s) and then opens mail for you, with your photo(s) attached to a new mail message. (Sometimes it's kind of difficult to not feel a little lazy when using these awesome applications!) Simply enter the address of the person you want to send the photo to and click Send to zip your memories across the Internet.

Set Desktop

Choosing Share | Set Desktop simply makes the selected photo your Mac's desktop picture. The number of people you share the photo with is limited to how many of your friends, family, and colleagues walk by your Mac and take time to look directly at your screen.

Order Prints

Sometimes it's good just to do things the old-fashioned way. In this case, the "old-fashioned way" is to get physical pictures in your hands. Choose Share | Order Prints, and you will see an order screen like the one shown in Figure 11-11, enabling you to order your prints. Those family and friends without computers will be most grateful when they receive your prints!

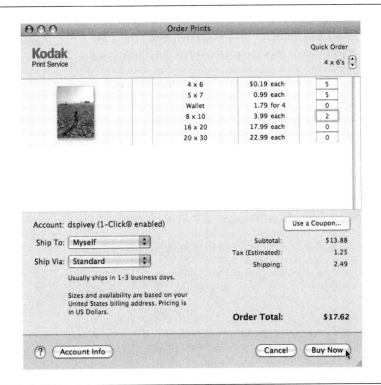

FIGURE 11-11 Ordering prints from iPhoto

Web Gallery

Choosing Share | Web Gallery is another method of publishing your pictures via a .Mac account. Your Web Gallery albums are available to anyone using iPhoto or through an RSS reader. Also, any changes you make to your Web Gallery albums are automatically updated for those viewing it.

You can specify who can view your published photos by using the choices in the "Album viewable by" menu. The "Edit names and passwords" option lets you create usernames and passwords for people that you want to view your albums. The Options check boxes enable you to allow visitors to your published album to download or upload photos to it. Click the Publish button when you've set the options to your liking.

Your published album appears in the Sources list. Select it to the see the published photos as well as the URL (web address) for accessing the published photos on the Internet. Click the "Tell a Friend" button to send an email to the people you want to view your photos.

Send to iWeb

If you have a personal webpage through your .Mac subscription, you can use iWeb (Share | Send to iWeb) to add your pictures to the site, either on your photo page or your blog. iWeb allows you to fully customize the way your photos are viewed on your site.

.Mac Slides

Use your .Mac account to publish pictures as a slideshow that others can access by viewing your webpage. Select the pictures you want to publish and choose Share | .Mac Slides. When prompted, click the Publish button to send your pictures to your .Mac account.

Send to iDVD

Choose Share | Send to iDVD to export your slideshow or album to iDVD, which creates a slideshow for the custom DVD you're designing.

Burn

Burning photo CDs is a great way to share your pictures as well as to archive them for safe keeping. Select the photos that you want to burn and choose Share | Burn. iPhoto prompts you to insert a blank CD, if you haven't already done so.

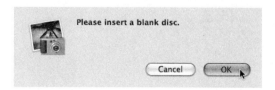

Once you insert the CD, iPhoto will burn the photos to it.

Export Slideshows

This option isn't available in the Share menu but is a really neat to way to share memories. Exporting your slideshow to a QuickTime movie allows you to e-mail it to people or post it on your website, complete with any audio you may have added to the slideshow.

Select a slideshow you want to export in the Sources list, and then choose File | Export. Name the exported slideshow something descriptive, choose the location to which you want to export it, choose a size for the slideshow, and then click the Export button.

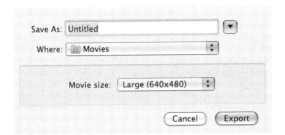

Print Your Pictures

iPhoto makes it really simple to print your photos on your own printer. Click a picture that you want to print, and then click the Print button in the toolbar to see the Print dialog box.

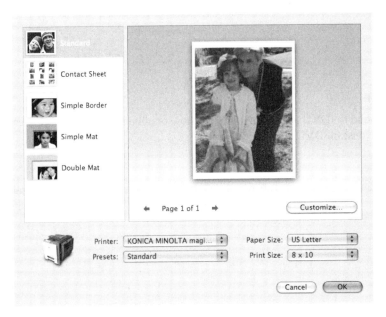

Choose border and layout options in the left pane, choose the printer you want to send the job to, choose the size of the paper you're printing on and the printed size of the picture itself (for example, 8 × 10 or 5 × 7). Click the Customize button to see other options for your printed photos, such as borders, themes, and backgrounds. Click OK to send the print job to the printer.

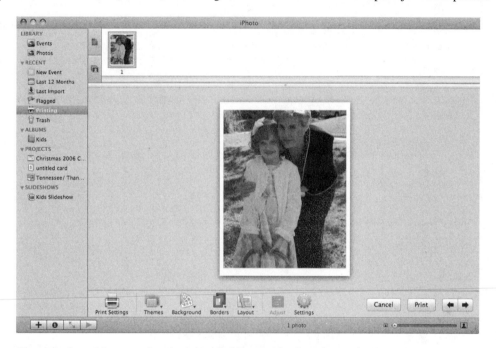

You can also add text to the photo by clicking the Settings button in the toolbar, or adjust the colors, brightness, and contrast by selecting the picture, and then clicking the Adjust button. Make any changes necessary, and then click the Print button to send the job.

You've got your own photo lab right on your desktop!

Summary

Sharing, organizing, and archiving your photos has never been easier, and the options for doing such are amazing. Apple has done a great job with iPhoto, which has become an absolute essential for all Mac users. Now that you've become familiar with it, use it to impress your family and friends. Even if you're not a professional photographer, with iPhoto you'll have fun fooling everyone into thinking you are.

Chapter 12

Well, Turn it Up, Man! Get In Tune with iTunes

How to...

- Use iTunes for all your music, spoken word, and movie needs
- Import songs into iTunes
- Burn CDs of your music
- Share your music (legally!)
- Sync your music with your iPod
- Navigate the iTunes Store

It seems that everybody and their mother has an iPod these days, or has at least heard of the iPod. If you've ever used an iPod, you probably are familiar with iTunes as well, since the only way to get music to and from your iPod is through iTunes.

iTunes is the best music software on the planet, bar none. This is the 21st-century way of doing everything musically. From listening to your tunes to organizing them, there is no easier way. iTunes has evolved into more than just a music application, though. You can also download video, such as movies and television shows, via iTunes for viewing with your Mac, iPod, iPhone, and now Apple TV!

It's Your Party *and* You're the D.J.!

Open iTunes by choosing Go | Applications in the Finder and then double-clicking the iTunes icon. In order to get around in iTunes, you need to know where all the goodies are. Figure 12-1 breaks it down.

Some of the items listed in Figure 12-1 need further explanation:

- **View**   Choose your favorite way to view your iTunes tracks and album artwork. The options are Cover Flow view (the coolest and, therefore, my favorite), list view, and grouped with album artwork.
- **Search**   Type any information you have for a song, and iTunes lists every item it finds that meets the criteria. This is really helpful if you have a huge list of tracks.
- **Status window**   View the name of the track that is playing, as well as the amount of time elapsed and remaining.
- **Track list**   View all of the tracks in your Library, sorted by the column headings. Click a column heading, such as Name, Artist, or Album, and your tracks will instantly be arranged alphabetically in that column.

■ **Library**   Look here to find every track stored in your iTunes folder.

■ **Browse**   Click this icon to see the Browser, which is an easy way to zip through your music collection by either Genre, Album, or Artist.

■ **Full Screen**   Click this icon to see your tracks in full screen, an awesome iTunes alternative view, as illustrated in Figure 12-2. This interface is rather limited, but is still oh so very cool. Click-and-drag the Cover Flow slider back and forth to find tracks, as well as to dazzle friends and enemies alike!

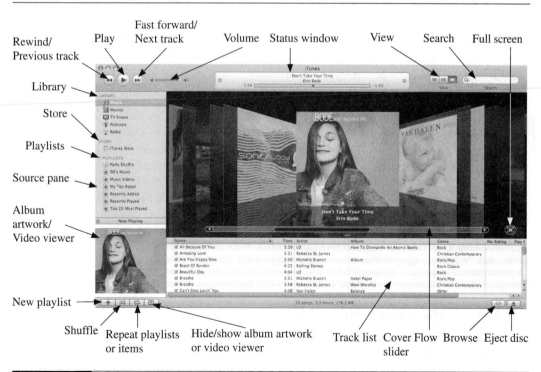

| FIGURE 12-1 | Tunes is ready to rock! |

Rewind/   Play   Fast forward/   Cover Flow   Volume   Exit full-
Previous track   Next track   slider   screen mode

FIGURE 12-2   iTunes in all its full-screen glory

Use the Mighty iTunes Store

The iTunes Store is your one-stop-shop for your multimedia needs (see Figure 12-3). You can download audio books and music tracks, listen to or watch university lectures, see movie trailers, check out celebrities' lists of favorite songs, get games for your iPod, and much more. One look and it's easy to see why the iTunes Store is the best in its class. To access the iTunes Store, click its icon in the source pane.

Browse the "storefront" of the iTunes Store and you will see many categories to choose from, lists of the most popular items in those categories, the most recent items added to the Store, links to your iTunes account, favorite items of Apple's staff, and items exclusive to iTunes. If you're not careful, you can get lost in here!

Find Much More Than Just Music

iTunes was originally intended as a management tool for your music library, but lately it has morphed into so much more. iTunes handles so many different types of multimedia now that Apple might do well to consider renaming it to iMedia, but hey, that's just my opinion. A look at the Source pane shows five options under the Library heading: Music, Movies, TV Shows, Podcasts, and Radio.

FIGURE 12-3 The iTunes Store: a world of multimedia is yours with a few mouse clicks.

Music

Music is the primary reason for most visits to the iTunes Store, so just because it's "old hat" doesn't diminish its importance. Browse the vast library of tracks or use the search field to quickly find the song or artist you're looking for.

How to ...   **Purchase Items from the iTunes Store**

While there are plenty of free items available in the iTunes Store, the bulk of the goodies must be purchased. To make a purchase, you need to create an iTunes account, which is easy enough. Once you've found an item you simply can't live without, click its Buy button and iTunes will immediately prompt you to either create an account or log on using an existing account.

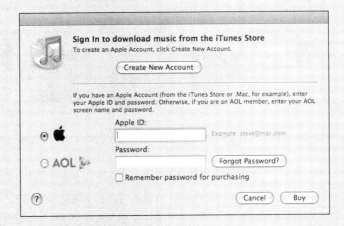

If you have a .Mac account, you can use it to log on and purchase items from the iTunes Store, or just enter your information as prompted to create a new account. You can also use your AOL (America Online) screen name as an alternative, if you happen to have one.

Movies

Trips to the video store are becoming less commonplace with the advent of online downloads of the latest releases. Download movies from the iTunes Store to view them on your Mac, iPod, iPhone, or Apple TV. This is a concept that has DVDs shaking in their cases.

See the movies you've downloaded by clicking Movies under Library.

TV Shows

In today's fast-paced world, it's tough to be home every time your favorite TV show is on. The iTunes Store comes to the rescue by allowing you to download TV shows so that you can view them at your leisure on your Mac, iPod, iPhone, or Apple TV.

TV shows that you purchase can be seen by clicking TV Shows under Library.

Podcasts

The iPod is so embedded in the culture that new words have sprung up around its existence. *Podcasts* are radio shows or videos that are available for download via the iTunes Store, most of them for free. You can find podcasts in the iTunes Store for almost any type of show imaginable, from political talk to religion to home or car repair.

A great feature associated with podcasts is the ability to subscribe to them, automatically downloading new broadcasts so that you never miss a show. When you find a podcast you like, always keep up with the current discussions by clicking its Subscribe button, thereby adding it to your Podcasts collection in the Library.

Radio

The Internet and radio are completely separate beasts to most people, but you can actually find great radio stations broadcasting through the Internet by using iTunes. Click Radio under Library and you see more than 20 different categories to select stations from. Everything from Ambient to Folk to Reggae is available for your listening pleasure.

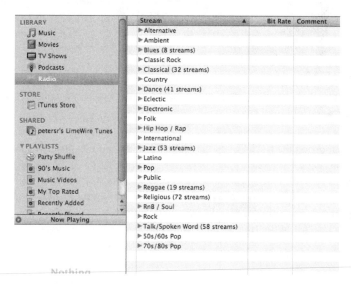

Import Tracks to Your Library

iTunes is one heck of a program, but without music, there just isn't much to it. So, how do you add music to iTunes? There are two basic ways: buy the tracks via the iTunes Store, as already described, or import them from another source, such as a CD.

Import Tracks from CDs

Copying tracks from a CD isn't nearly as tough as it may sound, especially to someone who has never done so before. As with most tasks, Apple actually makes it downright easy. By default, iTunes is set up to ask whether or not you would like to import the CD. If you want to see how this process works, click Yes.

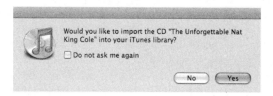

FIGURE 12-4   See the orange circle with the squiggly line (highlighted)? That's the song currently being imported (green circles with checks have already been successfully imported).

iTunes begins importing the tracks from the CD, and shows you its progress (see Figure 12-4). This is *really* difficult, isn't it? NOT!

Did you notice how iTunes recognizes the track numbers and song titles for your CD? That's because iTunes accesses the Gracenote Media Database via the Internet, finds the title of the CD you are importing, and downloads the list of tracks and songs for it automatically, provided you are connected to the Internet at the time you are importing.

Did you know?

Add to Library or Import?

Click the File menu and notice that the keyboard shortcuts for "Add to Library" and Import are very similar, the only difference being that Import requires you to press the SHIFT key. The reason these keyboard shortcuts are so similar is that the corresponding commands perform a very similar function, which is to add tracks to your Library. However, there's one major difference in the way they operate. Import *automatically* makes a copy of the track in your Music folder—period, end of story—whereas copying the track is *optional* with the "Add to Library" command. Mind you, the "Add to Library" function does add the track to your track list, and by default it does make an actual duplicate of the track file in your Music folder, but it doesn't have to be that way. To turn this option off, choose iTunes | Preferences | Advanced | General, and uncheck the "Copy files to iTunes Music folder when adding to library" box.

Why would you not want a copy of the track added to your Music folder? To save precious disk space, of course! If you already have the file in a separate folder, or a separate partition for that matter, making a copy of the file only takes up that much more room on your hard drive. My suggestion? Make a copy of the file in the Music folder and delete the original. That way, all your tracks are located in one place, making it much easier to back up your iTunes Library.

Import Files

Importing music and other tracks from audio files is just as easy as the other methods of importing to your Library. One of two methods will easily do the trick: either drag-and-drop the file into the iTunes track list, or choose File | Add to Library, browse your Mac for the file, click to highlight it, and click Open. Ta-da! The file is now added to your list of tracks.

Check Out iTunes' Preferences

iTunes has lots and lots of preferences to streamline your multimedia adventures to your tastes. Choose iTunes | Preferences and we'll get started.

General

The General preferences cover basics such as the size of text in iTunes, which types of items to display in the Source pane, the name of your shared iTunes Library, and whether iTunes should check for updates for itself automatically.

Podcasts

The Podcasts preferences enable you to specify when to check for new episodes of your favorite podcasts, and what to do with them when they're found.

Playback

In the Playback preferences pane, set how iTunes plays your music and videos, and choose how to shuffle the songs when the Shuffle option is on. A few of these preferences need a bit more explanation:

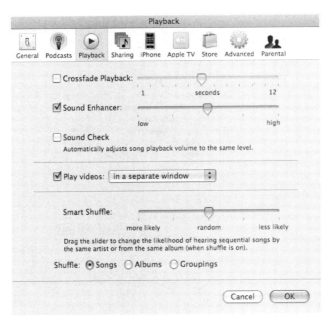

■ **Crossfade Playback** Causes songs that are currently playing to fade out at their end, while the next song in the playlist fades in.

■ **Sound Enhancer** Adds depth and enlivens the quality of music.

■ **Sound Check** Automatically adjusts the volume level of songs so that all songs play at roughly the same volume.

Sharing

The Sharing preferences allow you to decide whether to search for shared libraries of other users on your network, as well as what files, if any, that you want to share. Also choose whether people who access your shared files need a password to access them.

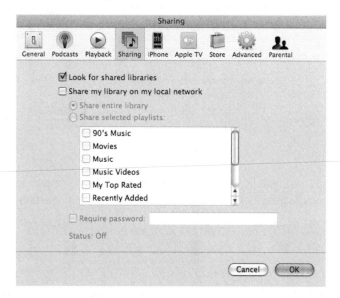

iTunes limits sharing to a maximum of five computers a day.

iPhone

You can synchronize your iPhone's settings and contents with your Mac by simply connecting it to the Mac. Contacts, music, photos, web bookmarks, email settings, calendars, podcasts, movies, and TV shows can all be synchronized. This preferences pane shows which iPhones have been backed up, or synchronized, with this Mac. You can also disable automatic syncing from here.

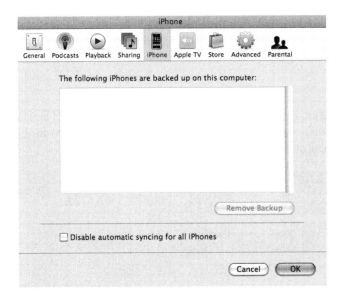

Apple TV

Apple TV syncs with iTunes, gaining access to all the multimedia you've purchased through iTunes. Use this preferences pane to see the Apple TVs that are currently synchronized with iTunes.

Store

These preferences control how you purchase items from the iTunes Store, whether prepurchased content is automatically downloaded, and whether a new playlist should be created when entire song collections are downloaded.

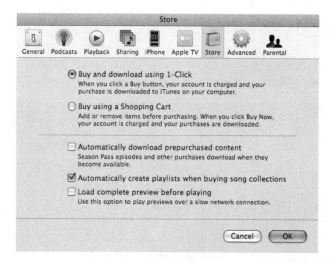

Advanced

The Advanced preferences pane has three tabs: General, Importing, and Burning.

General Tab

The General tab, as shown here, enables you to choose whether iTunes should organize your iTunes Music folder automatically, decide whether iTunes should make a copy of your imported files in the Music folder, configure Internet music streaming, and select options for the Visualizer.

Did you know?

You Can "Watch" Your Music

iTunes has an awesome feature called Visualizer, which quite literally visualizes the sound waves of your music. To see the Visualizer in action, begin playing a song and then choose View | Turn On Visualizer (or press ⌘-T). How cool is that? Very, very cool. Want to see something even cooler? Choose View | Full Screen (or press ⌘-F).

Importing Tab

The Importing tab, shown next, of the Advanced preferences pane enables you to configure how iTunes imports music from CDs. Decide how iTunes should behave when a CD is inserted into your Mac, what encoding to use when importing the tracks (the default is AAC, and is the best encoding method for most uses), and what quality to use for the encoding. These settings do not apply to music you download from the iTunes Store.

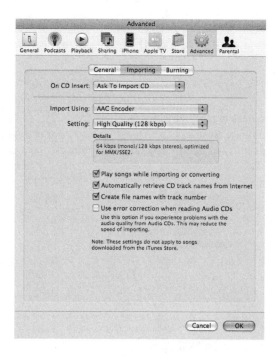

Burning Tab

The options on the Burning tab control the speed with which discs are burned, as well as what format is used to burn them.

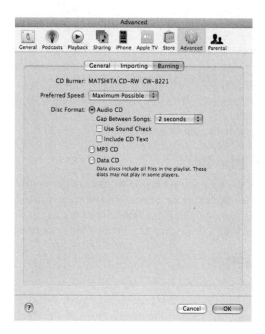

Audio CDs play on standard CD drives and can hold roughly 20 songs. MP3 CDs can only play in your Mac or on CD players that support MP3 playback; they can hold approximately 150 songs.

Parental

The purpose of these preferences is fairly obvious: to give parents the ability to limit their kids' use, or possible misuse, of iTunes. Restrict access to various sources such as podcasts and the iTunes Store, and limit availability of multimedia based on ratings.

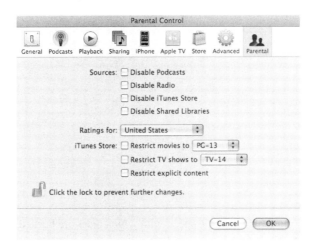

Create Playlists

Playlists are groupings of tracks that you create and customize. You can create playlists of your favorite slow songs, dance tunes, country hoedowns, or break-dancing grooves (yes, I grew up in the '80s, but no, I can't break dance). Playlists have no limits, unless you plan to burn the playlist to a CD (discussed in the next section), which would limit the total playing time of items in the playlist to typically 80 minutes.

There are two types of playlists: standard and Smart.

Create a Standard Playlist

To create a standard playlist, click the New Playlist button in the lower-left corner of the iTunes window, or choose File | New Playlist. Type a name for your playlist in the Playlist source pane, and then add tracks to it by dragging them from your Library to the playlist. Don't worry, this doesn't move the tracks from your Library, it just adds a copy of the track to your playlist.

Create a Smart Playlist

A Smart Playlist watches your Library for tracks that meet the criteria you specify for it. When a track is added to the Library that matches that criteria, a copy of the track is added to the Smart Playlist. There are several predefined Smart Playlists included with iTunes, such as Recently

Added and Top 25 Most Played. The Recently Added Smart Playlist is on the lookout for tracks that have been added to your Library during a specified period of time; its default is set to the last two weeks. The Top 25 Most Played Smart Playlist checks to see which of your tracks have been played the most, and then ranks them based on the number of times they have been played. To see these criteria, right-click or CTRL-click Recently Added or Top 25 Most Played in the Playlists source pane and choose Edit Smart Playlist from the options. Recently Added should look like this:

Top 25 Most Played uses these criteria:

To create a Smart playlist of your own, choose File | New Smart Playlist, and then manipulate the criteria to suit you. Click the + or – button to add or remove rules, respectively.

Burn, Baby, Burn!

My favorite feature of iTunes is the ability to create my own unique playlists and burn them to a CD. As with everything else in iTunes, this is not a tall task.

To burn a playlist to a CD, right-click or CTRL-click the playlist you want to burn and choose "Burn Playlist to Disc." Alternatively, you can select the playlist and then choose File | "Burn Playlist to Disc." Insert a blank CD, if you haven't done so already, and iTunes will soon pop out a CD containing the tracks from your playlist. iTunes will warn you if the number of tracks exceeds the space on the CD, in which case you would need to either whittle down the number of tracks or burn the playlist to multiple CDs.

Take Your Tunes on the Road: Connect Your iPod

Special thanks to my beautiful niece, Kelsey, for the use of her iPod (it even has her name engraved on the back of it) for this part of the chapter!

If you don't know what an iPod is, put this book down (gently now…oh, so gently), walk to your front door, open said front door, slowly crack open your eyes, and take what must be your first peek at the outside world in many a moon.

Even people who've never touched a computer before know that an iPod totally revolutionized the music world, hand-in-hand with iTunes of course. In this arrangement, the iPod is the sexy in-your-face superstar and iTunes is the silent but equal partner who likes to work behind the scenes. The two are inextricably intertwined, as designed by Apple. The iPod/iTunes partnership opened the door for Apple to give a whole new segment of the world, Windows users, a gander at the wonder and goodness of its software.

Before connecting your iPod to your Mac, know this: you can synchronize your iPod with only one Mac at a time! This means that if you have synchronized this iPod with another Mac and already have items on it, those items will be erased and replaced by the items contained in iTunes on the second Mac. iTunes will prompt you before doing anything to your iPod, but I thought it only fair to warn you now. This does not mean that you can't use your iPod with multiple Macs. See the upcoming How To sidebar "Use Your iPod with Multiple Macs" for more information.

Connect your iPod to your Mac now. Should your iPod's software be out of date, you will see a similar prompt to this one:

Decide whether to download and install the update immediately, just download the software and update later, or cancel the update entirely.

If you have synchronized your iPod with another Mac, you may see a message similar to this one, telling you that you have previously synced with another photo library and asking whether you're sure you want to sync with this one:

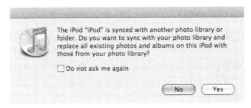

Make whatever decision you like, but understand this is irreversible.

Once your iPod is connected, its name displays in the Devices source pane, and your iPod's information is shown in the iTunes main window, on the Summary tab. The following are the five tabs in the iTunes window:

- **Summary**   Gives you the basics of your iPod, showing you its name, memory capacity, software version currently installed, sync options, and a visual breakdown of how the memory on your iPod is used.

- **Music**   Enables you to select which audio tracks and playlists to sync with your iPod.

As mentioned in the previous Caution, if you have synced your iPod with another Mac, you see a prompt such as this one:

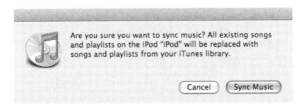

■ **Podcasts**   Offers similar options to the Music tab. Simply select which podcasts to sync with your iPod, and enjoy your favorite radio broadcasts anytime you like.

■ **Photos**   Presents you with options for syncing your photo library, as shown in the following illustration.

■   **Contacts**   Allows you to sync not only your contacts from Address Book, but also your iCal calendars.

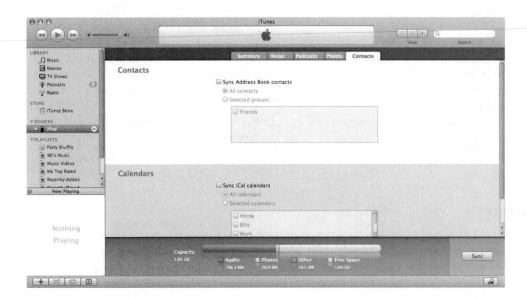

How to ...   **Use Your iPod with Multiple Macs**

The first time I heard you couldn't sync your iPod with more than one Mac, I thought it was a joke. Well, it wasn't a joke, which really drew my ire, but then I found out that I only knew half the story. It turns out you *can* sync with more than one Mac, you just can't sync *automatically*! You can sync with as many Macs as you want as long as you do so *manually*!

To make this magic happen, click your iPod in the Devices source pane, and then check the box next to "Manually manage music" (or "music and video" if you have a video iPod) in the Summary tab. iTunes tells you that you must manually eject your iPod to properly disconnect it from the system.

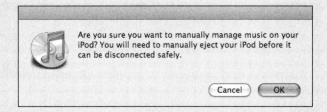

Don't worry about that message. It sounds so terrifying, like the Mac will blow up in your face if you don't properly disconnect your iPod from it, but I assure you that's not the case. All this message means is that you need to click the Eject iPod button in the lower-right corner of the iTunes window, or click the Eject button next to the iPod in the Devices source pane; after the iPod is no longer listed in the Devices source pane, you can disconnect the iPod from your Mac.

To transfer tracks and playlists manually, just begin dragging-and-dropping them from your Music Library to your iPod's icon in the Devices source pane. That's it!

Summary

iTunes is a huge part of the Mac experience for must users. Computers are no longer for business and the Internet only, but have firmly infiltrated the entertainment ranks. I never thought geeks would take over Hollywood and the music industry! Then again, us Mac users aren't garden-variety geeks; we're the coolest geeks on the planet!

Chapter 13

iLights! iCamera! iAction!: Using iMovie

How to...

- Navigate the iMovie interface
- Bring your digital movies into iMovie
- Edit a movie
- Add music and titles to your movie
- Apply cool special effects
- Share your movies

Computers have certainly come a very long way since I first sat down in front of one in the early 1980s. Back then, playing a game that consists of a couple of blocks and some text was an incredible feat. It was also one that could take you days of typing in code from a magazine just so you could enjoy such an experience.

Sounds pretty archaic, doesn't it? But today, with a Mac, I can do things that truly amaze. I can connect a camera to my Mac, import the digital movies and images from the camera, create and edit my own movie *myself*, and share it with family and friends hundreds of miles away. Better yet, in some cases that process may only take *minutes*!

When Apple introduced iMovie, it was a godsend for people who love to take video of their families and events, and even for those who make a living with their digital video camera. The ease with which you could get your movies onto the computer, and then get them off the computer edited, titled, and complete with a soundtrack, boggled the mind.

If you've never used iMovie before, get ready for a treat. This chapter gives you just enough of a taste for what iMovie can do that you won't want to stop here.

iMovie: Your Personal Editing Room

iMovie's interface is designed so that what used to be such a complicated task, editing video, is now something that absolutely anyone can do without requiring a degree from the University of Southern California film school. Let's see what's what in Figure 13-1.

Import Video into iMovie

Talk about flexibility! iMovie can import from your digital video camera, import movie files already on your Mac (formats include MOV, MPEG-4, DV, and others), and import iMovie HD projects from earlier versions of iMovie. iMovie can also import 1080i video.

iMovie can indeed import movies from your video camera, but do not *insert mini-DVDs, or any other nonstandard disk, into your Mac's CD/DVD drive. You could seriously damage your Mac's CD/DVD drive.*

Project library   Project window   Toolbar   Viewer

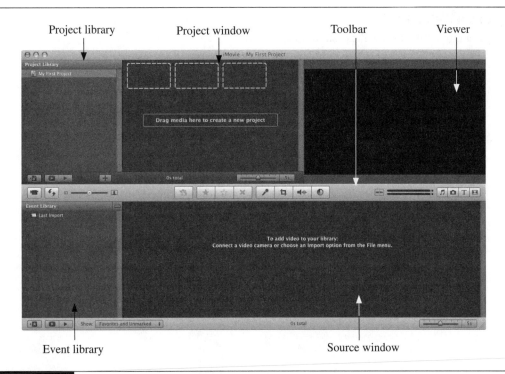

Event library   Source window

FIGURE 13-1   iMovie's interface layout makes a normally difficult job a cinch!

What's This "1080i Video" Stuff?

Some camcorders can record digital video in a high-definition format called 1080i, which can save the video in sizes up to 1920 × 1080 pixels (trust me, that's pretty big). This makes for some beautiful widescreen videos! However, something that large is going to take up huge amounts of hard drive space. iMovie gives you the option of importing 1080i video at its full size (1920 × 1080 pixels) or a large size, 960 × 540 pixels.

Check the documentation that came with your camera to see if 1080i is a format that it supports.

Import Movie Files

To import a movie file, follow these simple steps:

1. Choose File | Import Movies and browse your Mac for the movie file you want to import.

2. Select the movie file you want to import and choose a drive from the Save To destination if more than one hard disk is installed on the Mac.

3. Choose whether this is a new Event or part of an Event that exists already (more on Events in the next Did You Know? sidebar).

4. Choose at what size to save the file (if it is in the 1080i video format).

5. Choose whether to copy the movie files or move them from their original location.

6. Click Import and you will see a new Event in your Event Library. To see the clips (snippets of video) contained in the Event, just click its name in the Event Library and the clips display in the source window on the lower right, as shown in the following illustration.

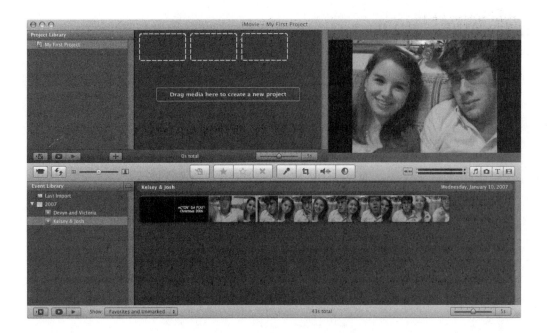

Did you know?

A Quick Word about Events

iMovie uses an Event Library to keep track of the movies you've imported. The Event Library organizes your movies into Events that can easily be browsed to find the clips you need. For example, when you import video from a Christmas family gathering sometime in the future, you could create an Event called "Christmas 2009." The Christmas 2009 Event would appear in your Event Library, ready for viewing or adding to a new iMovie project.

Events are great for one main reason: you can add as many clips from as many different sources as you like. In other words, if your cousin Jarrod e-mails you movies that he took with his cell phone at the Christmas gathering, you can add those to your Christmas 2009 Event, along with the video you imported from your camera.

Import iMovie HD Projects

You import an iMovie HD project in much the same manner as you import movie files:

1. Choose File | Import iMovie HD Project and browse your Mac for the iMovie HD project you want to import.

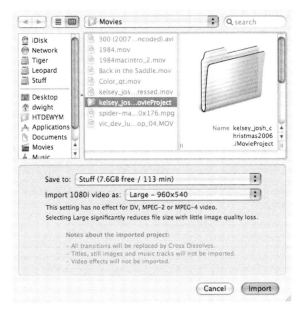

2. Select the project folder and choose a Save To location.

3. Choose at what size to save the file (if it is in the 1080i video format).

4. Click Import.

 None of the effects, titles, still images, or music tracks from the old iMovie HD project will be imported into iMovie.

Once iMovie has finished the import, a new project is listed in the Project Library, a new Event is added to the Event Library, and the clips are automatically added to the Project window, ready to be transformed into a customized movie, as shown next.

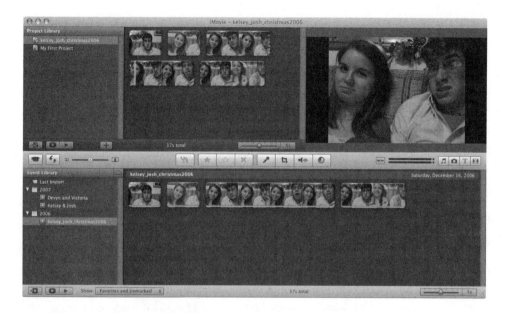

Import from a Video Camera

Traditionally speaking, importing with a camera is probably the typical way most people will import items into iMovie. There are two types of digital video cameras available today:

- **Random Access Devices (RADs)** RADs are cameras that use DVDs, hard disk drives (HDDs), or flash memory to store your digital movies. They connect to your Mac with USB cables. They are deemed Random Access Devices because you can import video clips selectively without having to play through the entire recording.

- **Tape-based digital video cameras** Tape-based camcorders (such as mini-DV format) must have a FireWire connection to work with your Mac. While you can also select which portions of their recordings you want to import, you must do so by playing through the recording.

NOTE *Importing video from a camera into iMovie* does not *erase it from your digital video camera.*

Import from a RAD

To import video from a random access device:

1. Set the device to PC or computer mode, connect it to the Mac, and the Import window opens.

2. To import all the clips on the device, select Import All. To import most of the clips, select Manual from the left side of the Import window, uncheck the boxes below the clips you do *not* want to import, and then click the Import Checked button. If you want to import

only a few clips, select Manual on the left side of the Import window, click the Uncheck All button, check the boxes only under the clips you *do* want to import, and then click the Import Checked button.

3. Choose a Save To location. The disk you use must be a hard drive in your computer or one that is connected externally with a FireWire cable. Be aware that USB drives will not work!

4. Decide whether to create a new Event or add the video to an existing Event. If you create a new Event, be sure to give it a descriptive name.

5. Choose the size of your 1080i video, if this applies to your clips.

6. Click OK to begin importing your video. This process can take quite a while, possible longer than an hour, depending on how much of the device's video you decided to import.

Import from a Tape-based Digital Video Camera

To import video from a tape-based FireWire digital video camera:

1. Set the camera to Play, VTR, or VCR mode.

2. Connect the camera to your Mac via a FireWire cable, and the Import window opens.

3. If you want to import the entire contents of the tape, make sure the selection on the left side of the Import window is set to Automatic, and then click Import. iMovie stops importing automatically when it reaches the end of the recording.

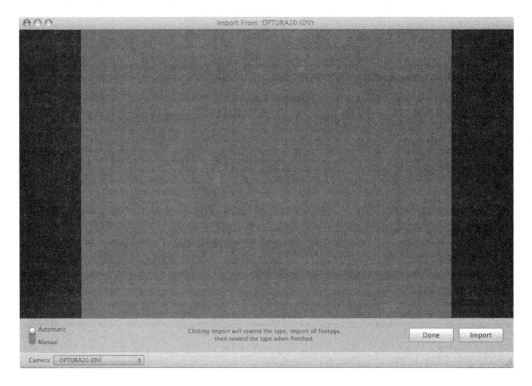

To import only portions of the tape, change the selection on the left side of the Import window to Manual, use the controls in the Import window to rewind or fast-forward the tape to the portion you want to import, and click the Import button. To stop importing, just click the Stop button.

4. Choose a Save To location, and whether to create a new Event or add the imported clips to an existing Event.

5. Choose your 1080i video size, if applicable.

6. Click OK, and then turn off your camera and disconnect it from your Mac.

View Your Imported Video

After your import is complete, it appears as a new Event in the Event Library. Click the new Event, and the video you just imported appears in the source window, as shown in the following illustration. Isn't it cool how it looks like a roll of film that's been stretched out? The "film" is a clip of video; clips begin where you started recording and end where you stopped. These clips contain all the images and sounds of the imported video; these images are called frames.

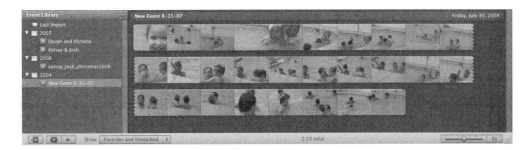

You can browse the contents of the video by dragging your mouse pointer over the clips; the images in the clips move, and you can hear the sounds, too. The images are also displayed in the viewer window. This technique is called "skimming."

You can play your video in its entirety by clicking a point in the video clip and pressing the SPACEBAR or double-clicking the mouse button.

Play an Event in full screen by clicking this button under the Event Library window:

Press ESC to stop full-screen playback.

Select Video to Work With

Click an Event in the Event Library to see its video clips. To select video for the project, click anywhere in the video clip, and iMovie places a yellow border box around a four-second section of the clip.

You can shrink or expand this selection by clicking-and-dragging the selection handles on either side of the yellow box.

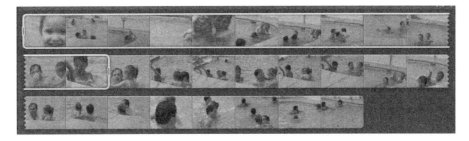

To select an entire clip at once, hold down the OPTION key while clicking the clip.

How to ... Play Favorites with Your Clips

I was always told it wasn't nice to play favorites, but when it comes to video, some is great and some is just plain bad. My Mac only has so much hard drive space, and I only have so much time; I don't want to spend either working with bad video.

iMovie lets you mark the really great video as a favorite, and it also lets you mark the bad video for rejection (such a harsh term!). Before continuing, make sure the source filter selector in the lower-left corner of the window is set to All Clips.

The marking buttons used to mark video selections are located in the iMovie toolbar. The black star is the "Mark as Favorite" button, the white star is the Unmark button, and the "X" is the Reject button.

Select the portion of video you want to mark, and then click the appropriate marking button for the task: mark it either as a favorite selection or as a selection that needs to be deleted (rejected). Favorites are denoted with a green bar that runs across the top of the frame range, and rejected clips are marked with a red bar. You can remove a mark by selecting the marked range and then clicking the Unmark button.

Create an iMovie Project

Now that you've imported your video, you need to begin creating a movie with it, so break out your director's chair, beret, and megaphone! First, you need to create a new project. Apple has been kind enough to provide a project called "My First Project" for us, but you're going to politely pass on that and create your own. Press ⌘-N or click the + button beneath the Project Library window. Give the project a descriptive name, choose the aspect ratio you want to use (Standard, iPhone, or Widescreen), and click Create. You are now ready to add video and music to your new project.

Add Video to Your Project

A project won't be much good without video. To add video clips to your project:

1. Select an Event from the Event Library, and then make a selection from the clips associated with it.

2. To add your selection to the project, click the Add to Project button in the toolbar.

You can also drag the selection to the Project window and drop it in.

3. Continue this process until you have added all the video clips you want to use for your project. You can choose as many clips as you want and can select them from any of your Events. You are the director, and as such you have unbridled freedom to do with your movie what you will.

4. Arrange the video clips in any order you like by dragging-and-dropping clips to any position in the Project window.

5. Click the Play Project button below the Project Library to see your project in action.

Add Music and Sound Effects to Your Project

You can add music and sound effects to any iMovie project you create. Open your new project, if it isn't still open, and then open the "Music and Sound Effects" pane in the lower-right corner by pressing ⌘-1 (or choosing Window | "Music and Sound Effects").

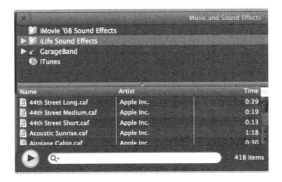

You can choose music or sound effects for your movie from any of the sources listed. Choose one from the iMovie or iLife options, and then drag the selection to the background of your project. Be careful not to drop it onto your video clips; it should go behind them. When you drop the music in the background, it is displayed by a green box.

The green box's length is indicative of the song's length compared to that of your video clips. If your song is longer than the video clips, it will fade out during playback of the project.

To lengthen or shorten the playing time of the music track, click the green box to highlight it, and then choose Edit | Trim Music. Drag the selection handles at the beginning and end of the song to adjust its length.

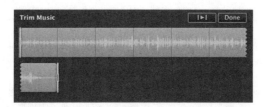

Remove the background music by clicking the green box in the background of your project and then pressing DELETE.

You've just created a very basic iMovie project! There is so much more you can do with your iMovie project, such as adding titles and placing transitions between video clips (fade in and out, wipes, and so forth).

Share Your Masterpiece

What good is it for a star director to create a masterpiece and not share it with the world? Naturally, iMovie makes the act of sharing your project simple, by publishing it to your .Mac Web Gallery, by publishing it to YouTube, or by exporting it to another format, and then e-mailing it or uploading it to the Web.

Publish to Your .Mac Web Gallery or to YouTube

iMovie can publish your movie to the Internet, where others can view it wherever they may be. Any Internet-enabled PC or Mac in the world can access your movie via your .Mac Web Gallery or YouTube.

Publish to Your .Mac Web Gallery

If you have a .Mac account, iMovie can publish your movie to your .Mac Web Gallery:

1. Choose Share | .Mac Web Gallery to open the Publish Your Project to Your .Mac Web Gallery window, shown next.

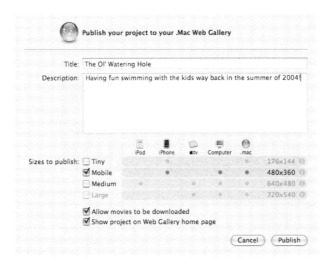

2. Name your movie, add a short description if you wish, choose the sizes you would like to make available (some sizes work better with certain devices, such as an iPod, iPhone, or Apple TV), choose whether to allow viewers of your movie to download it, and choose whether the movie should appear on your Web Gallery home page.

3. Click Publish.

When you have published a movie to your .Mac Web Gallery, a small icon of a broadcast shows up next to the project in your Project Library. You can discontinue publishing your video by choosing Share | Remove from .Mac.

Publish to YouTube

You may also have heard of little thing called YouTube. If not, it's one of the most popular sites on the Web for watching videos online. To publish your iMovie project to YouTube:

1. Create a YouTube account by visiting www.youtube.com.

2. Choose Share | YouTube to open the Publish Your Project to YouTube window, shown next.

3. Enter your YouTube account name, pick the YouTube category in which you want your movie listed, name your movie, add a short description if you wish, enter tags (search terms by which others can find your movie), choose a size, and choose whether to make the movie private (which enables you to control who can view it).

4. Click Next, agree to the YouTube terms of service, and then click Publish.

When you have published a movie through YouTube, a small icon of a broadcast shows up next to the project in your Project Library. You can discontinue publishing your video on YouTube by choosing Share | Remove from YouTube.

Export Your Movie

Choose Share | Export to execute a standard export of your project into an MPEG-4 file, playable in iTunes or QuickTime, as shown in the following illustration.

Choose Share | Export Using QuickTime to export the project as a QuickTime movie.

Click the Export and the Use pop-up menus for tons of QuickTime export options.

When you're done exporting your creations, you can upload them to the Web or email them to friends and family.

Summary

iMovie is one of those applications that I consider to be a "head turner": videos created with iMovie do turn heads! As soon as you show someone (particularly a Windows user) the movies that you created by your own hand, with a little help from iMovie, they can't help but be blown away.

This chapter has helped you get your feet wet with iMovie, but there is so much more to learn. iMovie has a great Help file, and you must check out the Getting Started PDF (click the Help menu and choose it from there). Video tutorials are also available on Apple's website at www.apple.com/ilife/tutorials/#imovie.

Dig into the closet and pull out those boxes full of mini-DV tapes and get to work, Spielberg!

Part IV

Time to Geek Out! Digging Deeper into Your Mac

Chapter 14

Making Sense of the System Preferences

How to...

■ Understand what all those options in the System Preferences are

■ Change the preferences to fit your needs

System Preferences is where you make your Mac bend to your will. With each change you make to the System Preferences, you shape and mold your Mac so that it will do your bidding without hesitation and exactly to your specifications. It's good to be the king!

To get started on your tour of Mac OS X's myriad of preferences panes, choose Apple | System Preferences. As Figure 14-1 shows, the preferences are divided into four categories: Personal, Hardware, Internet & Network, and System.

We'll explore the four categories and cover the preferences within each of them. Some of these preferences have been discussed in detail in previous chapters, so they receive only cursory treatment in this one. And for obvious reasons, self-explanatory preferences are given a very brief summary, if one at all. We've got lots to cover so let's get to it!

Personal

As implied by the name, the preferences in this category relate to customizing, or personalizing, your Mac. The seven preferences panes in this category are described in turn in the following sections.

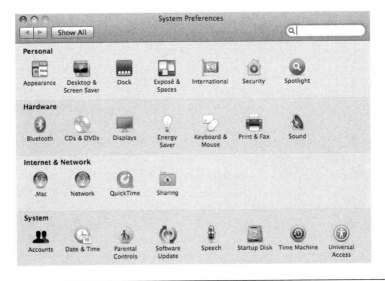

FIGURE 14-1   A view of your Mac's System Preferences, from the top

Appearance

The Appearance preferences pane was discussed already in Chapter 4, but we'll give it another quick look. Changes made in the Appearance preferences pane affect the general look and feel throughout your Mac.

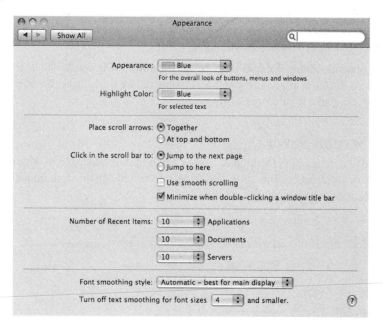

- **Appearance** Choose between Blue and Graphite for the basic look of elements in the Finder.

- **Highlight Color** Choose the color used to highlight text.

- **Place scroll arrows** Keep the arrows in the scroll bar together at the bottom or at separate ends of the scroll bar.

- **Click in the scroll bar to** Determine your Mac's actions when you click the scroll bar in a multiple-page document.

- **Jump to the next page** Choose this option if you want your document to scroll up or down one page, respectively, when you click above or below the "thumb" (the bar in the scroll bar), regardless of how far above or below the thumb you click.

- **Jump to here** Choose this option if you want your document to scroll to the corresponding place that you click in the scroll bar. For example, if the thumb is toward the bottom of the scroll bar in a lengthy document and you click the top of the scroll bar, your document scrolls to the first page, not just one page up.

- **Use smooth scrolling** Check this box if you want the contents of a window to scroll by smoothly instead of jumping.

- ■ **Minimize when double-clicking a window title bar**   Check this box to make your windows minimize when you double-click their title bar.

- ■ **Number of Recent Items**   Select the number of your most recent applications, documents, and servers that appear in your Apple menu.

- ■ **Font smoothing style**   Choose the way fonts are displayed on your screen using the preconfigured settings in the list. You may not notice any big differences (if any), depending on what type of screen you have.

- ■ **Turn off text smoothing for font sizes 'x' and smaller**   Choose at which size font smoothing is disabled. If you use small text, you will like this setting, because font smoothing can make smaller text hard to read.

Desktop & Screen Saver

Chapter 4 covered both tabs of the Desktop & Screen Saver preferences pane in detail, so consult that chapter for more information. Basically, this is where you change the desktop picture and the screen saver defaults for your Mac.

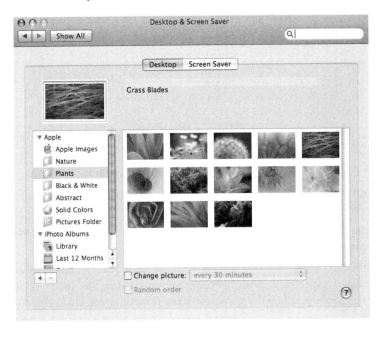

Dock

Chapter 3 covered the Dock preferences pane, shown next, in detail.

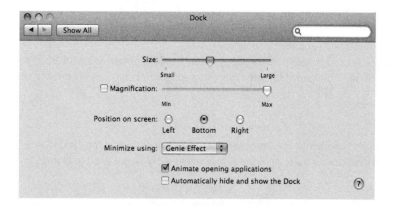

Exposé & Spaces

Chapter 3 also covered both tabs of the Exposé & Spaces preferences pane in detail.

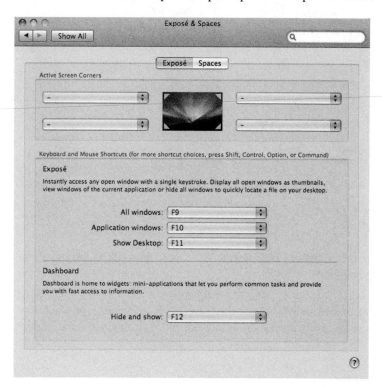

International

Finally, a preferences pane we haven't seen!

The International preferences pane broadens your worldly horizons by localizing your Mac's languages and formats. This pane has three tabs, Language, Formats, and Input Menu, described in turn next.

Language

Some applications let you change the languages used to display their menus and dialog boxes. Set your language preferences for these apps here. You most likely won't need to change these options.

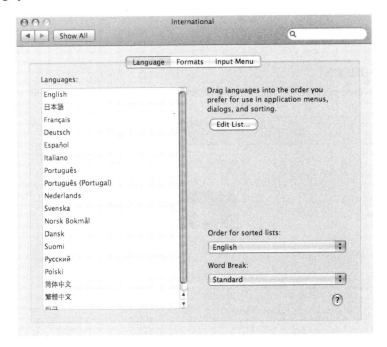

- ■ **Order for sorted lists** The language you choose here affects how windows handle their sorting options.

- ■ **Word Break** This setting changes what happens when a word is double-clicked. Leave this set to Standard, unless you installed Mac OS X in Japanese, in which case you should choose Japanese. Only programmers (developers) will want to use the English setting.

Formats

Many nations around the world format dates differently from how it's done in the United States, as well as use different currencies. The Formats tab of the International preferences pane lets you adjust these formats to your needs, as shown in the following illustration. Measurement format choices for U.S. and metric are also available here.

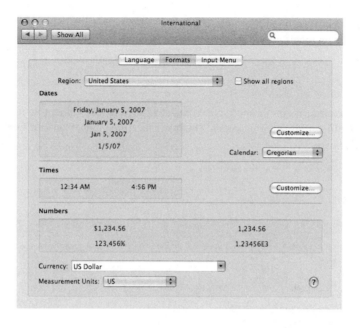

Input Menu

As with time and dates, a keyboard's formatting is different in many other countries from how it is formatted in the United States. Changing the Input Method here remaps your keys to match the format of other nations.

To easily switch between Input Methods, check the "Show input menu in menu bar" box to add an icon for the Input menu to the menu bar. The icon looks like a flag.

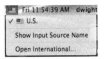

Security

Setting options in the Security preferences pane makes your Mac less vulnerable to attack by a hacker or someone else with malicious intent. This pane has three tabs, General, FileVault, and Firewall, described next.

General

These settings limit access to your Mac:

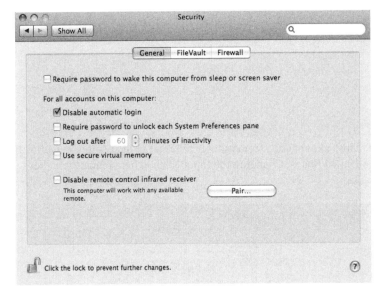

- **Require password to wake this computer from sleep or screen saver**   Check this box to require users to enter their account username and password to get the Mac to wake from sleep mode or quit running a screen saver.

- **Disable automatic login**   Check this box to require a user to log into the Mac to get it to boot completely.

- **Require password to unlock each System Preferences pane**   Check this box to lock every System Preferences pane and require a user to enter a username and password to be able to make any changes.

- **Log out after 'x' minutes of inactivity**   Check this box to cause your account to automatically log out after the amount of time specified. This is particularly useful to prevent other users from staying logged on when they have not used the computer in a while.

- **Use secure virtual memory** Check this box to secure information written to virtual memory. Sometimes your Mac uses space on your hard drive as RAM (random access memory); this technique is known as virtual memory. By default, any information written to virtual memory is unprotected, but checking this box secures that information by encrypting it.

- **Disable remote control infrared receiver** Check this box to turn off your Mac's built-in infrared port, if it has one, preventing any remote control from working with your Mac. This option doesn't show up if your Mac doesn't have an infrared port.

FileVault

Turning on FileVault will encrypt all contents of your home folder. Encryption keeps other users from seeing your data.

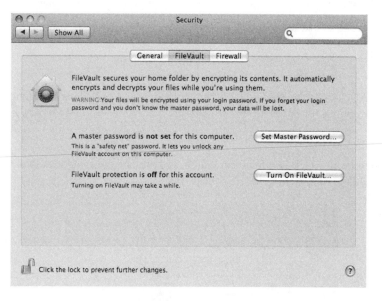

 Heed the WARNING in this preferences pane. You must set a master password to use FileVault, and if you lose or forget your account's login password and the master password, you won't be able to retrieve your files.

Firewall

Firewalls block people from accessing your Mac via the Internet or a network. Mac OS X has a firewall conveniently built into it, so buying third-party software to handle this for you is unnecessary (see following illustration).

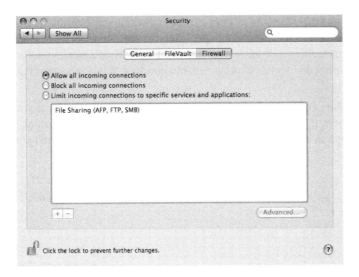

Spotlight

Chapter 3 afforded a look at the Spotlight search feature of Mac OS X. This preferences pane is where you set the options for Spotlight. Its two tabs are Search Results and Privacy.

Search Results

Choose the categories in which Spotlight can search, and arrange the categories in the order in which Spotlight should be searching them.

Privacy

Sometimes you may not want people to be able to find files in certain folders. To prevent Spotlight from searching those locations, add them to the Privacy list in this preferences pane.

Hardware

The preferences in this category (see Figure 14-1) determine how your Mac's hardware interacts with other aspects of your system. This category's seven preferences panes are described next in turn.

Bluetooth

Bluetooth is a common wireless communications protocol typically used for connecting devices that are in close proximity to your Mac, such as a cell phone, PDA, or even some printers.

This preferences pane allows you to configure your Bluetooth settings and displays a list of devices that are connected or have been connected to your Mac.

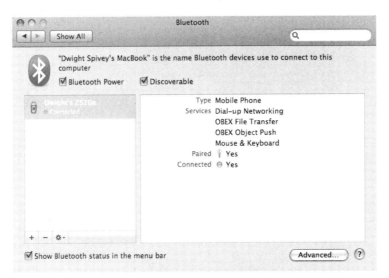

- **Bluetooth Power**   Check or clear this box, respectively, to enable or disable Bluetooth on your Mac.

- **Discoverable**   Check or clear this box, respectively, to specify whether other Bluetooth devices can find your Mac.

- **Show Bluetooth status in the menu bar**   Check this box to place an icon for Bluetooth in the menu bar, allowing you to easily and quickly make changes to your Bluetooth settings.

- **Advanced**   Click this button to access optional settings for Bluetooth. The options are all self-explanatory, as shown next.

CDs and DVDs

The options on this pane tell your Mac how to react when you insert a CD or DVD into its drive.

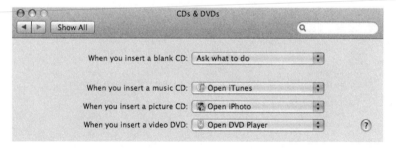

Displays

You use this pane to set your monitor and display preferences. Both the Display and Color tabs of this preferences pane were covered in detail in Chapter 4, in the "Change Monitor Preferences" section.

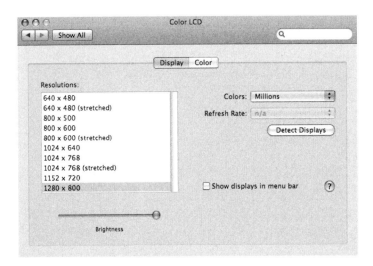

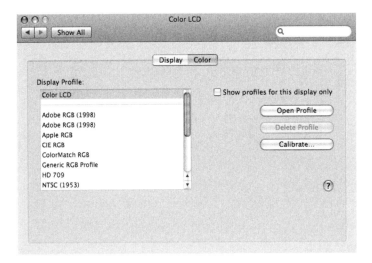

Energy Saver

Your Mac will go into sleep mode after a certain period of time in order to save energy. This is especially useful when using a laptop without a power adapter. Laptop batteries can run out of juice pretty quickly, so if you're not using the laptop, it's a good idea to have it go into sleep mode as quickly as possible. The "Settings for" option allows you to customize your settings depending on whether you're running your laptop with a power adapter or from the battery.

If you don't see the Sleep and Options tabs, as illustrated in Figures 14-2 and 14-3, click the Show Details button on the left side of the pane. Click the Schedule button to set a schecule for your Mac to wake and sleep at specific times.

Keyboard & Mouse

Control your input options with this preferences pane, which has five tabs: Keyboard, Trackpad (for laptops only), Mouse, Bluetooth, and Keyboard Shortcuts.

Keyboard

Adjust the Key Repeat Rate using the sliders provided.

All keyboards have function keys (F1, F5, F12, and so on), but some of those keys lead a double life. For example, the F1 and F2 keys on a MacBook act as the brightness controls for the

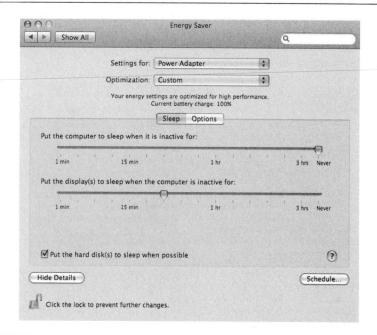

FIGURE 14-2   The Energy Saver preferences pane with all Sleep details revealed

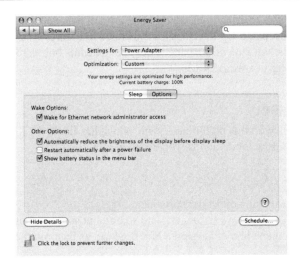

FIGURE 14-3 The Energy Saver preferences pane with all Options details revealed

display. Checking the "Use all F1, F2, etc. keys as standard function keys" box requires the user to hold down the FN key to utilize the keys' secondary functionality.

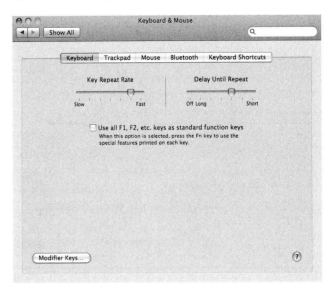

Click the Modifier Keys button to change the functionality of your modifier keys, as shown next. Modifier keys are keys you press simultaneously with other keys to perform a given function, such as using the ⌘ key with the O key to open documents.

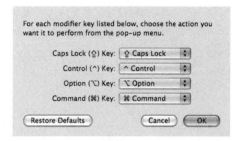

Trackpad

If you have a laptop, you will see the Trackpad tab, which you use to adjust your trackpad's tracking, scrolling, and double-click speeds. You can have your laptop ignore trackpad input when you have a mouse connected to it by checking the "Ignore trackpad when mouse is present" box.

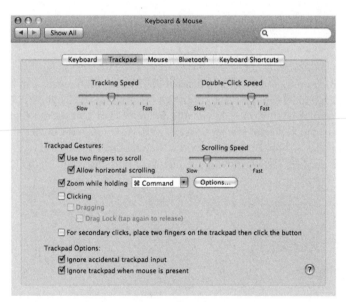

TIP *Trackpad Gestures are really helpful when using a MacBook. Checking the "Use two fingers to scroll" box lets you easily scroll through long documents by placing two fingers on the trackpad at the same time and dragging them together in the same direction. Checking the "Allow horizontal scrolling" box lets you scroll from right to left in your document using the same two-finger method.*

Mouse

Use the options on the Mouse tab, shown next, to modify your mouse's tracking, double-clicking, and scrolling speeds, as well as change your primary mouse button.

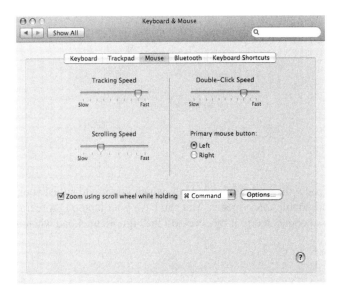

Bluetooth

There are so many Bluetooth options scattered about the System Preferences I'm beginning to think I've just eaten a blueberry pie! But I digress… This tab of the Keyboard & Mouse preferences pane is for use with wireless keyboards and mice. You can see the signal level of your Bluetooth mouse and keyboard connections, as well as set up a new device if needed. I recommend checking the "Allow Bluetooth devices to wake this computer" box. This allows you to wake your Mac from sleep just by moving the mouse or pressing a key on the keyboard.

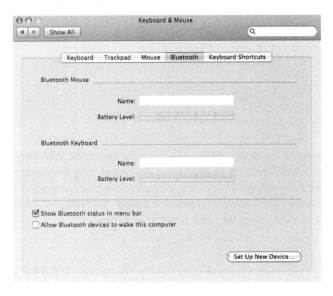

Keyboard Shortcuts

This tab enables you to view and modify the default keyboard shortcuts used by Mac OS X. Click the + button on the lower-left side of the tab to add your own custom shortcut.

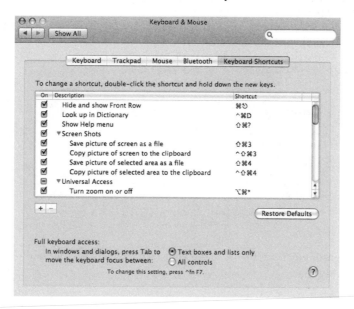

Print & Fax

Use these preferences for installing printers and faxes in Mac OS X. See Chapter 8 for in-depth discussion of this preferences pane.

Sound

Set your options for sound input and output using these preferences. Sound is thoroughly covered in Chapter 4, in the "Change Sound Settings" section, so go there to get all the goods.

Internet & Network

This category has only four sets of preferences (see Figure 14-1), but each set is chock full of options for, respectively, connecting your Mac to the Internet and your network, setting up QuickTime, and sharing with other computers.

.Mac

With .Mac, Apple offers to Mac users online services that are second to none. Sign in to your .Mac account and set up your .Mac services with this preferences pane. This section introduces the .Mac preferences options.

If you don't have a .Mac account, you can try one free for 60 days. Sign up from the .Mac preferences pane by clicking the Learn More button.

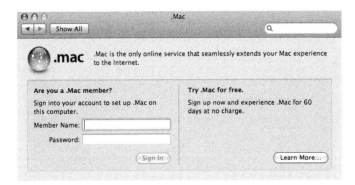

Once you've signed into .Mac, the .Mac preferences pane includes four tabs: Account, Sync, iDisk, and Back To My Mac.

Account

To change your account information and password, simply click the Account Details button, which whisks you away to the .Mac website, which you can make the changes.

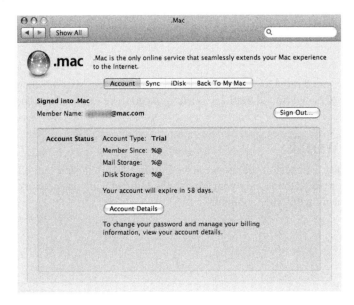

Sync

Sync is a great feature! Use the Sync tab to synchronize elements of your Mac with .Mac, such as contacts, mail settings, and preferences. What's even cooler is that if you click the Advanced button, you can set up multiple Macs to synchronize information with.

iDisk

Apple provides a certain amount of online storage for you when you open a .Mac account. You can store anything you like on your iDisk, just as if it were a regular hard drive, but with one great exception: you can access your iDisk from any computer anywhere. Use the iDisk tab of the .Mac preferences pane to see how much space you have available on your iDisk, to choose whether your iDisk's public folder can be a written to by others who may access it, and to choose whether to save a copy of your iDisk on your hard drive.

Back To My Mac

Here's probably the neatest option of the .Mac bunch. When enabled, Back To My Mac, shown next, allows you to access your Mac from any other computer you use with your .Mac account. Back To My Mac must be enabled on all the Macs you want to access and on the Mac you are currently using. You can share files and services between the Macs (as long as you enable those sharing options in the Sharing preferences pane) and use Screen Sharing to remotely control a Mac from anywhere you have an Internet connection.

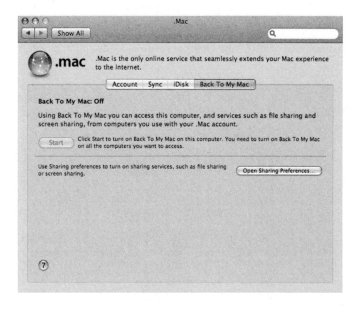

Network

The Network preferences pane is where you set up and maintain all of your Mac's connections to the outside world. Bluetooth, Built-in Ethernet, Built-in FireWire, and AirPort are all configured here. The details of all these preferences are covered in Chapter 15.

QuickTime

Chapter 10 introduces and discusses how to use QuickTime. This section covers your account's QuickTime preferences. The QuickTime preferences pane has five tabs: Register, Browser, Update, Streaming, and Advanced.

Register

If you have already purchased QuickTime Pro, you enter your registration information here to enable the professional tools for QuickTime. If you haven't purchased QuickTime Pro but would like to, click the Buy QuickTime Pro button to pay for it and get your registration information.

Browser

Use the Browser tab options to control how QuickTime downloads and opens movies in your web browser.

Update

Click the Install button on the Update tab to be spirited off to the QuickTime Components website, which showcases third-party utilities that you can obtain to increase the functionality of QuickTime.

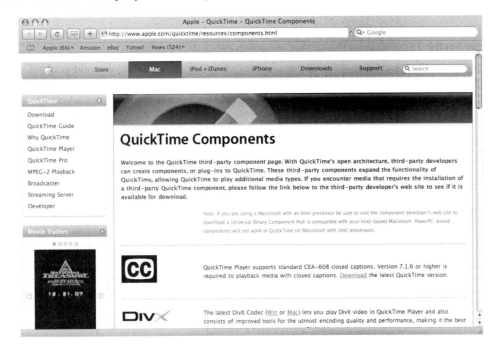

Streaming

The settings on the Streaming tab enable you to adjust the way your Mac downloads streaming media content from the Internet.

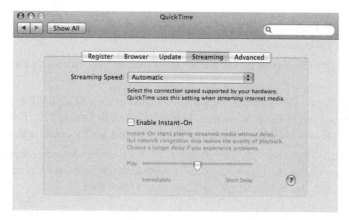

- ■ **Streaming Speed** Choose your Internet connection speed from this menu. QuickTime automatically detects your network speed, but if you are experiencing problems viewing video on the Internet, you can adjust your connection speed manually. If you don't know your connection speed, contact your ISP for that information.

- ■ **Play** Use this slider to adjust how quickly your Mac begins playing streamed video and audio.

- ■ **Enable Instant-On** Clear this check box to disable Instant-On if you experience jittery playback.

Advanced

Sometimes media playback may not be as automatic as you would like it to be, or you may need to make special settings for using QuickTime; the Advanced tab is the place to change these preferences.

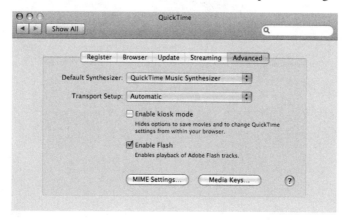

- ■ **Default Synthesizer**   QuickTime plays back files using its own built-in synthesizer, but if you have a different one you would like to use, change this option.

- ■ **Transport Setup**   Changes the protocol for your network connection, ensuring you get the best performance possible.

- ■ **Enable kiosk mode**   Check this box to keep users from changing your QuickTime settings and saving movies.

- ■ **Enable Flash**   Check this box to allow QuickTime to play movies that use Adobe Flash tracks.

- ■ **MIME Settings**   Every media file you download is assigned a MIME type, which tells the Mac what kind of file it actually is. QuickTime handles many MIME types, but you can add and remove MIME types to and from its repertoire by clicking this button.

- ■ **Media Keys**   Media keys are like passwords for accessing secured (encrypted) media files. The supplier of the file should provide you with the necessary key to view or listen to the file. Click this button to add media keys to QuickTime.

Sharing

If your mother is anything like mine (Hi, Mom!), she taught you to share with others from the earliest you can remember. Your Mac knows how to share, too—however, you need to be careful about what and with whom your Mac shares, which is exactly what this preferences pane is for.

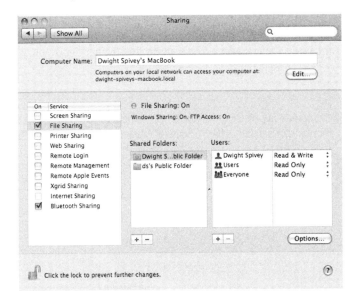

Check the box next to each service you want others to be able to access on your Mac, add or remove shared folders for each user account, and set access permissions for them.

Click Options to choose which communications protocols you use to share your files and folders. AFP is the Apple File Protocol, FTP stands for File Transmission Protocol, and SMB is for Server Message Block, which is what allows you to share with Windows-based PCs. Check the box next to each user account you want to enable these protocols for.

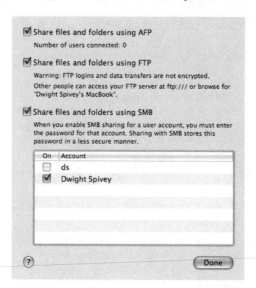

System

The preferences in this category (see Figure 14-1) apply to system-wide use of your Mac. This category includes eight preferences panes, several of which are covered in other chapters and thus are addressed only briefly here.

Accounts, Date & Time, and Parental Controls

Set up user accounts, configure your date and time preferences, and limit accessibility for some users with these preferences panes. Chapter 4 covers the details of these three preferences panes, so consult that chapter for more information.

Software Update

A great feature of Mac OS X is its ability to update itself when Apple releases software changes. The Software Update preferences pane has two tabs, Scheduled Check and Installed Updates.

Scheduled Check

Set up your Mac's schedule for checking Apple's servers for updates. You can have it check them immediately by clicking the Check Now button.

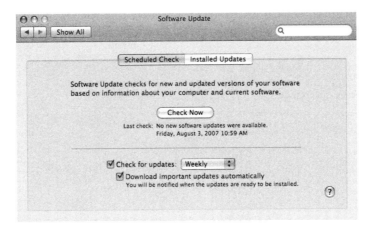

Installed Updates

Look at this tab to see your update history. This information can come in handy when troubleshooting system problems.

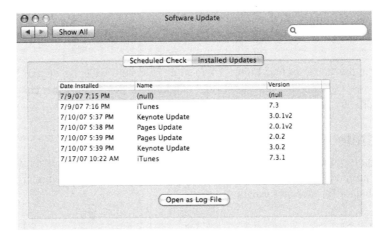

Speech

This preferences pane enables you to turn on a really cool feature of your Mac: the ability of your Mac to read the text on the screen to you out loud. But if that's cool, the next thing it can do is ice cold: do what you verbally command it to do! The iMac and MacBook come with a built-in microphone, which is what allows the Mac to hear you, and speakers, which allow you to hear the Mac. The Mac mini requires an external microphone.

The Speech preferences pane has two tabs, Speech Recognition and Text to Speech.

Speech Recognition

Click the On button to turn on Speakable Items, allowing your Mac to listen to your commands. This opens the speech feedback window, which is a round window with a microphone displayed in its top half.

When you turn on Speakable Items, you are given a list of tips for using this feature. These are well worth reading!

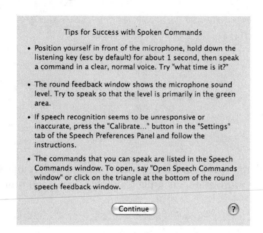

Tips for Success with Spoken Commands

- Position yourself in front of the microphone, hold down the listening key (esc by default) for about 1 second, then speak a command in a clear, normal voice. Try "what time is it?"

- The round feedback window shows the microphone sound level. Try to speak so that the level is primarily in the green area.

- If speech recognition seems to be unresponsive or inaccurate, press the "Calibrate..." button in the "Settings" tab of the Speech Preferences Panel and follow the instructions.

- The commands that you can speak are listed in the Speech Commands window. To open, say "Open Speech Commands window" or click on the triangle at the bottom of the round speech feedback window.

Continue

NOTE *Keep in mind that technologies such as Speakable Items are not perfect. In order for your Mac to hear your commands properly, it's best that you be in an otherwise quiet environment. The microphone is unable to filter the sound of your voice from other sounds in the room or office, so your ten-year-old daughter's slumber party may not be the best setting to use this feature. Your Mac may blow a gasket from trying to interpret all the screams and giggles! A microphone headset may help the Mac understand your commands.*

The Speech Recognition tab of the Speech preferences pane has two subtabs:

- ■ **Settings** This subtab enables you to change the listening device (if you want to use something other than the built-in microphone). The Listening Key is a key you press to activate your Mac's "ears," telling it to pay attention and execute the commands you are about to give it. You can set the Mac to listen only while the Listening Key is pressed, or to listen continuously, with or without a keyword. A keyword is a word that tells your Mac to listen up, that the next thing you say is a command that it is to implement.

For instance, you could say "Computer, what time is it?" to have your Mac tell you what time of day it is.

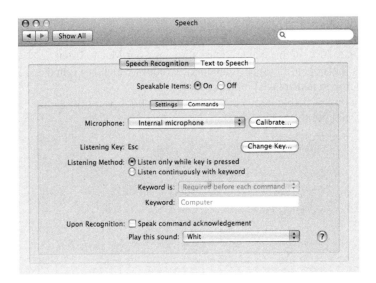

You may need to tweak the way your Mac listens to your speech to optimize its ability to do as you say. To achieve this optimization, click the Calibrate button and follow the instructions.

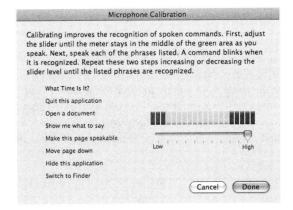

■ **Commands** Use this subtab, shown next, to configure the commands your Mac responds to. Some items in the list can be changed by clicking the Configure button.

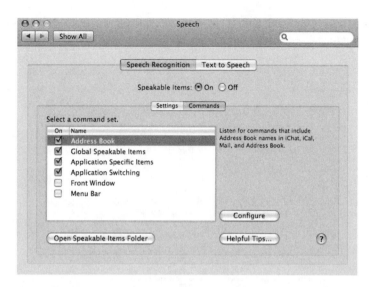

Click the Open Speakable Items Folder button to see a list of all the system-wide commands your Mac can perform.

Text to Speech

Your Mac can actually talk to you when you want it to. You can even have it read out loud what you've typed. The Text to Speech tab of the Speech preferences pane enables you to choose which voice your Mac uses to speak with (there are several to choose from) and choose exactly what it is you want it to say.

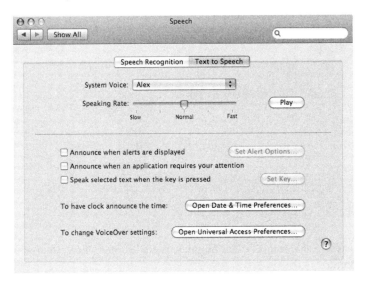

Startup Disk

If your Mac has multiple Mac OS X installations on it, you can select which installation to boot your Mac with by using this preferences pane.

Time Machine

Time Machine is one of Mac OS X's newest and most talked about features. Chapter 24 discusses in depth how to use Time Machine, so for now we will just take a quick look at its preferences pane, which is where you turn on Time Machine. You click the Choose Backup Disk button to tell Time Machine which volume, or disk, to back your data up to, which files on your Mac not to back up, whether to skip system files, and whether to back up automatically.

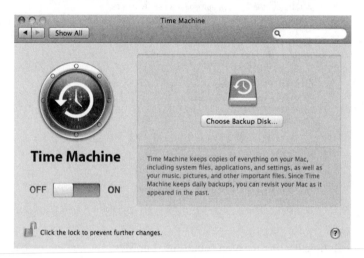

Universal Access

Universal Access makes your Mac much more user-friendly for those who have difficulty in seeing, hearing, or otherwise controlling their computer. The Universal Access preferences pane has four tabs: Seeing, Hearing, Keyboard, and Mouse & Trackpad.

Seeing

These options are designed to benefit Mac users who may have a hard time seeing what is displayed on their screen. Turning on VoiceOver causes your Mac to speak everything your mouse pointer crosses on the screen. Turning on Zoom makes selected areas of the screen appear larger.

The Display preferences enable you to reverse the color values on the screen, to use grayscale, and to reduce or increase contrast.

Hearing

If you have a difficult time hearing the alert sounds of your Mac, you can increase the volume in the Sound preferences pane, of course, but you also can check the box on this tab to have your Mac flash the screen when an alert sound occurs.

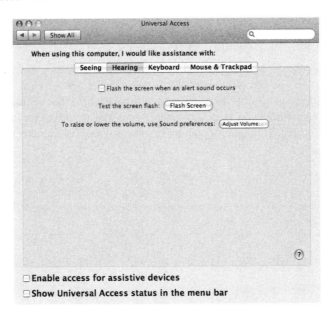

Keyboard

These preferences are great for users who have difficulty pressing more than one key at a time, such as is needed with modifier keys. Sticky Keys and Slow Keys are great aids in overcoming these limitations.

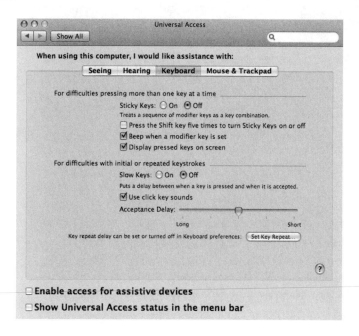

Mouse & Trackpad

Use these preferences to turn on Mouse Keys, which allows you to use your numeric keypad in place of your mouse, and also to resize your mouse pointer.

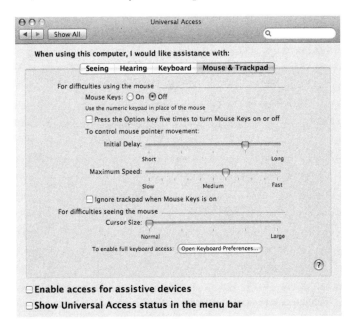

Summary

You've now seen all the options and features that are literally at your fingertips. After going through the System Preferences, your Mac should cruise along according to your wants and needs, your likes and dislikes. It's nice that something in your life is like that, isn't it?

Chapter 15

Making Your Mac Play Pretty with Other Computers: Networking and Sharing

How to…

- Decide whether to connect wired or wirelessly (or both!)
- Get going with the Network Setup Assistant
- Use AirPort Utility
- Configure Internet connections
- Share files and Internet connections

Sharing and connecting are things we humans don't do quite as well as we once did, and that's a shame. However, it seems that computers, especially Macs, are going in the opposite direction. Connecting to a network and sharing files, photos, movies, and music have never been easier than with Mac OS X. Mac OS X connects more easily to more types of networks than any other operating system, hands down.

If you've read Chapter 5, you've probably already used the Network Setup Assistant to quickly get onto the Internet, but Chapter 5 didn't go into much detail about networking. You're probably thinking that everything's running fine and you might just skip this chapter. I would advise you to read this chapter in its entirety, even if you do so at a later time, so that if a problem or situation calls for it, you will be educated on the basics (and some of the not-so-basics) of using your Mac on a network.

Wired or Wireless? That Is the Question!

Apple installed a wireless network adapter in your Mac called an AirPort card, which allows the Mac to communicate sans cable with a wireless network router or switch. They also included a built-in Ethernet port for connecting your Mac with a cable to a network router or switch. The question, then, is "Which way to go, wired or wireless?"

A Look at Wireless Connections

Wireless is the way lots of people want to network these days. The obvious advantage to wireless networking is explicit in the name: you are wirelessly connected to the Internet and other computers on your network, freeing you from being tied to your desk like it's a ball and chain. Wireless routers have become speedier over the years, so much so that you can surf the Web reasonably fast wirelessly, depending on your network, of course.

Those are the major pros, but as with everything in life, there are some cons, too. The first is that wireless Internet connections aren't as stable as wired connections. Second, while wireless Internet connections are faster than they used to be, generally speaking, they still aren't as fast as wired connections. The third, and perhaps biggest, drawback is security, or lack thereof. A wireless router is beaming signals, or broadcasting, in all directions, not just within your home or office. If you're not diligent about reading the documentation that came with your wireless router and educating yourself on how your wireless network works, you may be providing free Internet

Research Wireless Routers

Do your homework! Before you purchase any brand of wireless router, do research on the Web and ask tech-savvy friends and family for their advice. Most wireless routers can get the job done, but try to be as educated as possible about the brands and models available before you hand over your hard-earned cash. The reputation of a company's technical support should weigh heavily in your decision.

Be warned: companies with the biggest names don't always make the best products (I speak from personal experience). Check out Apple's own AirPort products. They are more expensive than the average router, but you know by now that you get what you pay for.

access to everyone in your apartment building, not to mention allowing unfettered access to the information on your Mac's hard disk. While that may sound like you'd be doing a good deed, you really would not be, when you consider that the guy downstairs may be a hacker just waiting to get whatever personal information he can from your computer and those of other people around you. Wireless is much easier to infiltrate than a wired network.

Wires Are Good, Too!

While wireless may be the "hot new thing," wired networks have been around for decades and continue to be used today, for several good reasons: they are faster, much more reliable, and more secure than wireless networks (as mentioned in the preceding section).

Wired connections have one major con, though. When you are connected to an Ethernet cable, you can't surf the Web from the sofa one minute and from the bed the next (at least not unless you have a 500-foot Ethernet cable towing around behind you).

If you get used to the freedom of wireless, it's *tough* to go back to a hard-wired connection. *Really* tough. One time I had serious problems maintaining a wireless connection, so I had to go wired to finish my work. There were at least two instances where I almost dropped my MacBook because, forgetting that I wasn't using wireless, I attempted to move to another room, and the Ethernet cord wasn't as long as my destination was far. When the length of cable ran out, it almost jerked my MacBook to the ground!

Network Setup Assistant Revisited

As previously mentioned, Chapter 5 covers how to use the Network Setup Assistant, so I won't use the space here to cover the same ground. Please refer to the "Use the Network Setup Assistant" section of Chapter 5 for instructions on using it to set up a basic network connection for your Mac. Choose Apple | System Preferences | Network and click the "Assist me" button to open the Network Setup Assistant.

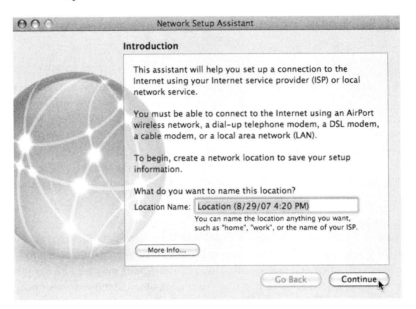

You've got three main connection types: dial-up modem, cable or DSL, and LAN (local area network). If you use a different method from these three, such as a satellite connection, consult your ISP for information on setting up your Mac.

Soar with AirPort

Sending data through the air with the greatest of ease is a breeze with your Mac. AirPort is Apple's all-encompassing name for all things wireless, in terms of a network, of course. The AirPort card in your Mac hooks up through the air with an AirPort Base Station (Apple's own brand of Internet routers), or any other wireless network router, to give you the freedom to surf the Web in your kitchen, on the sofa, or in your hammock, without the hassles of wires strapping you to your desk.

This chapter concentrates on connecting your Mac to an AirPort network and doesn't go into much detail regarding the setup for your AirPort Base Station. Your AirPort device comes with outstanding information for setting it up and connecting it to the Internet.

TIP
If you need step-by-step instructions for setting up AirPort Extreme Base Station, AirPort Express, or any other AirPort model, check out Apple's AirPort Base Station and Network Setup Guide online at http://docs.info.apple.com/article.html?artnum=305293. This guide walks you through the process of setting up your AirPort device fairly simply. (Of course, you must have an Internet connection to access this site.) Apple provides this information for customers who are wired to the Internet and want to break free of those tethers by using an AirPort Base Station.

Connect Wirelessly with Your Mac

If you used the Network Setup Assistant and are connected to the Internet (open Safari and try to access a webpage to find out), then you are already connected wirelessly if there are indeed no Ethernet cables going from your Mac to the router.

Choose Apple | System Preferences | Network to check your connection to the Internet.

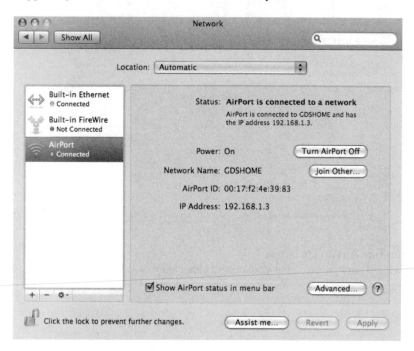

The Status section tells the story. If you are connected, it tells you so, and lets you know the name of the wireless network you're using, which in my case is GDSHOME.

If instead you see this Status message,

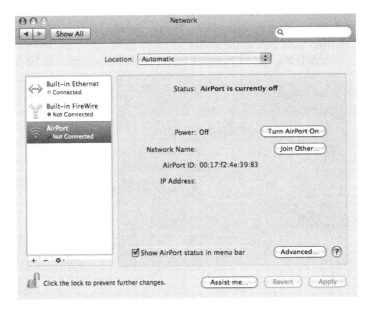

simply click the Turn AirPort On button.

Okay, so what if AirPort is on, but you aren't connected to a network? You see the following Status message:

In this case, you need to use the Network Setup Assistant to get connected, as follows:

1. Click the "Assist me" button at the bottom of the pane and then click the Assistant button to open the Network Setup Assistant.

2. On the Introduction screen, enter a descriptive name for the location and click Continue.

3. On the How Do You Connect to the Internet? page, choose "I use AirPort to connect to the Internet wirelessly," and click Continue. Your Mac scans the area for a wireless network and displays what it finds in the next window:

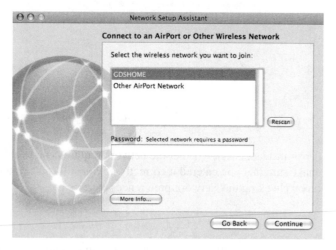

4. Select the network you want to join, enter the password for the network if one is required, and click Continue.

5. On the "Ready to Connect?" page, click Continue again.

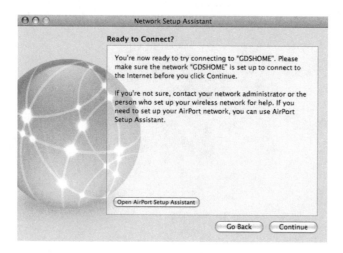

6. If you see this window, you are almost a bona fide wireless network guru—click Done
and you are ready to surf the Web wirelessly.

If you received an error instead, check whether the network requires you to enter a password
to access it, and if so, make sure that you entered it correctly. If you still can't connect, be sure
that AirPort is turned on by checking the Network preferences pane again.

AirPort Utility

NOTE   *You may disregard this section if you are using a non-Apple router.*

AirPort Utility is a tool for configuring and updating your AirPort Base Station from your
Mac. Choose Hard Drive | Applications | Utilities and double-click the AirPort Utility icon to
open AirPort Utility.

How to ... Easily Check AirPort's Status

There must be an easier way to check the status of an AirPort connection than to open System Preferences and then open the Network preferences pane every time, right? Right! But to do so, you need to open that very preferences pane first. Select AirPort in the connection pane on the left to see its settings in the main settings window on the right, and then check the box labeled "Show AirPort status in menu bar."

Look in the menu bar and you see a neat little icon that looks like radio waves ascending; that's the AirPort status icon, which indicates that AirPort is connected and is working like a champ. The higher the black waves go, the stronger your signal is.

When AirPort is turned off, there are no waves in the icon.

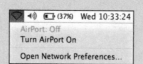

If no network is selected, the icon displays gray waves with a black arrow point up, like this:

Gray waves with no arrow means that AirPort is turned on but has lost its connection.

AirPort Utility scans your network for AirPort Base Stations and displays its findings in the pane on the left. Select a base station from the list to see its information.

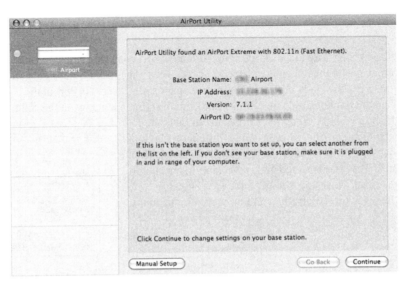

To make automatic changes to that base station's configuration, click Continue and follow the onscreen instructions. But if you're like I am—afraid that the world is ripe for takeover by evil robot overlords—you may prefer to do some things for yourself instead of letting automation rule the day. If you suffer from that particular neurosis, or one similar to it, click the Manual Setup button to see the banquet of settings available for your choosing in the AirPort Utility pane, which has five tabs:

■ **AirPort**   This tab, shown next, is where you can make changes to the way the base station works, as well as download any update you may have skipped earlier.

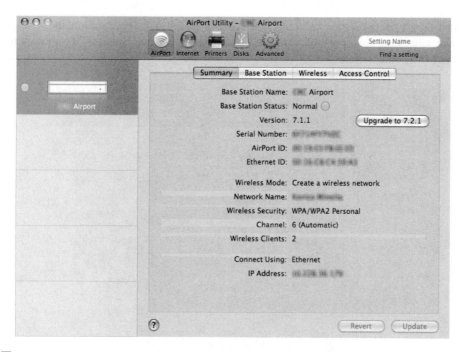

■ **Internet**   Use this tab to configure how your base station connects to the outside world.

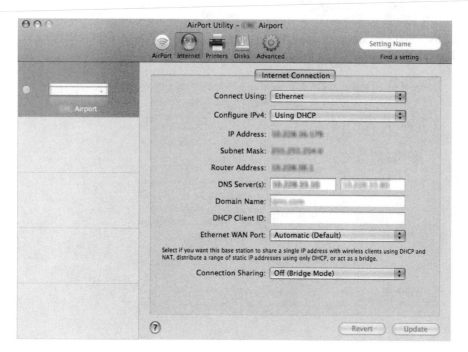

■ **Printers**   If there are any printers connected via USB to your base station, they show up here. Check the box entitled "Advertise printers globally using Bonjour" if you want to share the printer wirelessly.

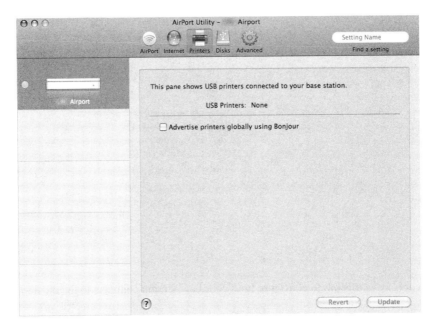

■ **Disks**   You can connect hard drives to your base station to share them with other Macs. This tab helps you to set up the options for sharing the drives.

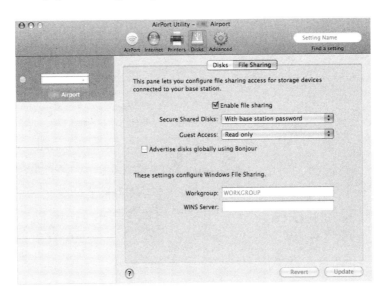

How to ... **Update Your AirPort Base Station**

AirPort Utility automatically checks Apple's servers for updates to your AirPort Base Station when it opens. If it finds an update, you must decide whether to implement it at this time by clicking Download or Cancel. If you'd like to see more details, click the Show Details button to see the firmware that was found and what model it's for.

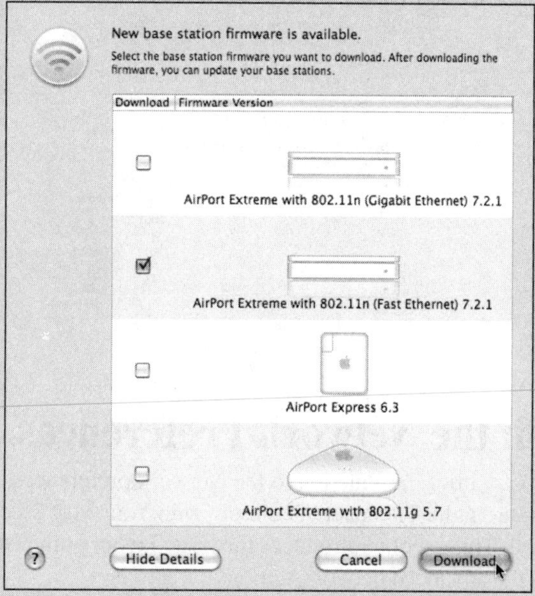

New base station firmware is available.

Select the base station firmware you want to download. After downloading the firmware, you can update your base stations.

Download | Firmware Version

AirPort Extreme with 802.11n (Gigabit Ethernet) 7.2.1

AirPort Extreme with 802.11n (Fast Ethernet) 7.2.1

AirPort Express 6.3

AirPort Extreme with 802.11g 5.7

Hide Details   Cancel   Download

Click Cancel to forgo the update (you'll be prompted again the next time you open AirPort Utility), or click Download to install the update. Follow the instructions onscreen and in your AirPort Base Station's documentation to complete the process.

■ **Advanced**   This tab allows you to keep a log of problems, check the number of clients that are connected wirelessly, and configure Bonjour access and IPv6 addresses.

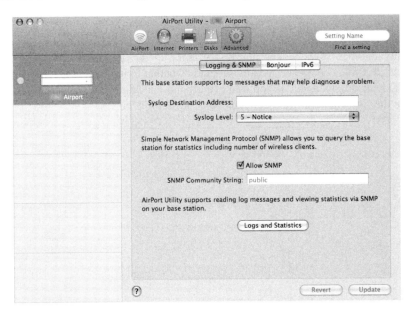

Become Pals with the Network Preferences

Chapter 14 gave you a very brief introduction to the Network preferences, and you got a sample of them earlier in this chapter in the "Connect Wirelessly with Your Mac" section, but you're about to get to know them well. This section introduces the basic layout of the Network preferences pane and then presents the advanced network settings.

Meet the Basic Network Preferences Pane

Open the Network preferences pane by choosing Apple | System Preferences | Network. Figure 15-1 shows the layout of the Network preferences pane, several elements of which are described next:

■ **Location selector**   Create settings that pertain to how your Mac connects to the Internet in different locations. For instance, create a location for Home and another for Work, and set the options necessary for your Mac to gain Internet access from each location. When you go to your workplace from your home, the only thing you need do to get back on the Internet is change your Location choice.

■ **Connection pane**   Look here for a list of the hardware connections your Mac can use to connect to the Internet. Typically, Built-in Ethernet and AirPort are most frequently used, but there are options for Bluetooth and FireWire as well (if you don't see them in the connection pane, click the + button under the pane to add them to the list). This pane also shows your current status for the hardware connection.

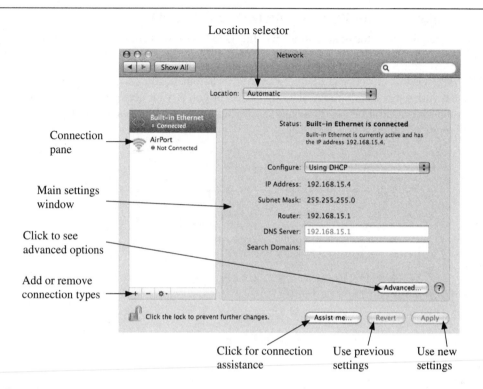

Location selector

Connection pane

Main settings window

Click to see advanced options

Add or remove connection types

Click for connection assistance

Use previous settings

Use new settings

FIGURE 15-1   The Network preferences pane gives you the low-down on your network connections.

- **Main settings window**   Look to this window to find the connection's basics, such as how your Mac gets IP addresses and what those addresses are. Your ISP or your router's documentation can help with any questions you may have about address configuration.

- **Advanced**   Click this button to see detailed settings for each connection type. More details on the advanced settings are provided in the next section.

- **Assist Me**   Click this button to have your Mac diagnose connection problems or to help you set up a new connection.

Meet the Advanced Network Settings

Typically, the settings that were automatically assigned to your network connection are sufficient, but occasionally that may not be the case. Check with your network administrator, ISP, or your router's documentation to see if there are any special requirements needed to access parts of your network.

Built-In Ethernet and AirPort use mostly the same settings options, so I'll briefly go over those common options first before introducing the settings that are specific to Built-In Ethernet or specific to AirPort.

Settings Common to Both Built-In Ethernet and AirPort

Click the Advanced button in the main settings window (see Figure 15-1) of either the Built-In Ethernet connection or the AirPort connection to see these preferences:

■ **TCP/IP**   On this tab, choose whether your Mac is automatically assigned an IP address by a network's servers or a router (Using DHCP), or you or your network admin should enter the address information (Manually). Ask your network admin about the other configuration options if you are unsure.

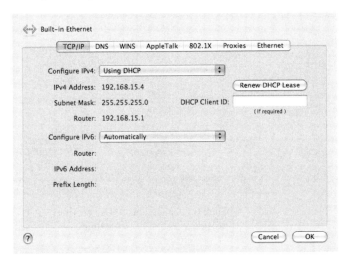

■ **DNS**   This tab shows Domain Name System servers for your network, if there are any. This is a configuration best left in the hands of capable IT folks if it's not already set up automatically.

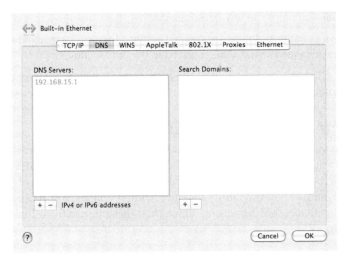

■ **WINS** WINS stands for Windows Internet Name Service, and is something you need not worry about at all if you don't have Windows-based PCs on your network. If you do have PCs on your network and would like for them to communicate with your Mac, very simply stated, this is where you can choose the name of your Mac and the Workgroup that it is part of so that the PCs see it when they browse their network. If you're not knowledgeable of such things, this one is basically screaming for the help of a network admin (and you might be, too).

■ **AppleTalk** AppleTalk is an older communications protocol developed by (guess who?) Apple back in the 1980s to allow Macs and other devices running the protocol, such as printers, to easily connect to one another with little or no configuration settings. If you have older Macs running Mac OS 9 or earlier, or if you have older printers that don't use Bonjour, check the AppleTalk Active box so that you can communicate with them.

■ **802.1X**   802.1X is a form of access control implemented on some networks. Ask your network admin if your network requires 802.1X authentication; if so, they should probably enter these settings for you.

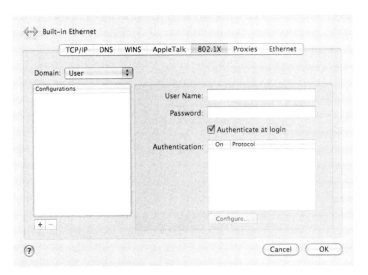

■ **Proxies**   Many corporate networks use proxy servers to control access to certain network functions, such as the Internet and using FTP (File Transfer Protocol). These servers may require authentication before allowing access to a particular function. Your IT department or ISP will provide you with these proxies if needed. If you have a home network, you can safely leave these settings alone.

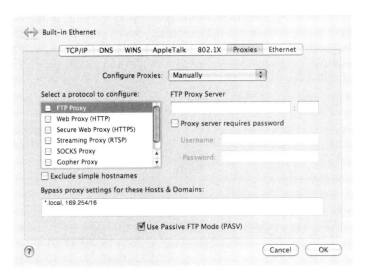

Built-In Ethernet

The Ethernet tab is unique to the Built-In Ethernet advanced settings.

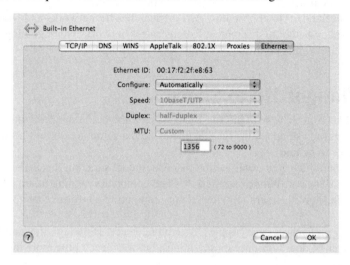

This is another case where the automatic settings should suffice, but occasionally they may need to be altered, depending on your network configuration. For instance, if your network is a Gigabit Ethernet network, it runs at incredibly fast speeds, but if you don't have an Ethernet cable capable of handling those speeds, you may need to manually change the Speed and Duplex settings here. If you have problems staying connected to your network or if things seem to be running really slow, consult your IT staff.

AirPort

The AirPort tab is unique to the AirPort advanced settings.

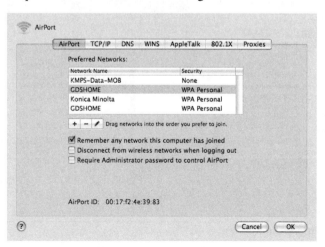

The Preferred Networks pane lists wireless networks you've connected to. You can add or remove items from the list by clicking the + or – button, respectively, below the pane. Drag the network names into the order in which you would like to join them.

Also, use the check boxes to choose how AirPort searches for networks and what it should do when it finds them, whether to disconnect from wireless networks when you log out, and whether an admin password is required to change AirPort settings.

Mom Always Taught Me to Share

Share and share alike. You share with me and I will share with you. Sometimes those concepts are hard to teach kids (and some adults, for that matter), but a computer doesn't need to be taught to share; it just needs to be told!

Your Mac can share files quite easily with other Macs to be sure, but it can also share with, and access the shares of, Windows-based PCs and computers running other, UNIX-based operating systems. In short, there are very few, if any, computing platforms that your Mac can't share with.

Open the Sharing preferences pane (Apple | System Preferences | Sharing), shown in Figure 15-2, to get started. Chapter 14 does introduce these settings, but we'll get a little more into them here.

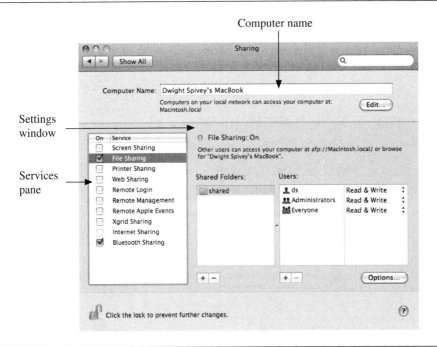

FIGURE 15-2   Your Mac is so kind to share!

Services

Services are functions that let your Mac use or allow various tasks, such as networking, printing, and sharing. Mac OS X is capable of many such services, but the services we are concerned with here are strictly for sharing different facets of the operating system. These services, listed in the Service column of the services pane, are described next. You turn on a service by checking its corresponding check box in the On column of the services pane, and turn off a service by clearing its check box.

Screen Sharing

Enabling Screen Sharing allows other computers (only those that you grant access for) to remotely view and control your Mac.

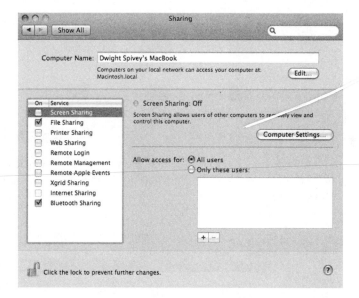

Control access to your Mac by selecting which users can connect. Click the + and – buttons at the bottom of the preferences pane to add and remove users, respectively.

File Sharing

With File Sharing enabled, you can share files on your Mac with other users on your network. Figure 15-2 shows the main options for the File Sharing service.

The Shared Folders pane lists which folders on your Mac you've set up to share files from. The Users pane displays exactly who can access said shared folders and enables you to limit the type of access they have to the files and folders within it. Click the + and – buttons beneath both panes to add and remove shared folders and users.

How to ... Access Network Shares

To access the shared files and folders on your network, choose Go | Network in the Finder; a Finder window opens to show you all the computers on your network that have sharing enabled.

Double-click the computer you want to access, and you will either be connected as a Guest (if that kind of access is granted on this computer) or be prompted for a username and password to gain permission to see shared items. You see this window when connected as a Guest:

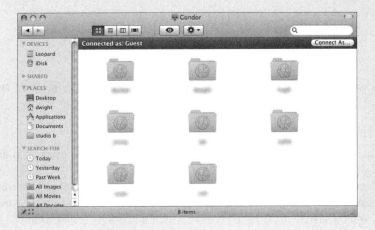

To log on as a registered user of the computer, click the Connect As button in the upper right of the Finder window to see the login window:

Enter your name and password to access files and folders you have permissions for.

Clicking the Options button lets you decide what network protocols can be used to access your shared files and folders:

■ AFP, or Apple File Protocol, allows you to share files using the aging AppleTalk protocol.

■ FTP is another old-school method for transferring files and folders, particularly over the Internet.

■ SMB stands for Server Message Block, which is the networking protocol primarily used by Microsoft Windows. If you want to share files with your PC brethren, check this box and check the box next to your user account.

Printer Sharing

Printer Sharing simply allows other computers to print to printers connected directly to your computer. See Chapter 8 for more information.

Web Sharing

Your Mac can act as a website server if you have built a site and are storing it in the sites folder in your user account's home directory. A good reason for doing this would be to easily share files on an internal network. Click the Help button (?) in the lower-right corner to learn how to host a website from your Mac.

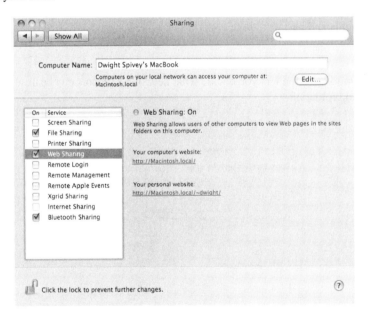

Remote Login

Secure Shell (SSH) is yet another network protocol your Mac has mastered. Remote Login allows other computer users to access your Mac using this protocol. Click the + and – buttons at the bottom of the preferences pane to add and remove users, respectively. For security reasons, keep this service turned off unless otherwise directed by your IT personnel.

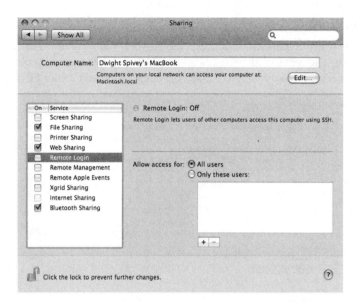

Remote Management

Remote Management allows a network admin running Apple's Remote Desktop software to have full access to your Mac from their own computer. This is a great tool for troubleshooting from across the office or across a university campus. Don't turn on this service unless you are told to by your IT department. Click the + and – buttons at the bottom of the preferences pane to add and remove users, respectively.

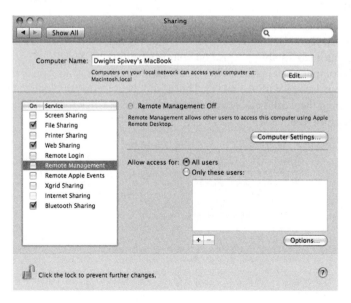

Remote Apple Events

Apple Events are basically commands, or scripts, that tell your Mac to perform certain tasks, such as open a file or print. This service allows applications on other Macs to send Apple Events to the applications on your Mac. Keep this service turned off unless directed by your IT staff to use it.

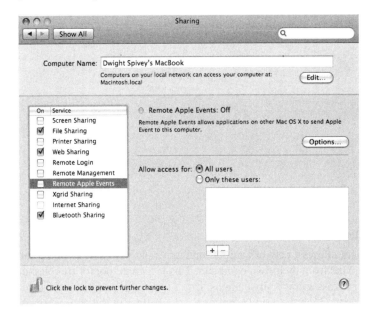

Xgrid Sharing

Here's another one of those "what the heck is this?" items. Actually, as obscure as it is to most home computer users, Xgrid is a pretty cool feature that's meant for computationally intensive environments such as a lab. Enabling Xgrid on your Mac allows an Xgrid server on your network to use your Mac's computational power when you're not using your Mac. You are essentially sharing your Mac's processor with the server. This allows heavy computations to be performed much faster by sharing the workload between many computers. Click the Configure button to set up the Xgrid options for your Mac.

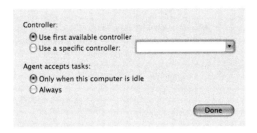

Internet Sharing

This service quite simply lets you share the Internet connection of your Mac with other computers on your network. Use this service if you have only one Mac connected to your ISP. For instance, one Mac can connect directly to the cable or DSL modem, and use the Internet Sharing service to allow other Macs to access the Internet through it. Choose which connection you want to share from in the pop-up menu, and choose which protocols other Macs can use to access your Internet share.

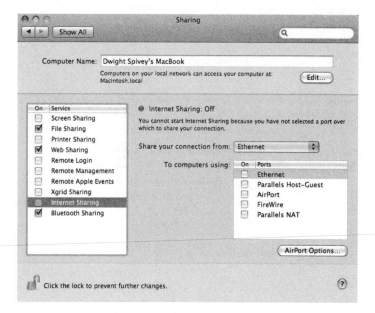

CAUTION *For various reasons, enabling Internet Sharing may be a big no-no with your ISP, so check with your ISP before you turn on this service.*

If you have a slow Internet connection, I would advise you to not enable Internet Sharing, unless one of your pastimes is watching moss grow while waiting for websites to load.

Bluetooth Sharing

Choose how your Mac interacts with other Bluetooth devices. What actions should the Mac take when receiving items from other devices? Which folder on the Mac should those items be saved to? Are other devices allowed to browse your Mac, and if so, which folders?

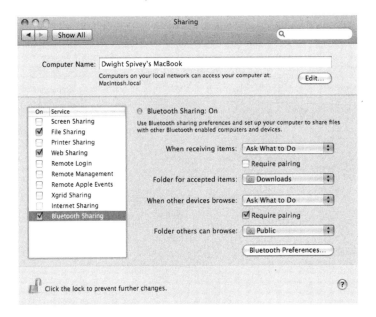

Summary

You now should be able to share any file and any folder on your Mac with any computer you want. Being able to move and copy files from and to other computers is what makes a network a near necessity in most homes and an absolute necessity in a business. Being able to share with Windows-based PCs means your Mac will feel right at home in any network, and it won't be the oddball in the group because those PCs will all be able to share their files with your Mac, too.

Chapter 16

Deeper into the Internet Jungle with Safari

How to …

- Learn the advanced features of Safari
- Use bookmarks to organize your surfing habits
- Set up Safari's preferences to your liking
- Use tabs for more efficient browsing
- Use RSS feeds
- Search the Internet for information

It's time once again to visit the World Wild Web. Yes, I know the Internet is Wide, but it's equally Wild, and Safari is perfect for touring the depth of its jungles. We barely skimmed the surface of Safari's capabilities in Chapter 5, but we're about to get much deeper into its rich features. First, open Safari and get a refresher on the layout of its interface by examining Figure 16-1. This is the same shot of Safari as Figure 5-2, but to prevent you from getting "page-turners thumb," I've added it to this chapter as well.

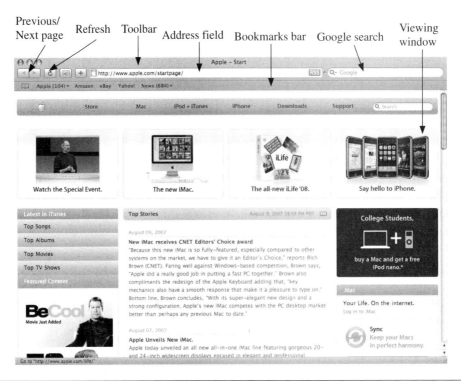

FIGURE 16-1 Another look at Safari's layout

Embark on Advanced Safari

Safari has tons of features that the brief overview in Chapter 5 didn't touch upon, but we're going to tackle several of the more useful ones now:

- **Private browsing**   Private browsing allows you to surf the Web without other users of your computer knowing what you've been up to. This option certainly has its uses (you don't want your wife to know you've been setting up her dream vacation via the Internet) but it has its quite obvious misuses (Junior doesn't want Mom to know what he's been checking out on the Web after she's gone to bed). To turn on this feature, choose File | Private Browsing from the menu bar and click OK in the window shown here.

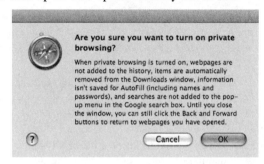

> **Are you sure you want to turn on private browsing?**
>
> When private browsing is turned on, webpages are not added to the history, items are automatically removed from the Downloads window, information isn't saved for AutoFill (including names and passwords), and searches are not added to the pop-up menu in the Google search box. Until you close the window, you can still click the Back and Forward buttons to return to webpages you have opened.
>
> Cancel   OK

TIP   *Private browsing remains on only during your current Safari session; when you quit Safari, private browsing is turned off again.*

- **Reset Safari**   Resetting Safari is kind of like using private browsing, only after the fact. Resetting Safari clears searches, items you entered into forms, cookies, and pretty much every other trace of your Internet activity. Choose File | Reset Safari, check which settings you want cleared, and then click the Reset button.

- **Empty the cache**   Safari keeps a copy of each webpage it visits in a file called a cache so that the page loads faster the next time you go to it, assuming no changes have been made to the site. Emptying the cache clears those pages from the cache, which is a good idea if the page isn't loading correctly. Choose File | Empty Cache and then click the Empty button.

> Reset Safari
>
> **Are you sure you want to reset Safari?**
>
> Select the items you want to reset, then click Reset. You cannot undo this operation.
>
> ☑ Clear history
> ☑ Empty the cache
> ☑ Clear the Downloads window
> ☑ Remove all cookies
> ☑ Remove all website icons
> ☑ Remove saved names and passwords
> ☑ Remove other AutoFill form text
> ☑ Clear Google searches
> ☑ Close all Safari windows
>
> Cancel   Reset

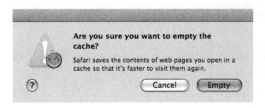

> **Are you sure you want to empty the cache?**
>
> Safari saves the contents of web pages you open in a cache so that it's faster to visit them again.
>
> Cancel   Empty

■ **Customize the toolbar** Choose View | Customize Toolbar to add or remove items to or from Safari's toolbar. To add an item to the toolbar, drag-and-drop it in the location you want it to be displayed. To remove an item from the toolbar, drag it out of the toolbar and release the mouse button. Easy! Click Done when you're finished customizing.

■ **History** Safari keeps a list of all sites you visit. To see these sites, click the History menu, or to see your history going way back, choose History | Show All History.

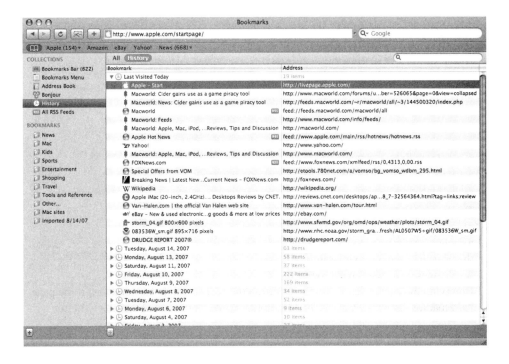

TIP
You can delete individual items from your history by choosing History | Show All History, clicking the item you want to delete so that it's highlighted, and then pressing DELETE.

■ **Activity**   You can monitor Safari's activity by opening the Activity window. As you open pages in Safari, its current process (typically which images and graphics are being downloaded so you can view the page) is tallied in the Activity window. To see this window, choose Window | Activity.

Use Bookmarks

Bookmarks are essentially placeholders for your favorite websites. Creating a bookmark for a website makes it easily available from the Bookmarks menu, saving you the time and effort of typing in the address or searching for it with a search engine like Google.

Create Bookmarks

To create a bookmark for a site you have opened in Safari, choose Bookmarks | Add Bookmark. When prompted, enter the name you want to use for the bookmark, choose the location in your bookmark folders (collections) in which you would like it saved, and then click Add.

Your new bookmark is available by clicking the Bookmarks menu and selecting it from the location you saved it in.

Lightning-Fast Bookmarks!

Are you the impatient type? One of those folks who think that blinking your eyes is a perfectly good waste of reading or television-watching time? If so, you must be gathering cobwebs over the time it takes to create a bookmark the "old-fashioned" way.

When you run into a site that you just can't live without, you can quickly add a bookmark to Safari by dragging the address for the site to the Bookmarks Bar and dropping it there. Sweet!

Keep Bookmarks Organized

Eventually you may have so many bookmarks that you have a difficult time finding what you are looking for. The best thing to do is organize your bookmarks from the get go. To see and organize all of your bookmarks, choose Bookmarks | Show All Bookmarks, or click the Bookmarks icon in the Bookmarks Bar.

The Bookmarks window opens, shown in Figure 16-2, allowing you to organize your bookmarks any old way you would like.

The Bookmarks/Collections pane shows all of your bookmark collections, some of which are represented by folder icons. Collections are given descriptive names of their categories, such as Kids and Sports. As you can see, Apple has provided you with some preconfigured categories and bookmarks, which you can feel free to do with as you please.

When you create a bookmark, part of the process is to choose a bookmark collection in which to store the bookmark. That bookmark should be listed under the Bookmark title column, with its corresponding address under the Address column.

You can later move a bookmark from one collection to another by simply clicking the collection the bookmark is currently residing in and then dragging-and-dropping the bookmark onto the desired collection. To keep a copy of the bookmark in both locations, just hold down the OPTION key while dragging-and-dropping onto the new collection.

To delete a bookmark or a bookmark collection, select it and then press DELETE. To create a new bookmark collection, click the + button in the bottom-left corner of the window, and to add a new subfolder to a collection, click the + button under the Bookmark title and Address pane.

NOTE *You can edit the Bookmarks Bar and Bookmarks Menu collections like most other collections, but you cannot edit the Address Book, Bonjour, History, and All RSS Feeds collections.*

Bookmark title   Bookmark address   Search bookmarks

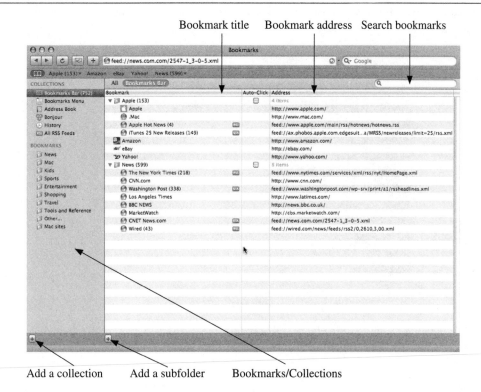

Add a collection   Add a subfolder   Bookmarks/Collections

FIGURE 16-2   Organize your bookmarks with ease with Safari's Bookmarks window.

Import and Export Bookmarks

Backing up your bookmarks is as good an idea as backing up your data, especially when a bookmark is a critical part of your daily life and work. Over time (much faster than you might think), you can build a vast collection of bookmarks that would take many hours to recompile should you lose your bookmark list for any reason.

Exporting your bookmarks saves the list of links to a file that another browser can import, instantly moving your lengthy list of addresses from one browser or Mac to another. To export your bookmarks, choose File | Export Bookmarks, name your bookmarks, choose a location in which to save them, and then click Save.

To import bookmarks into Safari, choose File | Import Bookmarks, browse for the bookmarks file and select it, and then click Import.

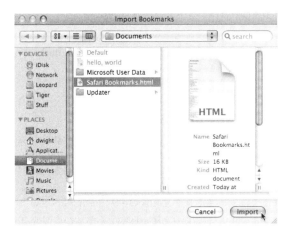

Your imported bookmarks are shown as a collection in the Bookmarks/Collections pane, and the name of the collection includes the date on which the bookmarks were imported.

Configure Safari Preferences

Safari's preferences enable you to customize Safari to your own style of web browsing. Access Safari's preferences by clicking Safari in the menu bar and choosing Preferences. We'll go over each of Safari's preferences panes one by one:

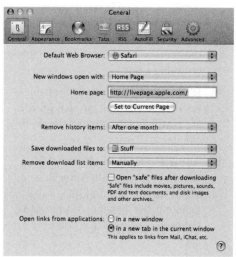

- **General** Choose how new windows open, what site to use for your home page, when to delete items from your history, where to save files downloaded from the Internet, and what to do with those files once downloaded. The Default Web Browser pop-up menu lets you choose which browser (if you have a third-party browser, such as Firefox, Camino, or Opera, installed) opens when you click a webpage link in an email or document.

■ **Appearance** Choose font styles for Safari here. Clear the "Display images when the page opens" check box to make webpages load faster by not showing pictures and graphics on the page. Of course, if you do this you will miss a great deal of content on most sites. You should change the Default Encoding option only if you notice garbled text on a webpage.

■ **Bookmarks** Choose yet more options for organizing your bookmarks. You may also choose to sync your bookmarks from this Mac to your .Mac account, which in turn can sync the list with other Macs of your choosing. This keeps your bookmarks consistent across multiple Macs, making it that much easier to browse like a champion!

■ **Tabs** Determine how to use tabs in your Safari experience. Tabbed browsing is the best thing to hit web browsers since…well, the advent of web browsers! Tabs allow you to open multiple sites without opening multiple windows. It's much more convenient to have one window open with ten tabs than to have ten separate windows open. The keyboard shortcuts in this window make tabbed browsing a breeze.

■ **RSS** Configure options for using RSS feeds within Safari. RSS feeds are covered in the next section in this chapter.

■ **AutoFill** Choose whether and when to use AutoFill. AutoFill is a neat feature of Safari that is able to automatically populate common fields on webpages that you have

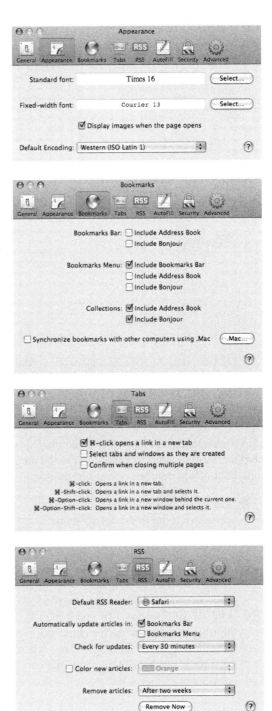

filled out in the past. For instance, if you've filled out a registration form to receive alerts from a news site, then you go to another site to register for movie updates, information such as your name and e-mail address that you entered into the name and e-mail address fields from the news site will

automatically show up in the corresponding fields of the movie site if you configure these preferences to allow Safari to use this option.

CAUTION   *I highly advise against checking the "User names and passwords" box. You probably don't want just anyone to walk up to your Mac and be able to access your bank accounts, private email accounts, and the like. Checking this box causes Safari to remember usernames and passwords for every secured site you visit.*

■ **Security**   Tell Safari whether it should enable plug-ins and Java-related content, block those annoying pop-up windows, or accept cookies from websites. Plug-ins are used by Safari to display multimedia content, such as pictures and video. Java is used by many interactive websites (sites that require user input) and for animations. JavaScript is present in most websites, and is used often for buttons and interactive forms.

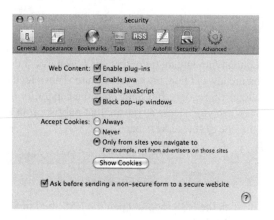

TIP   *Accepting cookies from a website doesn't mean that the administrator of that site is going to have his mother bake you a batch of chocolate chip cookies for visiting his webpage. Cookies are simply small text files that some sites use to track your browsing behavior or authenticate users. Choosing whether to accept cookies or not is entirely up to you. Some people are concerned that cookies are an invasion of privacy since they do keep up with your browsing habits, but on the flip side, some websites, such as those that employ shopping carts for purchasing items, may not work without cookies enabled.*

■ **Advanced**   Configure the way smaller font sizes are displayed, what style sheet to use, and what proxy settings are needed. Ask your network administrator whether proxies need to be set up in your browser if you are unable to surf the Web and know that you have a working network connection. Most users, under normal circumstances, won't need to change these settings.

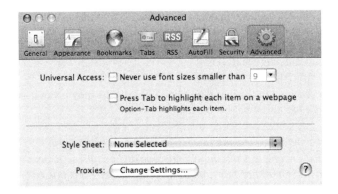

Get RSS Feeds

RSS stands for Really Simple Syndication, which is a format used for viewing webpages that frequently update their content, such as news sites and blogs. RSS feeds update automatically so you are always kept up-to-the-minute. These feeds have usually been accessed using programs called RSS readers, but Safari has the capability to utilize RSS built right in.

When you access a website that publishes an RSS feed, Safari displays an RSS logo on the right side of the address bar.

Click the RSS logo to open the RSS feed in Safari. The following image shows the RSS feed for the Apple Hot News site.

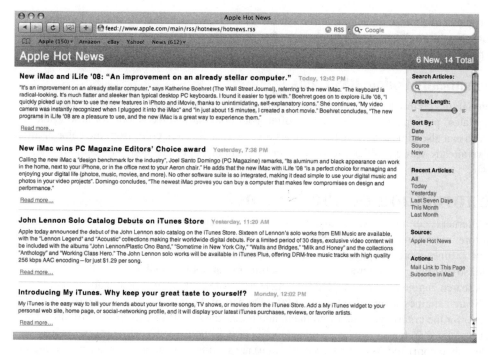

The upper-right corner shows the number of articles in the feed. The right side of the RSS feed window gives you several options for viewing the feed:

- **Search Articles**   Search the articles in the feed
- **Sort By**   Sort the articles using different categories
- **Recent Articles**   View a range of articles for this feed going all the way back to last month
- **Actions**   Mail links to the page to friends and family

You can bookmark RSS feeds in the same manner as you bookmark a standard webpage. If you save the bookmark in the Bookmarks Bar or the Bookmarks menu, Safari will display a number next to the bookmark title representing the number of new articles in the feed.

Automatically Update RSS Feeds

Open Safari's preferences and click RSS to set options for viewing RSS feeds. Use the "Check for updates" pop-up menu to choose how often your bookmarked feeds look for new articles.

You can also choose to have new articles display in a different color from the color of articles you've already viewed, which is especially convenient on pages that contain lots of articles.

Find Information on the Internet

The Internet is certainly entertaining, but its primary function is to enable users to find, gather, and store information. Where in the world do you begin to find the information you need? There are many times more webpages on the Internet than there have ever been people in the entire world, so searching the Internet one page at a time might not be feasible for you!

A search engine is what you need, and there are more of them available than you could ever use. Search engines scour the Internet (at least the part of the Internet they have indexed on their servers) for the criteria you enter into them, and return the results to you almost instantly. The most popular search engine of them all is Google (www.google.com), while others such as Yahoo (www.yahoo.com) and Ask.com (www.ask.com) are worthy of your attention as well. Keep in mind that if you don't find what you are looking for on one search engine, another may well have hundreds of links regarding the topic, so don't just limit yourself to one or two search engines. Sites such as Dogpile (www.dogpile.com) query multiple search engines at once, which is a huge help if you're having a difficult time finding information on a topic.

Apple has facilitated quick searching of the Internet by providing a Google search field in the upper-right corner of the Safari browser window. If you are searching for sites on ancient Rome, type the subject into the Google search field and press RETURN to be zipped away to Google's search results page, which should look something like the following image.

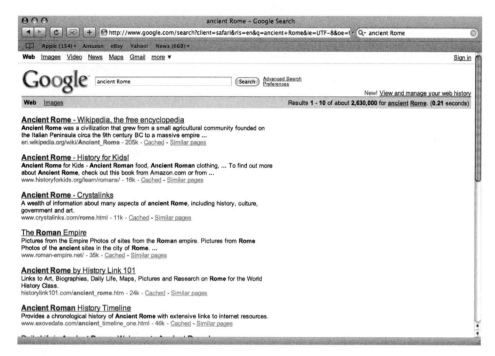

You've just found more information on ancient Rome than the Romans ever had!

When searching the Internet, remember to be as specific as possible to ensure the most accurate results. For example, if you want to find out more on the Coliseum, entering "Roman Coliseum" would greatly narrow your search, as opposed to just typing in "Rome."

Summary

The Internet is an awesome tool the likes of which the world has never known. More information and entertainment than you could ever hope to find in one location is waiting for you in cyberspace, and Apple has provided the best browser in the world for you to discover it: Safari. Enjoy!

Chapter 17

Mail Call!

How to...

- Set Mail's preferences to suit your work and play habits
- Make your emails look amazing
- Add email contacts to your Address Book
- Create rules to govern Mail's treatment of certain emails
- Add and receive email attachments
- Add additional accounts to Mail
- Read RSS feeds from within Mail

Mac OS X's Mail application is so much more than just a plain-Jane email "sender/getter." Mail allows you to actually be creative with your email, to actually *design* the format of your emails, making them uniquely your own. Your friends and family will soon learn that whenever they see email from you in their Inbox, that email is going to look great (whether your grammar stinks or not!). But Mail isn't just for making your messages look pretty; it's for getting work (and play) done in a professional, yet intuitively easy, manner.

Chapter 5 got you up and running with Mail, but this chapter will up your status to world-class sprinter. So open the Mail application and let's get started.

Set Preferences for Mail

Choose Mail | Preferences to access Mail's nine preferences panes, described in turn in the following sections. These preferences allow you to "teach" Mail how you want it to behave in various circumstances. Let the training begin!

General

In the General preferences pane, choose your default e-mail program, how often to check for new mail, which sound alerts you to the presence of new mails, how to handle iCal invitations, and where to save downloaded attachments (files the sender of the email attached and sent along with the text of their email). You can also choose which mailboxes to include when searching your emails, and whether or not to synchronize email across various Macs using your .Mac account.

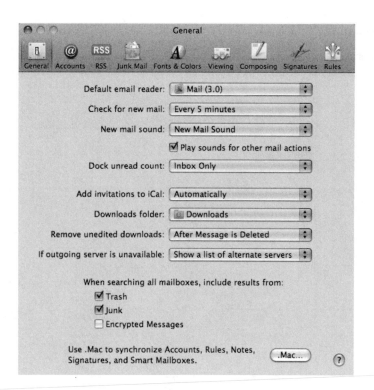

You can choose what email application to use as your Mac's default for receiving and sending email by changing the "Default email reader" option. By default, it is set to Mail, of course.

Accounts

The Accounts preferences pane enables you to create, edit, and remove email accounts, and control how Mail works with each individual account. Click the + and – buttons in the bottom-left corner to add and delete email accounts, respectively.

Click one of the accounts in your Accounts list to get the "low-down" on it. Make changes to the accounts in one of the three tabs available: Account Information, Mailbox Behaviors, or Advanced.

Account Information

The Account Information tab gives you all the settings information for each of your e-mail accounts. Change any settings that may be necessary to properly receive email from this account on your Mac.

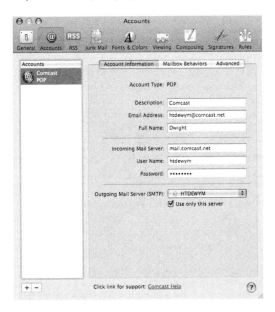

Check your Outgoing Mail Server options by clicking the aptly named pop-up menu, and select choose Edit Server List to see the settings used to communicate with your ISP's SMTP server.

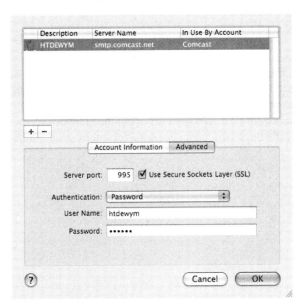

Check the "Use only this server" check box to allow mail to be sent only from the default SMTP server for the account. Otherwise, Mail will try to use one of your other SMTP servers, if there are any.

Contact your ISP if you are having difficulties sending or receiving emails. Now that you are familiar with the Account Information tab, you should be able to follow any instructions your ISP may give you.

Mailbox Behaviors

The options on this tab let you store your notes in your Inbox for even easier access, decide when Mail should erase Sent or Junk mail from their respective mailboxes, and choose how to handle deleted messages. The options may differ depending on the account type (IMAP or POP).

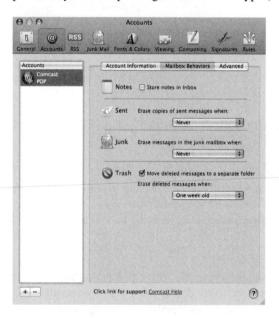

"Store draft messages on the server" keeps drafts on your ISP's mail server, where you can access it from other computers. This option is only available for IMAP accounts.

Advanced

The Advanced tab is where you turn the current account on or off, have Mail check the account for new mail automatically, decide whether or not to keep copies of emails on your ISP's server, have Mail skip messages that are larger than the size specified, and set what port number and authentication type are necessary for communication with your ISP's incoming mail server.

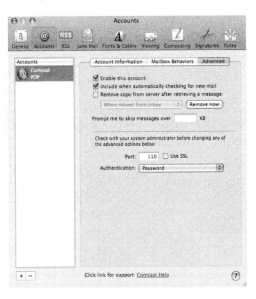

 *I highly recommend leaving the "Remove copy from server after retrieving a message" option unchecked. If you check this option, and you lose the emails that are stored on your Mac, you won't be able to retrieve emails from your ISP. Unchecking this box is a safeguard, keeping copies of emails on your ISP's server in case you need them in the future.*

RSS

Safari isn't the only application on your Mac that can function as an RSS reader: Mail fits that bill, too. The last section in this chapter details using RSS feeds with Mail. The RSS preferences pane includes the preferences that determine Mail's handling of those feeds. Use these settings to determine your Mac's default RSS reader, how often Mail should check for updates to RSS feeds, and how you would like to remove articles from the feed list.

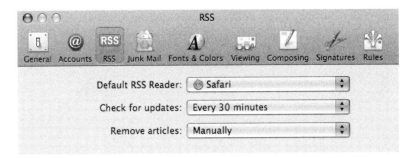

Junk Mail

You may know junk mail by its other nomenclature, spam, but a rose by any other name is still a rose, or in this case junk by any other name is still junk. Anyone who's used email to any extent has most likely received emails that they didn't solicit; this kind of email is considered junk mail.

Mail's Junk Mail preferences pane offers many options to protect you and yours from such potentially nasty intrusions. Mail has an excellent junk mail filter that can sift through your Inbox to find email that meets the requirements for junk mail. It marks that email as junk and, by default, leaves it in your Inbox.

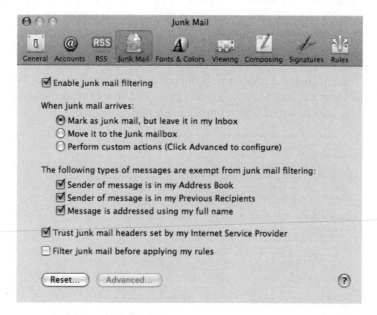

Use the Junk Main pane to turn junk mail filtering on or off, decide what Mail should do with the mail it has marked as junk, make sure that Mail knows some types of messages should never be marked as junk, choose whether to trust your ISP's junk filters, and decide whether to separate the junk mail from the rest before or after rules have been applied (more on rules later in this chapter).

How to ...   Create a Custom Junk Mail Filter

Junk mail is usually just harmless advertisements that, at the most, pose a serious threat to annoy you to death with their frequency. On occasion, however, you may run across a virus (yes, even on a Mac, even though the likelihood is extremely low) or the junk mail may be much more racy than you want Junior to be gawking at. While most of us are lucky enough to just be annoyed, don't let that get your guard down! The moment you're not careful is the moment you should be.

Sometimes it's necessary to get really specific about which email is junk in order to weed out particular items that may sneak past Mail's already-extensive filters. To set up a custom junk mail filter, click the "Perform custom actions" radio button in the "When junk mail arrives" section of the Junk Mail preferences pane, and then click the Advanced button at the bottom of the pane to see these configuration options:

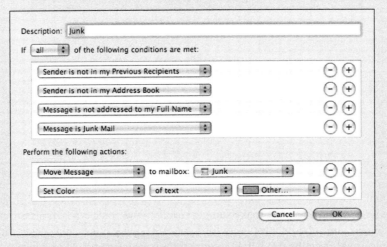

Click the + and – buttons to the right of the conditions menus to add and remove criteria from the list. Do the same for the actions to modify what happens to mail meeting the previous conditions.

Fonts & Colors

This preferences pane simply allows you to change Mail's default fonts and colors.

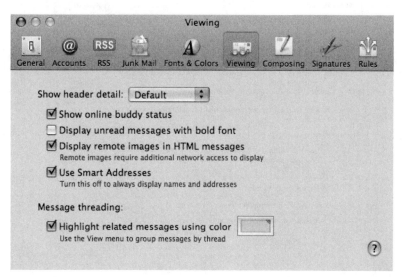

Viewing

It's your Mail, so mailboxes should show your email the way you want them to! That's exactly what these options are all about.

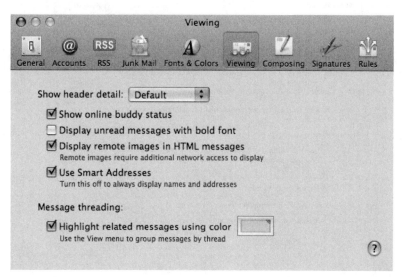

The Show Header Detail option enables you to tell Mail how you want the header information to appear in your emails. Headers are the information you see at the top of the email when you first open it, such as From, Subject, Date, and To.

The four check boxes under the pop-up menu enable you to specify whether to show the status of your iChat buddies in your e-mails, whether to show in bold font messages that haven't been read, whether to show pictures and graphics in emails, and whether Mail should use Smart Addresses (when an email is typed, the name of the recipient is automatically inserted into the address field, not the actual address).

Checking the last option, Message Threading, causes Mail to highlight all other emails that relate to the one you are viewing. This is a really handy utility when you're trying to find all the emails that pertain to a particular subject or conversation.

Composing

The Composing preferences pane has lots of options to configure, so we'll take the three sections of the pane one at a time.

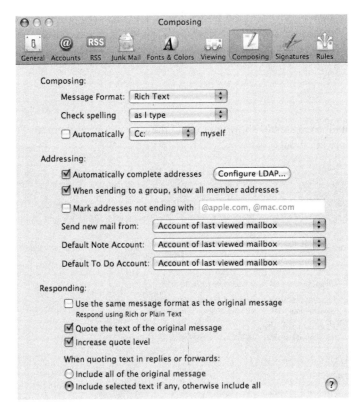

Composing

Decide which format to use when creating new email: rich or plain text. Rich text gives you the font selections and color changes that are needed to design an attractive message, while plain text is precisely what it says it is: plain old text. You cannot use the advanced graphics features of Mail, such as Stationery, if you choose to send email in plain text format.

This section also enables you to choose how to handle spell checking and whether to send a copy to yourself of the emails you send to others.

TIP *Why would you ever want to use plain text? Well, while most email applications are able to send and receive email with rich text and graphics, some of the people you send emails to may still use email applications that only allow plain text. Those people won't be able to read your email if you are using rich text.*

Addressing

The options in this section determine how your new emails display addresses, what account to use by default when sending email, and which accounts to make the defaults for Notes and To Do lists.

LDAP stands for Lightweight Directory Access Protocol, and is commonly used throughout businesses as a means to access the company-wide telephone and email directories. Ask your IT administrator if your company uses an LDAP server to help you find email addresses of other employees. If so, click the Configure LDAP button and add the required information to link Mail to the LDAP server (again, your IT department should be able to help with this).

Responding

Which format should you use when replying to an email? The best, and most courteous, thing to do is reply in the same format in which the original email was received, so the "Use the same message format as the original message" box is checked by default.

Checking the "Quote the text of the original message" box causes the original message and its subsequent exchanges to be listed beneath your reply, like so:

The quotes can be easily differentiated from one another by checking the "Increase quote level" box. Single message sequences are assigned a color line of their own, making them distinct from other sequences in the history of the email.

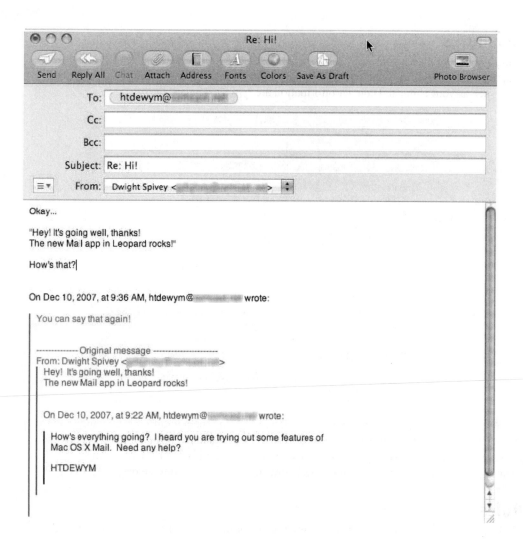

Signatures

Using a signature places your personal stamp at the end of every email you send, adding that final personal and professional touch. A signature can contain any information you want, but items such as your name and contact information are typical standard fare.

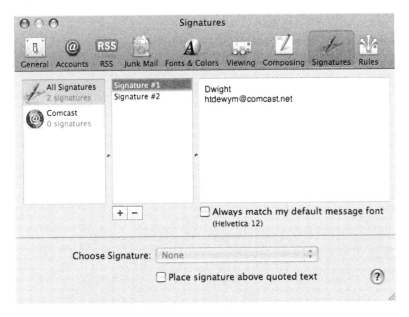

You can create as many signatures as you like, assigning them to different accounts and customizing them to fit your needs. Checking the "Place signature above quoted text" box puts your signature directly below your latest message when you reply to or forward a message. Clearing the check box puts your signature below the quoted text from the original message.

Rules

Mail lets you create rules used to filter your email according to the criteria you set up in them. Rules can be used to make copies of certain emails in folders specifically created for them, such as assigning all emails addressed from your spouse to a folder you created in your Inbox called Wife or Hubby. Another example would be to send all email whose subject contains information about your son's football team practices into a folder called Football Practice Info. You can make rules that automatically send certain emails to the Trash, or group them by dates in which they were sent or received. The options are mind-blowing! Okay, maybe mind-blowing is a bit strong of a term, but there's lots of possibilities, trust me.

The Rules preferences pane presents you with a list of all the rules that have been created for Mail.

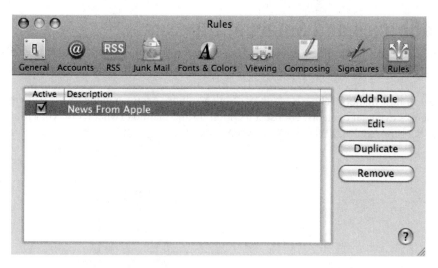

Select a rule from the list and then click the Edit button if you would like to make adjustments to it, or click the Add Rule button to make a new rule altogether.

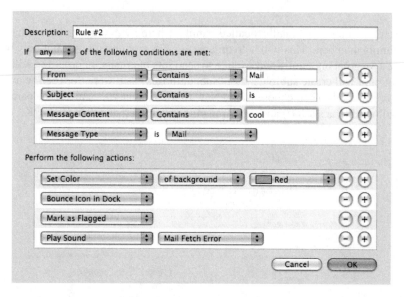

Give your new rule a descriptive title, and then configure it to your heart's content.

Create Mailboxes and Smart Mailboxes

Mailboxes are to Mail what folders are to Finder: they are places to store and organize emails of a certain variety. Creating a new mailbox is the equivalent of creating a new folder in a Finder window.

To create a new mailbox, choose Mailbox | New Mailbox. Assign a name that is descriptive of the mailbox's eventual contents, choose a location for the mailbox (whether on your Mac or on the mail server of an IMAP account), and then click OK.

For this example, I created a mailbox called Family, where I will organize email that I receive from family members. This will help organize emails from my family, but only to a small degree because I've got a big family and we like to send lots of emails. In order to facilitate better organization, I will create subfolders, or "submailboxes" as it were, for each segment of my family. To create a subfolder, choose Mail | New Mailbox, type the name of the parent folder (or mailbox) followed by a slash (/) and the name of the subfolder, and then click OK.

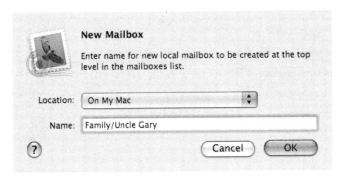

I created subfolders for Mom and Dad, Kelli and Keith, and Uncle Gary, as you can see in the following image.

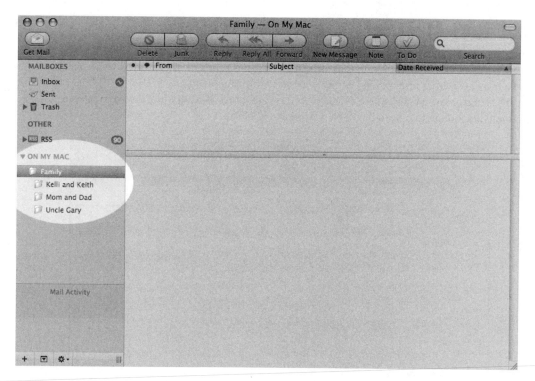

Smart Mailboxes are brilliant little buggers. They give a central location where you can view emails that meet criteria you've defined, without actually moving those emails from the original mailboxes in which they are stored. For instance, you can create a Smart Mailbox that shows all emails from a specific person that it finds in all your other mailboxes.

To create a Smart Mailbox, choose Mailbox | New Smart Mailbox, assign the Smart Mailbox a descriptive name that immediately tips you off to its contents, and then add or remove criteria using the pop-up menus and the + and − buttons on the right.

Format Your Messages

With Mail, you can create stunning messages to send to your colleagues and family. There's never been another email program that offers the design features of Mac OS X's Mail. You can make truly beautiful presentations within your New Message window.

To create a new email, choose File | New Message, press ⌘-N, or click the New Message button in the toolbar to open a blank New Message window.

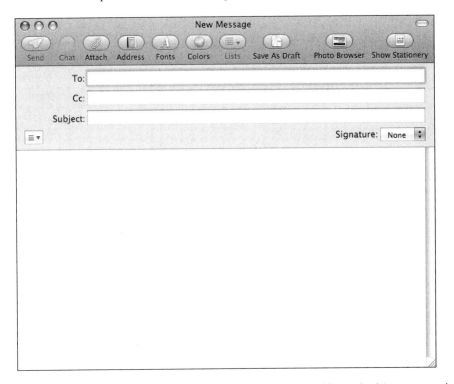

You already know how to enter email addresses (see Chapter 5 if you don't), so our main concentration here is on formatting the message itself.

Choose Fonts and Colors

A formatting element that is almost as important as the content of the email itself is your choice of fonts and their colors. Click the Fonts button in the toolbar to browse the fonts installed in Mac OS X.

Be sure that you choose a font and a size that are appropriate for the type of email you are sending. For instance, you probably

don't want to use the Comic font to send a presentation email to your boss, unless you work for a company that markets the wares of clowns, of course.

The colors you choose for your fonts or for the background of your email should also maintain the tone of the email's nature. Choose your colors by using the Colors palette, which you open by clicking the Colors button in the toolbar.

Choose your colors from a color wheel, color sliders, a spectrum of colors from an image, or from a selection of crayons.

Add Photos with Photo Browser

This component of the toolbar lets you add images to your email rather effortlessly. Simply click the Photo Browser icon in the toolbar and select the picture you want to include, either from your iPhoto Library or Photo Booth.

Select multiple items by holding down the ⌘ key while clicking the photos you want to use.

Use Stationery

Stationery is one of the best features to hit email in a very long time. It's such a simple idea, but one that hasn't been implemented, at least not on a large scale, until now. Stationery is a series of templates designed using HTML (the programming language used primarily for creating Internet websites), which enables the templates to easily incorporate images and other graphics to create a very polished appearance. These templates are prebuilt by Apple and are included in Mail.

Click the Show Stationery button in the toolbar to see the templates that are available. Browse through the many choices until you find the best one to suit the mood of the subject you are emailing about or until you just find one that strikes your fancy.

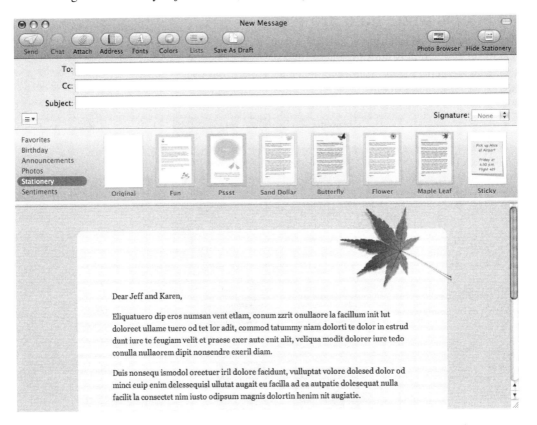

If you choose a template that has placeholder text in it, you can easily edit the text by clicking on the text and changing it as necessary.

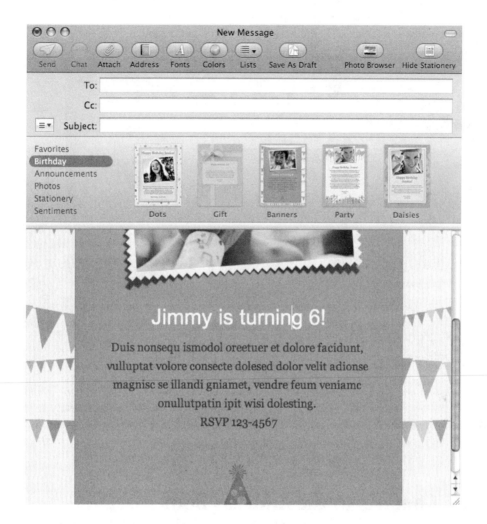

Add Attachments

Attachments are files you can send along with emails, sort of like adding an item, such as cash, in an envelope when sending a letter to someone. Attachments can be anything, from text files to pictures to entire applications, but be sure that the size of the attachment isn't too large for the server you are sending it too. Also check with your ISP to see if it limits the size of files that you can send as attachments. If the attachment is too large, the recipient won't get the attachment, and may not get the email at all. Either your ISP or that of the person you are sending the email to will notify you if the email is unable to be sent or received.

To attach a file to an email, click the Attachment button in the toolbar, browse the Mac for the file you need, click the file to highlight it, and then click the Choose File button.

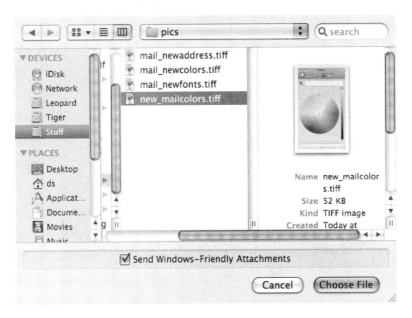

If you plan to send the email to one of your less-fortunate friends who may be running a Windows-based PC, be sure to check the box called "Send Windows-Friendly Attachments." This option encodes the attachment in such a way that it is readable by Windows email applications. It's always safe to use this option, whether the recipient has a Mac or not, because Macs can handle Windows-friendly attachments, too.

Add Email Contacts to the Address Book

Now that you can create one heck of a good-looking email, you need to have someone to send those masterpieces to. When you receive an email, it's quite easy to add the sender or others included on the email to your Address Book. Click the name of the person in the To or From field of an email and hold the mouse button down, and then choose the "Add to Address Book" option.

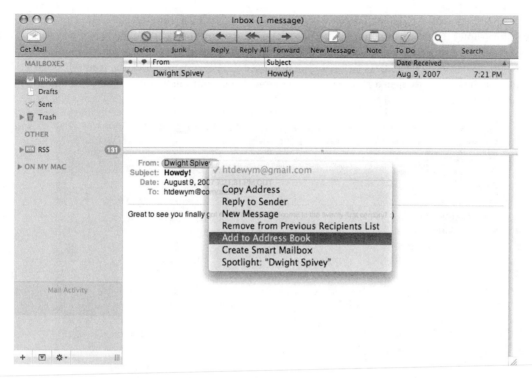

The next time you want to send an email to that person, their name and address will readily be available by simply typing the first few letters of either into the To field.

Use More Than One Account

You can use more than one email account with Mail. As an example, I have multiple email accounts set up with my ISP and another with Gmail (Google's free email service). I can open the Accounts preferences pane and add them all to Mail, providing one central location with which to manage all of my email. The Inbox section of the Mailboxes pane lists all the inboxes for your different accounts.

If you select Inbox in the Mailboxes pane, all messages from each of your accounts are displayed in the mail list. This can be tricky because you don't know which account goes with which email. To clear up any confusion, click the Inbox for each individual account to see email it contains.

Another potential pitfall can occur when creating new email. Be sure the New Message window shows the proper account you want to send the email from. Fear not, there is a way to be certain the correct account is used, thankfully; choose the correct account in the From pop-up menu underneath the address fields. If you don't see the From menu, click the New Message button in the toolbar to open a New Message window. Notice the small button on the left that looks like a list:

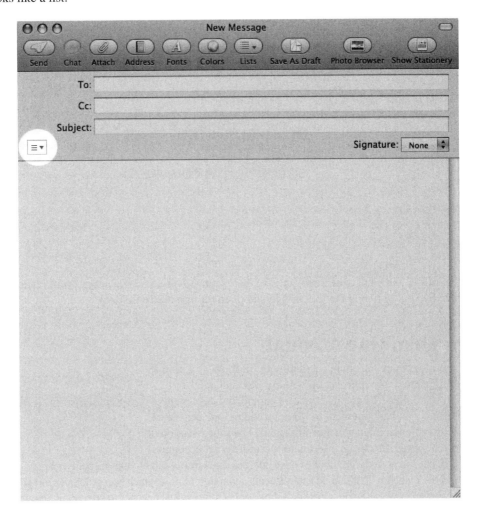

Click the list button and choose Customize, check the box next to the From field, and then click OK to add it to your New Message windows.

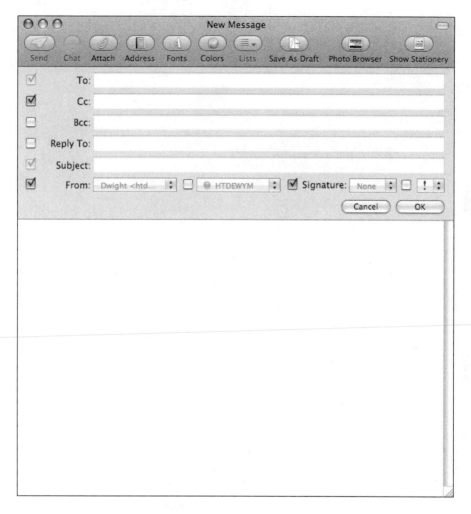

Now you can choose which account to send the new message from by clicking the pop-up menu next to the From field and making your selection.

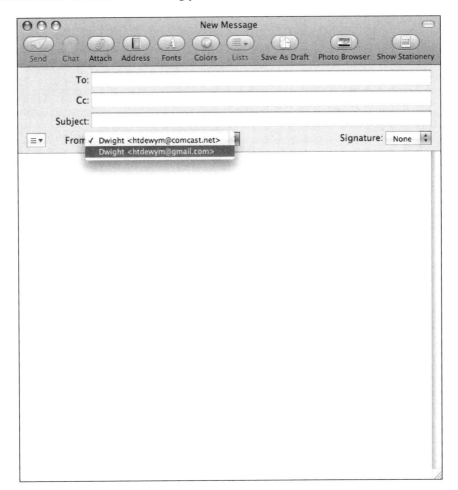

Read RSS Feeds

Add the reading of RSS feeds to all the other actions that Mail can handle. Having the ability to read RSS feeds in Mail keeps you from constantly switching between applications to keep up with the day's events in a separate RSS reader.

To add RSS feeds to the Mailboxes pane, choose File | Add RSS Feeds. This opens a window with more RSS feeds than you'll ever have to time to read! Choose your favorites from this precompiled list, or add your own feed by typing its address in the Feed URL field (click the Other button in the bottom-left corner if you don't see this field), and then click Add.

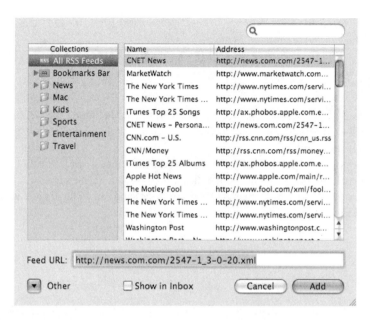

RSS feeds are displayed in the Mailboxes pane just like inboxes. To read a feed, just click it in the Mailboxes pane and select an article that interests you from the list. The article displays in the message viewer in the bottom pane.

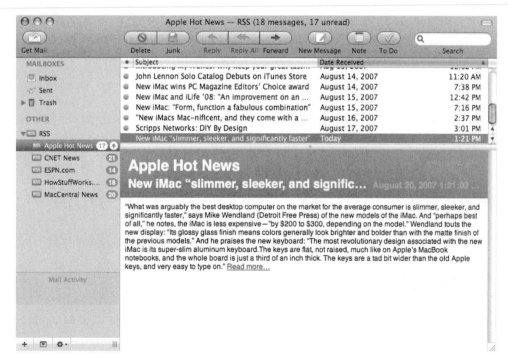

Mail Can Read Your Email to You

Mail is so intelligent that it can actually read your email to you, out loud. This feature is perfect for Mac users who have problems seeing text on the screen, or are simply too busy (or lazy) to read the email themselves.

Open the message by double-clicking it in the mail list window, choose Edit | Speech | Start Speaking, and your Mac will read the entire e-mail to you, headers and all. If you'd like Mail to shut up, just choose Edit | Speech | Stop Speaking, and the better-than-it-used-to-be-but-still-pretty-annoying computer voice will cease and desist.

Summary

By now you have a thorough understanding of how Mail performs its most basic tasks, but don't stop here. To discover more of Mail's capabilities, explore Mail Help (Help | Mail Help). Your personal post office should be humming along in no time, and don't be surprised when your friends and family start asking you for pointers on how to make their email look as good as yours (the answer's easy: tell them to get a Mac!).

Part V

Making Your Mac Even Better: Adding Microsoft Windows and Hardware

Chapter 18

ATTENTION! Welcome to Boot Camp, Private!

How to...

- ■ Prepare your Mac for a Windows installation
- ■ Install Windows
- ■ Dual-boot between Mac OS X and Windows
- ■ Use Windows without booting directly into it

There have been some great partnerships in the past. Peanut butter and chocolate, Abbot and Costello, The Captain and Tennille, and of course, Apple and Microsoft.

"I'm sorry, come again?"

Okay, that last one may have been a little whimsical, at best. Apple and Microsoft haven't always been the best of buddies, but they haven't exactly been the worst of enemies. Alright, maybe I'm stretching that a bit, too. Regardless, both companies are still around after decades of competing with one another. Apple makes software for Windows, Microsoft makes software for Mac OS X, and the world still spins on its axis and revolves around Sol.

The inclusion of Intel processors into the Mac lineup has opened up all kinds of possibilities for computer users. No longer are people who must use Windows for whatever reason forced to buy an inferior machine, and no longer are Mac users unable to run some Windows-only applications that some businesses insist on using (usually unnecessarily). How can I make such claims? Because of this one word: Boot Camp.

Boot Camp is a utility Apple developed to help Mac users install Microsoft Windows on their Mac.

TIP   *Apple doesn't provide you a copy of Windows! You have to obtain your own copy of Microsoft Windows to install it on your Mac. You can use Windows XP Home or Professional but the CD must include Service Pack 2 already; you cannot upgrade from an older version of XP later. You can also use these versions of Windows Vista: Home Basic, Home Premium, Business, Ultimate, or Super-Honking-Fantastic. (Okay, I made that last one up, but the others are legit.)*

Why Install Windows on Your Mac?

"Why in the name of all that is good and sacred would I want to desecrate my Mac with such tripe?"

If you're someone who just asked that exact question, verbatim, chances are good that there's nothing I could say to convince you of the benefits of installing Windows on your Mac. This chapter may just not be for you. But if you're the curious type, or sincerely want to know the pros of running Windows on your Mac, please carry on.

"Switchers" is a name some use to describe people who have made the jump, the evolution if you will, from Windows to Mac. Switchers are popping up all over because people are beginning to catch on to how great Apple's products really are, due in no small part to the iPod and iPhone. However, some potential switchers were unable to make the leap because they simply couldn't afford to dump their software libraries that were made only for Windows. Others simply were forced to stay with PCs because their company used a proprietary software that was written only for Windows. They were, for all intents, captives of Microsoft Windows and PC vendors.

But then something wonderful happened: Apple announced they were moving their entire line of Macintosh computers from the PowerPC processors that had served so well for so long to Intel processors. This decision took the computer world by storm, but people still wondered if Windows could be installed on a Mac. Apple silenced that question by providing Boot Camp, a utility that helps you configure your Mac for a Windows installation. PC users who have always admired the Mac but had to use Windows for one reason or another suddenly had no excuse to not buy a Mac with Apple's move to the Intel processor.

The coolest part of this whole "Windows on your Mac" thing? Windows doesn't replace Mac OS X on your hard drive; it's installed on your hard drive right along with Mac OS X, and you get to select which operating system to boot your Mac into!

Have the Best of Both Worlds:
Install Windows with Boot Camp

To install Windows on your Mac using Boot Camp, follow these steps:

1. Open the Boot Camp Assistant by choosing Hard Drive | Applications | Utilities and double-clicking its icon. Another way to get to Utilities is to choose Go | Utilities while in the Finder.

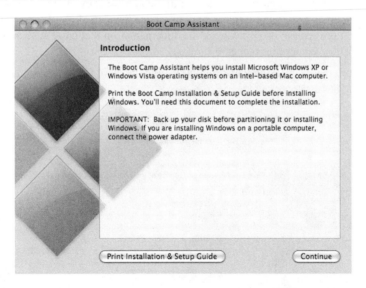

The Introduction window gives you some sound advice: print the Boot Camp Installation & Setup Guide, *so that you have it handy once you've booted your Mac into Windows, and back up your system before continuing the Assistant, so that you don't lose files if something goes wrong during the partitioning process.*

2. Click Continue to move to the partitioning options.

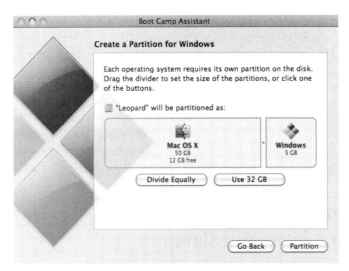

3. By default, your Windows partition is set to 5GB. Click the Divide Equally button if you prefer to split your drive between the two operating systems, or click the Use 32GB button to automatically set the Windows partition to occupy that much space on your hard drive. You can also customize the size of the partitions by clicking the tiny dot that separates them and dragging it to the right to reduce the size of the Windows partition, or to the left to increase its size. Check the documentation that came with your Windows CD or DVD for size requirements.

4. When you're ready, click the Partition button, and the Boot Camp Assistant begins partitioning the disk.

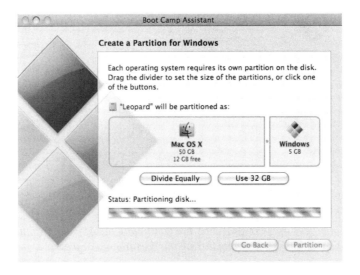

5. Once the disk is partitioned, insert your Windows installation CD or DVD and then click the Start Installation button.

6. Your Mac reboots into the Windows installation disc. Follow the onscreen instructions to install Windows, but be sure to compare the steps to those in the *Boot Camp Installation & Setup Guide* (you *did* print it, right?).

CAUTION   *Be* absolutely certain *that you pick the Boot Camp partition when prompted to choose a partition for your Windows installation. If you choose the wrong partition, you could wipe out your entire Mac OS X disk.*

7. Eventually you are asked to format your Boot Camp partition. Choose either the NTFS (recommended), FAT, or SLIM-N-TRIM file system for your Windows install. Once again, I must admit that I made up the SLIM-N-TRIM file system, but I don't see why Microsoft has to pick on overweight file systems by calling them names.

TIP   *If you want to be able to read files from and write files to your Windows partition while booted into Mac OS X, format the Boot Camp partition with FAT. Mac OS X can only read NTFS partitions, and cannot write to them. Keep in mind, though, that a partition larger than 32GB cannot be formatted with FAT.*

8. Once the installation process is complete, your Mac boots up into Windows. Insert your Mac OS X installation disc and wait for the Boot Camp installer to open. The Boot Camp installer installs drivers that are needed by Windows so that it can play nicely with your Apple hardware, such as your Mac's built-in iSight camera and video drivers.

9. Click Next to begin the installation.

10. Choose to install the Apple Software Update for Windows. Allow the installer to complete its process in peace; do not touch anything until the installer is finished! When you see the Finish button, click it, and then restart your Mac.

11. When your Mac boots back up, you see the Boot Camp Help window. It's a good idea to read through the Help window's contents to find out the little ins and outs of using Windows on your Mac.

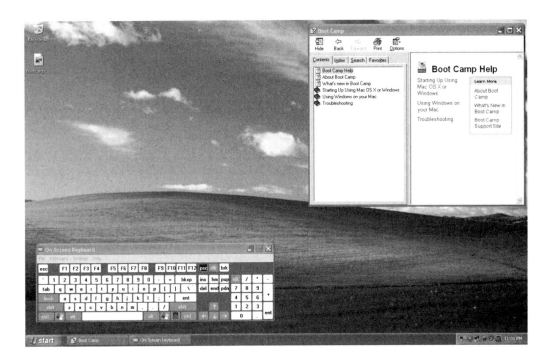

Choose Which OS to Boot Into

"Well, I've now got Windows installed, but how do I get back to Mac OS X?" Part of the Boot Camp installation is a control panel that it added to your Windows system. Open the Boot Camp Control Panel by choosing Start | Control Panel and double-clicking the Boot Camp Control Panel icon.

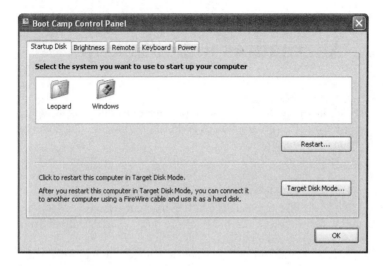

The Startup Disk tab lists the operating systems available for your Mac to boot from. The icon that looks like a folder with a blue X on it is the Mac system folder. Click it to highlight it, and then click Restart to boot into Mac OS X immediately, or click OK to reboot later.

To boot back into Windows from within Mac OS X, choose Apple Menu I System Preferences I Startup Disk, select the Windows partition, and click Restart to immediately reboot into Windows, or close the window to restart later.

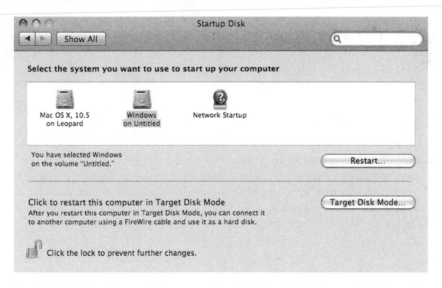

To choose which operating system opens when the Mac first starts up, hold down the OPTION key immediately after your hear the startup tone, and continue to hold until you see hard drive icons that represent each partition. Select the OS you want to boot into and click the arrow beneath it.

Alternatives to Boot Camp

Boot Camp is Apple's answer to installing Windows on a Mac, but there is an alternative: Parallels Desktop for Mac. This program helps you install Windows, DOS, and even Linux operating systems on your Mac.

Parallels uses a technology called *virtual machines* to store your Windows (or other) operating systems and applications. A virtual machine is, in basic layman terms, a "fake computer" created by the Parallels software that an operating system could be installed on and used just like an actual computer. The virtual machine uses your Mac's hardware, including its memory, networking, USB and FireWire ports, CD/DVD drives, mouse, hard disks, and almost any other device you connect to it.

Virtual machines don't quite run at your Mac's full speed, but they are remarkably close in speed, and more than adequate for most tasks. While playing most new graphics-intensive games may not work very well (this may be rectified as virtual machine technology improves), "normal" computer work won't be a problem in the slightest.

A big plus to using Parallels is that there's no need to partition your hard drive. Virtual machines can automatically adjust their size depending on the amount of data stored in them. If you add an application, the virtual machine size increases; if you remove an application, the size decreases.

Visit www.parallels.com/en/products/desktop/ to get more information, and you can also download a trial version of Parallels Desktop for Mac so that you can "kick the tires" before purchasing.

Summary

The ability to run Windows on a Mac is great for people who are moving to a Mac after having been stuck using Windows-based PCs for years. It allows the option of keeping all your old PC software around, and that's a definite plus after having plunked down the coins for all of it over the years. The chances are pretty good that you now have the fastest Windows machine in the neighborhood or office! But don't be surprised if over a period of time you find yourself booting less and less into your Windows partition.

Chapter 19

It's Alive! Adding Hardware to Your Mac(enstein)

How to...

- Understand what adding more memory can do for your Mac
- Know what kind of devices you can connect to your Mac
- Add external devices via USB and FireWire
- Understand the difference between USB and FireWire

Your Mac came out of the box ready to tackle your every command head on. How well it tackles those commands may differ from Mac to Mac, however, the factors behind this difference being just how well a Mac is equipped. Apple provides the option of upgrading certain aspects of your Mac before you buy it, such as installing a larger hard drive or bumping up the amount of memory—but of course, the purchase price of your Mac increases proportionally with the number of new hardware devices that you choose to add.

Some Mac users like to make their own modifications, however. Why pay Apple to do it when you can do it yourself? Be careful, though! The more options you add to your Mac and the more cables you have dangling out of the back of it, the more your nerd quotient skyrockets! Before you know it you'll be like those über-geeks you see in the movies, with rack after rack of hard drives and monitors all busily whirring away on who-knows-what.

In this chapter we'll take a gander at the basics of adding hardware to your Mac.

Understand Why Adding More Memory Is Never a Bad Idea

No axiom could be truer when it comes to computers: adding more memory is *never* a bad idea. There simply is no reason why adding more memory to a computer is ever a bad thing. Period. Nada. End of story.

By stating that it is never a "bad idea" or "bad thing," I mean that installing as much memory as the Mac can hold simply won't hurt it but there may be a point at which adding more memory doesn't help much either. For instance, if you use your Mac only for "the basics" (e-mail, Internet browsing, word processing), then anything more than 2GB is probably overkill, and you won't see much of a speed difference, if any. However, if you run memory-intensive applications such as Adobe Photoshop on a regular basis, the more memory you install the better.

Can you have too little memory (aka random access memory, or RAM)? Absolutely! Try running Mac OS X with only 128MB of RAM and you'll see just what I mean. S-l-o-w doesn't begin to describe it.

Discover What Adding Memory Does for Your Mac

Your Mac needs memory to run programs such as the operating system and the applications you use. The two types of memory used for running programs are the installed RAM modules and a portion of your hard drive that is set aside to act as a backup for your RAM, called virtual memory. When programs load on your Mac, the files needed to run them are loaded into RAM;

the more files that are needed to run a program, or the more programs you have running at one time, the more space that is taken up in RAM. When there is no longer any space left in RAM, your Mac brilliantly begins using the virtual memory space made available on the hard drive.

This all sounds like a genius way of handling things, and indeed it is, but it's not the optimal way, to be sure. RAM is much, much faster than a hard drive, so when your Mac accesses data for a program stored in RAM, it is blazingly speedy. On the other hand, if the Mac has to begin accessing that data from the hard drive, the operations get noticeably much slower. The more memory you add, the less chance your Mac will need to access virtual memory at all.

"I'm Convinced! How Do I Install More Memory?"

Each consumer Mac has different specifications regarding the type of memory it needs, so be sure to check the documentation that came with your Mac or consult Apple's support site (www.apple.com/support/) for your particular model. Those references are also the best places to learn how to install the memory once you purchase it.

 Apple gives plenty of instruction for upgrading memory on the iMac and the MacBook, but be careful with your Mac mini. Apple recommends taking your Mac mini to an Apple Authorized Service Provider or a brick-and-mortar Apple Store (if there's one in your area).

When it comes to purchasing memory for your Mac, Apple is one of the most expensive sellers to buy from. Visit www.ramjet.com or www.ramdirect.com to find the best memory prices for your Mac model.

Add External Devices

At some point you will physically connect an external device to your Mac. If you have a Mac mini or an iMac, you already have done so: your mouse and keyboard (unless they are wireless, of course).

What devices might you consider adding to your Mac? There are many options, and which devices you should connect depends on what kind of work or play you need to accomplish. Here's a list of devices you may need to pair with your Mac:

- **Printer** Whether laser or inkjet, at some point you will most likely need a printer to print school projects, self-publish a book, or print photos to share with others.

- **Scanner** Wouldn't it be great to get rid of all those papers on your desk, and not have to maintain drawers and drawers of files in filing cabinets? Scan that paperwork into your Mac and you can store it digitally instead! Scanners are also great for moving your old family photos to digital.

- **Hard drive** At some point you are going to have so much data on your Mac's built-in hard drive that it can hardly breathe, and it will tell you so. One solution is to delete some of your data, but what if it's all so important you can't afford to lose any of it? An external hard drive is the way to go. You can instantly increase your storage capacity without having to crack open your Mac's casing, and an external hard drive is portable, too. If you plan to use Time Machine (see Chapter 24) an external drive is a must-have.

■ **Digital video camera**   Your Mac, in conjunction with iMovie, is a whiz at editing digital video, so if you want to make movies on your Mac, you'll be connecting your digital video camera to it at some point.

■ **Digital still camera**   To get photos from your digital camera into iPhoto, you have to connect your camera and Mac. Apple hasn't quite perfected osmosis as a means of data transfer for the Mac, although I suspect someone in its secret labs is feverishly working on it.

■ **Speakers**   Computer speakers used to sound as good as tin cans, but today they can provide amazingly rich sounds, even deep, booming bass. A really good set of speakers is a must if you plan to use your Mac as an entertainment hub.

■ **Graphics tablet**   Graphics tablets are alternative input devices that let you "digitally draw" on your Mac. Graphic artists and photographers also use them to touch up photos.

■ **Trackball**   Trackballs are another alternative input device for your Mac. Remember the old-style computer mouse that used a small ball on the bottom whose movements controlled those of the pointer on your screen? Trackballs are kind of like those mice, except the ball is on the top. They are considered to be less harmful to your wrists than a standard mouse.

To add a device to your Mac, you simply need to determine the kind of connection it uses, and then attach its cable to its corresponding port on your Mac. Your Mac will recognize that a device has been attached to it. The first time the device is attached, you may be prompted to perform some action, or an application such as iPhoto may automatically open; the action, if any, depends on the type of device you connect.

Choose Between USB and FireWire

Devices you connect to your Mac generally use either USB or FireWire for communications, and a few offer both types of ports, allowing you to decide which connection best suits your needs. What's the difference between USB and FireWire, besides the obvious differences in the shapes of the ports? They are both fast connections, to be sure, but they each have their special reasons for existing. FireWire and USB use two different communication techniques, or topologies, meaning that FireWire devices have a distinctive way of talking to FireWire devices, and USB devices talk to other USB items in their own way.

USB

USB connects using a host-client topology, which means it must connect to a computer in order to communicate with other USB devices. USB comes in two varieties: USB 1.1 transfers data at the rate of 12 Mbps (megabits per second), and USB 2.0 is rated at up to 480 Mbps. USB 1.1 has passed into the great beyond with the advent of 2.0, but the two versions are compatible with one another, so if you have an older, USB 1.1 device, it will work with your new Mac, which only uses USB 2.0.

The two main types of USB connectors are Type A (see Figure 19-1) and Type B (see Figure 19-2). Cameras and some other devices often use a third type of USB connector called micro.

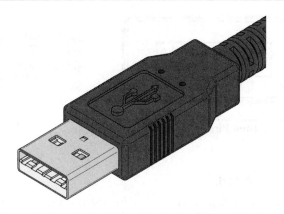

FIGURE 19-1   A-type USB connector

FireWire

The topology used by FireWire devices, called peer-to-peer, is optimum for transferring large amounts of data at a very fast rate. This makes FireWire the optimal way to transfer video in real time. Since FireWire is peer-to-peer, two FireWire devices can connect to each other without the aid of a computer.

Like USB, FireWire comes in two flavors: incredifast and superbad-incredifast, or FireWire 400 and FireWire 800, respectively. Data transfer speed is 400 Mbps for FireWire 400 and, you guessed it, 800 Mbps for FireWire. FireWire has two types of connectors, 6-pin and 4-pin, both shown in Figure 19-3.

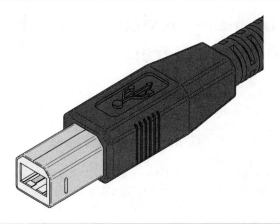

FIGURE 19-2   B-type USB connector

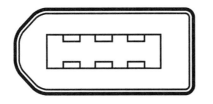 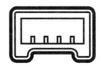

FIGURE 19-3   6-pin and 4-pin FireWire connections

"Which Is Best for My Needs?"

I think it's fairly obvious that FireWire beats USB in the speed wars. Don't be fooled by some of the data rates; even FireWire 400 is faster than USB 2.0 in practical use, despite the fact that USB 2.0's reported date rate is 80 Mbps faster than that of FireWire 400. The reason is because of the topologies used. When it comes to transferring large amounts of data, FireWire is the hands-down winner.

   "So why the heck is USB so prevalent?" Great question! Want a blunt answer? USB is cheaper to implement than FireWire, thereby lowering the cost of your Mac and your devices. Some may say that's too simplistic an answer, but it's the bottom line. There's much more history involved in the USB versus FireWire debate, but that's way beyond the scope of this book. If you're bored to tears one day, maybe you could research it on the Web. How do you think us computer-heads learn all this stuff?

Too Many Devices? Never Fear, Hubs Are Here!

Your Mac may only have one or two FireWire ports, but most people don't use more than one FireWire device at a time anyway. However, USB is a different story. Most devices that attach to your Mac use USB for connectivity, and five is the highest number of ports currently available for a consumer Mac. If you use a wired keyboard and mouse, the number of open ports instantly drops to three.

   What do you do if you have more USB devices than USB ports? What if you are one of those users who connect more than one or two FireWire devices at once? Hubs, my friends, use USB and FireWire hubs! Hubs are devices that provide multiple ports for USB, FireWire, or both, and they connect to your Mac through only one of its ports. Hubs operate on the same principle as electrical extension cords in that from one port you get many. Problem solved!

Summary

Adding external devices to your Mac is almost an inevitability. At some point you will want to print a document, connect an iPod, or use a scanner, and this chapter has given you the fundamentals so that connecting the device shouldn't be too daunting a task.

When you start adding devices to your computer, you have taken a big step in your quest for nerdiness. Remember, with each external device you connect, your geek quotient increases tenfold.

Part VI

Troubleshooting and Getting Further Help When You Need It

Chapter 20

What the Heck Just Happened?

How to …

- ■ Not have a cardiac arrest the first time your Mac acts up on you
- ■ Understand basic troubleshooting steps
- ■ Make sense of the problem so that you fix it easier and faster
- ■ Know the more common problems and their resolutions
- ■ Use alternative solutions for fixing problems
- ■ Start over by restoring or reinstalling Mac OS X, should it come to that

The title of this chapter is very appropriate because, having worked in a technical support capacity, I've heard this (and *far* worse!) more times than I remember. I was about to say I had heard that statement more times than I could count, but knowing how high I can count, I figured that saying I had heard it more than ten times wasn't very impressive … Onward then!

Don't Panic!

The first time a novice computer user realizes that their computer may be experiencing problems, it sends shockwaves of fear through them. Here you've got this great computer—no, you've got a Mac, so you've got the *best* computer—that you spent half a fortune to purchase, you've done *absolutely nothing wrong* (hopefully not, anyway), and this hunk of metal and plastic just went belly up on you. Yikes!

I'll be honest; when a computer has a glitch, it sends pangs of fear through even the most seasoned nerd, if only for a moment. I liken this to having a problem with your car. When that car won't start, even Henry Ford would experience a slight sinking feeling. You know this already, but let me state it for you anyway: things happen. At some point in your life you will stub your toe, or break a bone, or possibly even worse. There will be a time when your home's roof leaks, its tiles blow off, or a tornado decides the roof looks better on your neighbor's new motor home. And just as sure as the sun will rise tomorrow, somewhere down the line your computer will act a little funny, a program will begin crashing rather consistently, or horror of tech horrors, you hear a not-so-funny grinding sound that sounds suspiciously like your hard drive going down the tubes. A problem may occur a week after using your computer, or it may happen ten years down the road, but just like death and taxes, computer trouble is unavoidable.

The worst thing you can do is panic. Although it's hard not to sometimes, I've yet to see the problem that panic actually resolves. Please understand, I'm not preaching…I'm speaking from experience. My best advice is to tell you to ride out that first wave of panic, then settle down and solve the problem. You'll be happy to learn that most problems are easily resolved with very little muss or fuss.

Master Troubleshooting 101

Basic questions are the essence of troubleshooting. The first thing to ask yourself when a problem happens is, "Did anything change before this problem occurred?" Did you add anything to your Mac, such as more memory or an external device such as a scanner or printer? Did you recently install new software or a software update? Are all cables firmly connected? Was anyone else using the computer before you, and if so, did they make any changes? Did one of your kids pour chocolate milk into the slot-loading CD/DVD drive, or take a hammer to your keyboard? And the most important question of all, is the power on?

If you answered yes to the question you asked yourself, start there. If you connected a peripheral device, disconnect it. Installed new software? Uninstall it. Cables not connected? Connect them! Certainly some problems are not this easy to resolve, but the vast majority are.

How to ...   **Enable the Root User**

There is a hidden user account on your Mac called the root user. Root is the end-all be-all of user accounts, the head honcho, the big cheese, the godfather of your Mac. The root user is the real ruler of your Mac's kingdom. Admin or not, yours is but a puppet regime; not even your admin account has the privileges enjoyed by root. That said, it must be understood before you enable this account that if you choose to log in as that account, you can do absolutely *anything* to your Mac, for good or for bad. Consider yourself warned.

Now that I've properly frightened you, know that there are good reasons for enabling this account. What if your account has a serious problem (say, you can't even log in), and although there are numerous other accounts on the system you can log into, yours is the only admin account? If you enabled the root account, you're good to go. Log in as root to resolve the issue.

To enable the root account, open the Directory Utility (Hard Drive | Applications | Utilities | Directory Utility) and click the lock icon in the lower left to make changes.

Enter your admin account's username and password when prompted. Choose Edit | Enable Root User. Enter a password for the root user account, enter it again to verify it, and then click OK. If you ever need to change the root password, just choose Edit | Change Root Password. Quit Directory Utility when you're finished (press ⌘-Q).

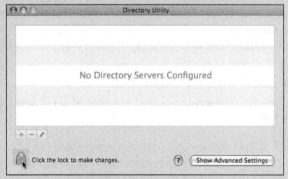

Rule Numero Uno: Restart

Quite simply, the single best thing to resolve most of your Mac-related headaches is a quick and easy restart. Restarting allows your Mac to collect its breath and shake any cobwebs it may have in its busy little noggin. If you find yourself spending more time waiting for your Mac to restart than you do productively using it, it's time to try something else.

Log Into a Different Account

A very basic approach to Mac troubleshooting is to log into another user account and see if the trouble occurs there as well. If it does, the issue is system software or a hardware problem. If it does not happen, then there is something wrong with your user account. In that one simple step you've eliminated quite a few possibilities.

If you only have one user account on your Mac, I strongly advise you to consider adding another account strictly for troubleshooting purposes. Should a problem arise, the first thing you should do is log into that account.

Back Up Your Stuff

Backing up your data is one of the most important things you can do. Backing up means to save copies of your files to another location, such as an external hard drive, CD, or DVD, or perhaps a server on your network. If there is a serious problem with your Mac, you'll be extremely glad you heeded this advice. Chapter 24 is all about backing up, and covers this procedure like a blanket, so feel free to jump on ahead before continuing with the rest of this chapter if you like.

Let's delve a bit more into the most common issues Mac users face.

Troubleshoot Typical Hardware Problems

Your Mac's hardware is some of the best in the industry, and that's no exaggeration. Everyone in the tech world knows the typical resale value of a Mac is much higher than that of other computers due to Apple's high standards of quality. But no matter how well Apple makes its products, they will break at some point. Usually, though, most hardware problems you may experience don't necessarily stem from a broken Mac. Simply restarting your Mac can often cure most of your Mac's ills.

This section looks at some typical hardware problems and possible fixes to those problems.

My Mac Won't Power Up!

You're pushing the power button, but your Mac refuses to come to life. Here are a few things to look for:

- *Check the obvious.* Are your power cables or adapters connected on both ends? If you're connected to a power strip, be sure to check that the power switch is in the on position.
- *Is the battery charged?* If you are using a MacBook, you have to be on the lookout for your battery's charge level. Connect your power adapter to see if the MacBook will

start with it. If your battery has a hard time holding a charge, you may need to have it replaced. Consult your MacBook's documentation for help.

■ *Is the power outlet you are connected to working?* Try connecting the power cord to a different outlet, or connecting a different device to the outlet your Mac is using.

■ *Have you connected another device to your Mac recently?* If so, disconnect the device and try turning the Mac on again. If it does come on, there may be a conflict of some sort with the device and your Mac. If it's a device that connects through USB, try connecting it to a different USB port to see if the port you were connecting to may have a problem.

■ *Did you recently add an internal device?* Adding memory or cards to your Mac's motherboard can cause startup problems if not installed properly. Remove the auxiliary part and try again. If the Mac boots normally, try once more to reinstall, being absolutely certain of the proper installation procedures.

■ *Is your display having problems?* Sometimes a display may not be working properly, making you think the Mac isn't on when it actually is. Did your Mac make its signature startup sound when you first turned it on? Do you hear any of its fans turning or are there any lights visible on the Mac? If the Mac is on but you simply can't see anything on your display, make sure the display is connected properly and that the brightness is turned all the way up.

■ *Reset the SMC.* The System Management Controller (SMC) is a chip in your Mac that controls all its power functions. Resetting this chip may resolve any power problems, including the inability to start. It may sound like you need to don a NASA spacesuit to perform this task, or better yet call Scotty from *Star Trek* to see if he can lend a hand, but there's no need for such with this simple routine. On the following page are two separate routines for resetting the SMC, depending on the model of Mac you have.

The Flip Side—Your Mac Won't Shut Down

You've learned what to try when your Mac won't start up, but what about those rare times when it won't shut down? There are two ways to exert your mastery of your Mac in this regard:

■ **Force a restart** Press CTRL-⌘ at the same time as the power button.

■ **Force a shutdown** Press and hold the power button down for ten seconds.

- **iMac or Mac mini** Power the computer completely down and disconnect all cables from it, including the power cord, mouse, and keyboard. Wait a minimum of 15 seconds, plug the power cord back in, but do not push the power button. Connect the mouse and keyboard and then push the power button on the computer.
- **MacBook** Turn off the MacBook, disconnect any cables, including the power adapter, and remove the battery. Hold down the power button for a minimum of five seconds, and then release it. Reconnect the battery and power adapter, and then press the power button normally.

External Devices Don't Work Properly

One minute you are printing that letter to Grandma, and the next minute your Mac acts like it's never seen the printer before. What gives? Suffice to say, "stuff happens." Let's try to figure out why.

- *Again, check the obvious.* Is the device turned on? Check all power cables, as well as the on switch for your power strip (if using one).
- *Check the cables used to connect the device to your Mac.* Make sure that the USB, Ethernet, or FireWire cable you are using to connect the device to your computer is firmly seated in the ports at both ends (the device and the Mac), and is unhindered (crimped, broken, cut, stepped on, and so forth). Be certain that the cable is not too long; no more than 16 feet is recommended for USB and shorter than 15 feet is recommended for FireWire. Try a different cable if you have one, or try connecting your cable to a different port.
- *Is there anything between the device and your Mac, such as a hub?* If you are connecting the problematic device to your Mac via a USB or FireWire hub (used to extend the number of USB or FireWire ports available for your Mac), try removing the device from the hub and connecting it directly to your Mac. If the device works properly without the hub, the likely culprit is the hub itself or a port on the hub.
- *Install the latest drivers for your device.* Check the website of the manufacturer of your device to see if it has released new drivers for your device. If it has not, try reinstalling the drivers that came with it.
- *Contact the manufacturer of the device.* When all else has failed, contact the manufacturer of the device in question. Oddly enough, the concept of calling the company that makes the problematic product is the last thing that comes to mind for some people. Of course, the opposite is also true; some people will contact the maker of the product over and over, never thinking that it may just be the Mac that has the real issue.
- *Check for device incompatibility.* Sometimes devices may conflict with one another, causing one or more of them to not work properly. To see if this is the issue, remove all devices except your mouse and keyboard, unless you have a MacBook, in which case remove any external mouse or keyboard you've attached. Restart the Mac and make certain the mouse and keyboard are working properly. Reattach each external device one at a time,

being sure that each connected device works properly before you add the next one. When or if you discover a problem after connecting a device, there is a conflict between that device and one of the others. Contact the manufacturer of the problem device for help.

System Profiler

Apple has included one handy-dandy utility in Mac OS X called the System Profiler. The System Profiler will tell you every delectable detail of your Mac's inner and outer workings. To open the System Profiler, choose Apple | About This Mac, and then click the More Info button. System Profiler displays your Mac's innermost secrets in this window:

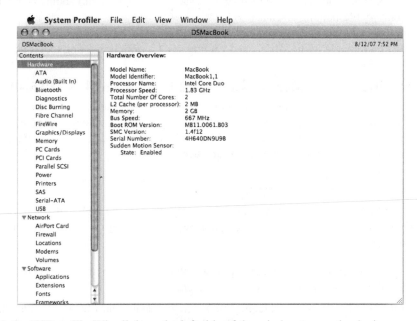

Click the USB or FireWire link on the left side of the window to see the devices your Mac sees on each port. If your problem device is listed there but you aren't able to use it, software is most likely the problem. If the device doesn't show up in the list, you most likely have a hardware problem of some sort.

Troubleshoot Typical Software Problems

Software can cause just as many problems with your Mac as hardware can, and such problems can be just as crippling. But thankfully these problems have another thing in common with hardware issues: they are usually easily resolved. This section looks at some of the most common issues you may run into, and shows you a few tricks to get your Mac up and running again.

The Mother of All Computer Troubleshooting Techniques

You've made it this far into the book, so I feel I must let you in on one of those secrets we geeks, as well as our nerd counterparts, like to keep tucked away until we really want to impress someone with our tech prowess. The technique I'm about to impart to you is one of the best-kept secrets in the world of high technology, so I share this information at no small risk to all that I hold near and dear. Okay, I guess I can trust you by now, so here goes...

Restart. Yep, just restart your Mac.

Restart and sit back in amazement as most of your Mac's ills and foibles just magically disappear into the air like so much smoke in a hurricane. Try this amazing feat at the first sign of trouble and chances are good that you'll resolve the issue. The simple restart should be the first shot fired in your troubleshooting arsenal.

Yes, this simple solution was covered earlier in this chapter in the "Troubleshooting 101" section, but this is a reminder of how basic and yet important a troubleshooting tool it is.

Check Whether Your Mac Is Running the Latest OS Version

Make sure your Mac is running the newest version of its operating system. Sometimes the very problem you are experiencing may have been resolved already in an update from Apple. Run Software Update by choosing Apple | Software Update to see if any updates are available; if so, download and install them to see if that corrects any troubles for you.

Troubleshoot Startup Issues

If your Mac powers up but Mac OS X won't start properly, chances are high that you have a software problem of some sort, even if only temporarily. Try these steps when experiencing a problematic startup:

- **Shut Down, then Restart**   Hold the power key down until the Mac shuts completely down, wait a few seconds, then power it back up.

- **Zap the PRAM**   Sounds frightening, but it's no big deal. Your Mac stores some of its settings using a chip, called parameter RAM (PRAM), that is powered by a small battery on your controller, or motherboard (the brains of your Mac). Sometimes resetting, aka *zapping*, the PRAM can correct startup problems. To zap the PRAM, restart the Mac and immediately press and hold the ⌘-OPTION-P-R keys; do not stop pressing these keys until you hear the Mac's startup sound at least twice. After the second chime, you can let go of the keys, having successfully zapped the PRAM.

- **Boot into Safe Mode**   Safe Mode is a special way to start Mac OS X running only the bare minimum of required software and kernel components. Boot into Safe Mode by holding down the SHIFT key immediately after you hear the startup chime—*not* before you hear it. When you see the gray Apple, you can let go of the SHIFT key. Your Mac automatically checks the directory on its hard drive and effects repairs, if necessary.

Once your Mac boots all the way up, restart it without holding any keys down to boot normally.

If these three options yield no positive results, it's time to bring out the big guns, described next.

Boot from the Mac OS X Installation Disc

The easiest way to see if the problem you are experiencing lies with your Mac OS X system software is to boot your Mac using the Mac OS X installation disc. Insert the disc into your Mac and restart. As soon as you hear the Mac's startup sound, begin holding the C key and do not let go until you see the boot screen.

If the Mac doesn't boot even when using the installation disc, hardware may be at fault. If hardware appears to be at fault, you should contact Apple Support or take the Mac to your local Apple Store for evaluation of the problem. If there is no Apple Store in your area, try searching Apple's support site or your local yellow pages for an Apple Service Provider in your area.

If the Mac boots up properly from the disc, the issue is most certainly one with the system software or the file system on your hard drive. Next step: run Disk Utility!

Run Disk Utility from the Software Installation Disc

Errors in the file system may be the culprit, so the next thing to try is to have Disk Utility attempt a repair. When the disc has fully booted, start Disk Utility from the Installer menu. Click the name of your Mac OS X volume in the disc pane, click the First Aid tab, and then click the Repair Disk button. Disk Utility first verifies your drive to see if there are any problems with the file system, and then repairs any damage that it may find.

After running Disk Utility, restart the Mac normally to see if the issue is resolved.

Overcome Kernel Panic

The kernel is not just a place to get good chicken; it's also the name of the core part of your Mac OS X operating system. If the kernel's not happy, nobody's happy. Should you be the unlucky recipient of a message that says, "You need to restart your computer," your Mac is experiencing a kernel panic. Most likely your Mac has had some kind of corruption to its operating system files; chances of a kernel panic being caused by hardware are pretty slim.

If you are certain that you moved or renamed your system folders before experiencing the panic, you have to reinstall Mac OS X. Take this as a huge, glaring hint: don't move or rename your Mac OS X system folder!

If you have no idea what may have happened to the system, try these things next:

- ■ **Restart** The venerable restart is of course your first step to take. This resolves the vast majority of kernel panics.
- ■ **Force Mac OS X to boot** Restart the Mac and then immediately begin holding down the X key. This should force your Mac to boot into Mac OS X. If the Mac boots correctly,

make sure your Mac OS X volume is set as the startup disk in System Preferences |
Startup Disk.

- **Boot with the OPTION key**   If starting up with the X key doesn't work, try starting up
  holding down the OPTION key. You should see icons appear in the middle of the screen of
  your Mac OS X startup disk. Click the disk icon and then click the forward arrow.

- **Zap the PRAM**   Zap the PRAM to see whether resetting it clears up the problem. As
  covered earlier in the chapter, to zap the PRAM, restart the Mac and immediately press
  and hold the ⌘-OPTION-P-R keys. Keep holding these keys until you hear the Mac's startup
  sound at least twice. After the second chime, you can let go of the keys to reboot normally.

If none of the preceding measures works to resolve the kernel panic, installation of the operating
system should be your next, and last, resort before looking into hardware possibilities.

Repair Disk Permissions

Can't delete a file or folder from the trash? Are applications locking up unexpectedly or not
launching correctly, or at all? Does your Mac seem to be slowing—down—or—getting—
really—sluggish? Your disk permissions may be having a bad day.

Every file and folder on your Mac has permissions associated with it. These permissions
determine who can read, write, and execute the file or folder. If these permissions become
corrupted for whatever reason, they need to be repaired.

To repair these permissions, use the Disk Utility program, which is located in *Hard Drive/*
Applications/Utilities. Open Disk Utility, click the icon of your hard drive in the disc pane, click
the First Aid tab, and then click the Repair Disk Permissions button. If Disk Utility finds any
corrupted permissions, it repairs them and resolves your problem.

NOTE   *In some instances, such as an unusable system, it may be necessary to boot your Mac
from your Mac OS X installation disc to run Disk Utility.*

My Application Just Crashed!

Applications allow your Mac to do what it does best, and that is to make your life easier and more productive. However, there's nothing easy or productive about an application that consistently closes (crashes) while in the middle of your work.

Try these techniques to heal an ailing application:

- **Restart**   Yet again, the mother of all troubleshooting tools rears its head!

- **Repair disk permissions**   Follow the instructions detailed in the preceding section for repairing disk permissions.

- **Install the latest updates**   Like Mac OS X, applications need updates, too. Check the website for the manufacturer of your application for any updates that may be available and install them.

- **Throw away preference files**   Each application on your Mac creates a preference file, which the application uses to keep track of its settings and any changes to them, such as default page sizes, default fonts, and so forth. Sometimes those preferences may become corrupted and need to be rebuilt. To rebuild them, close the offending application, throw its preference file in the Trash, and then restart the application. Consult your application's documentation to find where it stores preference files. If the application was made by Apple the preferences should be located in the Hard Drive/Users/Your Home Folder/ Library/Preferences directory.

- **Reinstall the application**   When all else fails you have to bite the bullet and reinstall the application. Consult the documentation of your application for any special instructions on uninstalling it.

Thaw Freezes

You're plodding along with your Mac, whistling while you work, of course, when all of a sudden it just stops responding. Time seems to be standing still, for your Mac at least. You've just experienced a "freeze," meaning that Mac OS X or the software you are using has come to a screeching halt. More often than not the software you were currently using is the problem, not the entire system.

When experiencing a freeze, test your mouse and keyboard. If the mouse pointer won't move or the keyboard won't work, check their connections to the Mac. If the connections are okay, move on to the following steps.

Stop a Stuck Process

You may request an action, or *process*, from your application that for whatever reason it can't follow through on, causing the application to stop in its tracks. Try stopping this process by holding down ⌘-PERIOD (⌘-.).

Force Quit

Forcing an application to quit when it is misbehaving can cure a freeze. To force quit, simultaneously press ⌘-OPTION-ESC, which opens the Force Quit Applications window.

Select the name of the problem application from the list and click the Force Quit button.

Try forcing the Finder to quit. The Finder is an application just like any other, and sometimes it may need a swift kick in the seat of the pants to get it running smoothly again.

Shut Down or Restart

On occasion, you simply have no alternative but to start from scratch. Hold down the Power button for ten seconds and your Mac should shut down. If not, you have to get downright nasty with it by forcing it to shut down or restart:

■ To force a shutdown, press ⌘-OPTION-SHIFT-POWER.

■ To force a restart, press ⌘-CTRL-POWER.

Confront a Blue Screen

I'm sure some of you former Windows users saw the title of this section and screamed in terror. Don't worry; this is not the Mac equivalent to the dreaded Windows "blue screen of *death!*" (Laugh maniacally at the end of this sentence for dramatic effect.)

If you see a blank blue screen at startup, you probably have a login item that isn't agreeable with the rest of the system. Boot into Safe Mode by holding down the SHIFT key as soon as you hear the startup sound, and continue holding until the gray Apple logo appears. After the Mac boots up, choose System Preferences | Accounts, and then click the Login Items tab of your account.

Write down your list of login items in case you want to add them back to the list later, because you now need to remove all of them by clicking the - button below the list. After they have all been removed, restart your Mac normally.

If you no longer see a blue screen, add login items back to the list one at a time to determine which one caused the problem. Once you've discovered which item is the culprit, you need to restart into Safe Mode to remove it from the list for good.

Evaluate Third-Party Solutions

This may come as a surprise to some of you, but sometimes (although not often) Apple may not have the best solution for your problem. There, I said it! Actually, that wasn't a hard thing to admit at all, because I've used many of the major third-party disk utilities and antivirus software programs. Some of these offerings by other companies (who aren't Apple but love the Mac as much as you and I) are fantastic first choices when it comes to troubleshooting Mac system problems. Mind you, these tools aren't free (developers have to eat, too, you know), but they're worth every penny when in a pinch, trust me (been there, done that).

Do your own research regarding third-party applications; some would argue that they are unnecessary on Mac OS X, but others swear by them. Make your own informed decisions before plunking down your hard-earned cash.

Consider Third-Party Disk Utility Software

Here are three of what I consider to be the best of the best when it comes to disk utilities:

- **Alsoft DiskWarrior**   Alsoft has made disk utility software for the Mac for more than 20 years, according to its website; I know they've been around as long as I've used Macs, which is going on 13 years now. DiskWarrior is a popular optimization and disk recovery tool, and it actually saved my bacon during the course of writing this book! Get more info at www.alsoft.com/DiskWarrior/.

- **Prosoft Drive Genius**   This is the "new kid on the block" when it comes to Mac disk maintenance and repair utilities, and it's quickly making a name for itself. I used Drive Genius extensively for various tasks while writing *How to Do Everything Mac*, and I must say it's an impressive utility. Go to www.prosofteng.com/products/drive_genius.php to learn more about this product.

- **Prosoft Data Rescue**   Data Rescue can retrieve information from a hard drive, even one that has crashed. Prosoft markets Data Rescue as "a hard drive recovery service in a box" because many data recovery companies actually use Date Rescue themselves. This is a utility that you may not use often (hopefully), but if you ever do need it, you'll be glad you've got it. Visit www.prosofteng.com/products/data_rescue.php for more information.

Consider Third-Party Antivirus Software

Believe it or not, there are antivirus applications for the Mac, although few and far between. Why so few? Well, there just isn't much of a threat from viruses when you're using a Mac. The reasons vary for this anomaly, but it's still the reality. Some may argue that the Mac is based on UNIX, and is therefore more difficult to write viruses for. Others would cry "Rubbish!" at that notion, arguing that since there are fewer Macs than Windows-based PCs in the world, malicious hackers would rather do a lot of damage than a little, so they concentrate all their efforts on bringing down Microsoft. More sensible folk tend to agree that it's probably due to a combination of both reasons.

Does this render antivirus software unnecessary? If you're someone who believes that "safer is better than sorry" you might want to pick up a copy of one of the following:

- **Norton Antivirus**   Symantec has been making antivirus software for the Mac for a long time. It is generally one of the most popular antivirus companies for both Macs and PCs. Visit www.symantec.com to learn more.

- **McAfee VirusScan for Mac**   McAfee is another major player in the Mac antivirus market. Check out VirusScan for Mac at www.mcafee.com.

- **Intego VirusBarrier X4**   Intego is a stalwart in the Mac antivirus arena, too. VirusBarrier is an excellent competitor to offerings from larger companies, and in the interest of full disclosure, I must admit that I use it myself. Give Intego a look at www.intego.com/virusbarrier.

When All Else Fails, Reinstall or Restore

To quote a famous song from long ago, "you got to know when to hold 'em, know when to fold 'em." With apologies to Kenny Rogers, that holds true for computer troubleshooting as much as it does for poker. Sometimes, when all else has failed, and your poor hair lies in clumps at your feet, some strands of which may still be clinging to the sweat of your palms after you so violently dislodged them from your scalp in frustration, it's simply time to start over entirely.

Or not! Apple has given you one more reprieve before you are limited to blowing the whole hard drive completely away. You can attempt to reinstall Mac OS X without erasing the disk.

CAUTION *Before doing anything else,* back up *if at all possible. Save as much of your information as you can before attempting a reinstall, no matter which one of the following two procedures you choose. Jump ahead to Chapter 24 to find out all about backing up your Mac.*

To reinstall Mac OS X and all the software that was bundled with your Mac, insert your Mac OS X installation disc and double-click the Install Mac OS X and Bundled Software icon. Follow the instructions to reinstall the operating system and bundled software, and everything else on the drive will be retained in its current state.

If that process doesn't resolve your woes, you've got to go for broke with a complete format of the drive and reinstallation of software. Insert the Mac OS X installation disc and double-click the "Install Mac OS X and Bundled Software" icon. Follow the instructions as before until you get to the "Select a destination" window, where you click Options, and then click the "Erase and Install" radio button. Once Mac OS X is reinstalled, you can begin reinstalling any third-party applications and bring over any other files and folders you may have backed up.

Things may be so bad for your Mac that you can't even double-click the "Install Mac OS X and Bundled Software" link from the disc. If that's the case, boot the Mac from the disc and follow the installation instructions from there.

Summary

This chapter is full of information to help keep your Mac chugging along happily. I hope you never have to use any information in this chapter, but it's here for you just in case.

Chapter 21

Helpful Resources for Your Mac

How to ...

- Get help from Mac OS X
- Navigate Apple's superb support website
- Know who and how to call when you need extra support
- Find the best Mac sites on the Web

This book, like almost all others of its kind, is designed to help you get the most out of your Mac. However, there are only so many pages that can be dedicated to troubleshooting problems. Where do you go if the tips given in *How to Do Everything: Mac* don't resolve the issue, or the issue is something *really* funky that isn't discussed at all? The purpose of this chapter is to point you in the right direction for help when you encounter such issues, beginning with the help system provided by Mac OS X itself.

Consult Mac OS X's Help System

Mac OS X has a wonderful help system that's actually helpful! There's a surprisingly large amount of help offered within Mac OS X, for both the operating system and the applications your Mac shipped with, so you may be able to solve most of your riddles without even leaving the friendly confines of the world's best operating system.

Typically the last heading in an application's menu bar is Help. Click the Help menu and choose Help for the application you are using. For instance, if you're in the Finder, the Help menu displays Mac Help, and if you're in Safari, you see Safari Help (along with a few other selections).

Figure 21-1 shows the Safari Help window. Other Help windows are similar in layout, with links to frequently asked questions and main topics, as well as an index of the subjects broached in the help system.

Browse the help topics listed to learn more about the particular application, or type a subject into the search field to find specific information. You can also click the Index button to see the index of help topics available listed by the first letter of the topic.

What if you need help with another application or operating system question? Click the Home menu button and choose the help system you need. Simple as that!

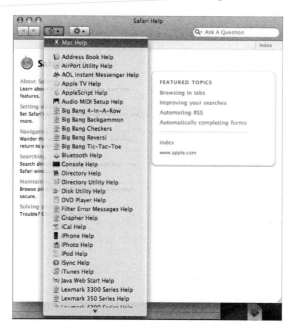

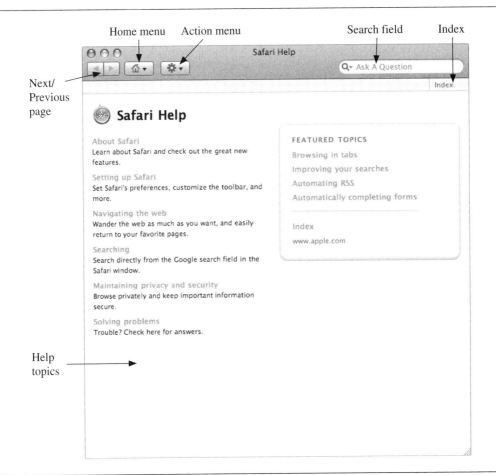

Home menu   Action menu   Search field   Index

Next/
Previous
page

Help
topics

FIGURE 21-1   Safari's Help window, which has the typical look of most Help windows.
Layout of graphics and links may differ between applications' help systems, but
functionality and navigation is the same.

Exploit Apple's Support Pages

You simply won't find better online technical support than you get from Apple. Open Safari and
go to Apple's support website (www.apple.com/support) and you will be greeted with so many
options your head may swim!

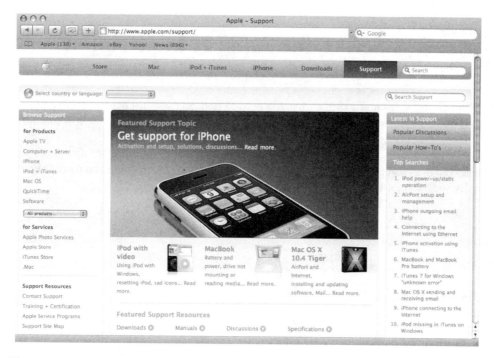

If you aren't a native English-speaker, you can select from more languages than I even knew existed (what's Sverige?) by clicking the "Select country or language" pop-up menu in the upper-left corner of the page.

The right side of the main support page links to the newest support documents available, lists the most popular How-To's, searches, and discussions, and links to more information about AppleCare (Apple's extended support program). You can also register your product, view the status of a repair, and learn more about Apple's exchange and extension programs for recalls and known issues.

The left side lets you browse the support pages of a particular product or service, and links to support resources such as alternative contacts for support, training and certification information, and service programs. Links to popular solutions are also available on the left side of the page.

Don't know if your product is under warranty? Enter the serial number of the product in the "About Your Support Coverage" section to find out its status. If you don't know where to find your serial number, there's a handy link just to the right of that section that you can click to find out its location on your product.

The center column of the main support page is where featured topics are shown. There is a section called Featured Support Resources that lets you choose from downloads (such as upgrades to software), manuals, product specifications, and access to the discussions area of the site.

How to ... Search for Support Information

Sometimes you may know exactly what you need to find, and you just need to be able to search for it. The main support page has a Search Support field in the upper-right corner for you to enter your question or topic.

Type **printing** in the Search Support field and press the RETURN key to see the results. When I did this search I came up with 280 results! You will probably find even more than that due to additions to the support site since this was written.

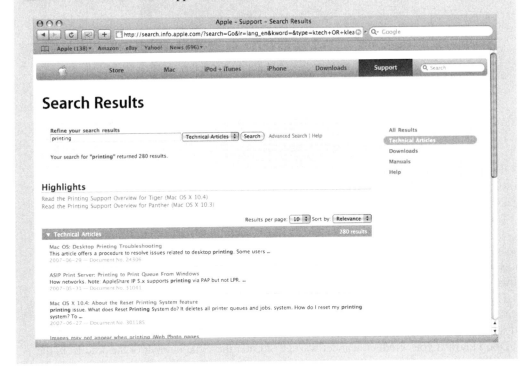

You can narrow searches by being as specific as possible. For instance, if you are having problems printing from iPhoto, type **print iPhoto** and the number of results should decrease quite dramatically (I whittled mine down to only 46), making your search far more effective.

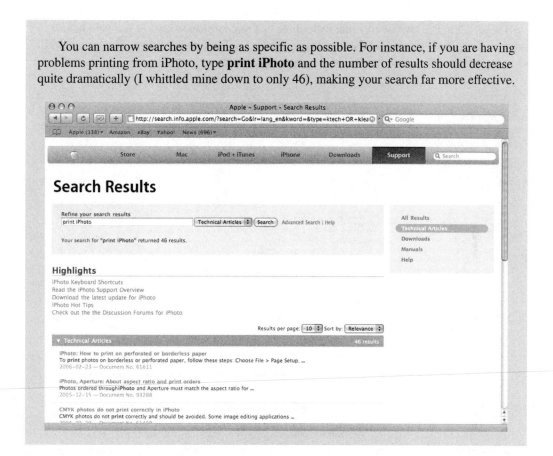

My favorite part of Apple's support site is the Discussions section. Other real users of Macs are there, discussing problems, trading tips and advice, and simply trying to help one another get more from their Mac and its software. It's a beautiful thing!

To access Discussions, click its link under Featured Support Resources, or just type **http:// discussions.apple.com/index.jspa** into Safari's address field and press RETURN. You are greeted with many different topics, or forums, in which you can peruse or participate.

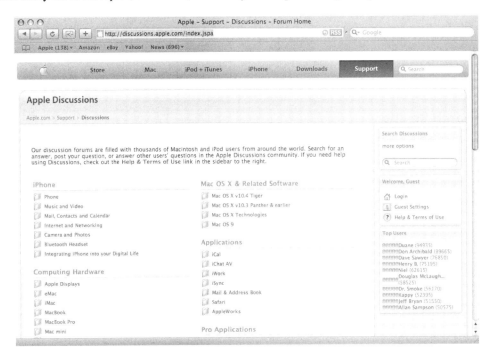

To explore Discussions, click the Safari forum under the Applications heading. You will see links to Safari support pages and tutorials, and a little further down the discussions pick up, as shown in the following image.

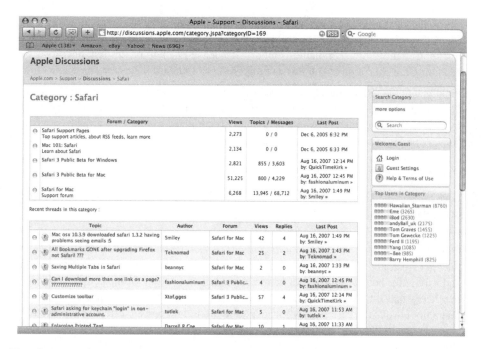

Type in a question or topic in the search field to see if other users are experiencing the issue. More often than not you will find that others have already resolved the problem you're now seeing, or that someone in the forum knows how to perform a task you've been curious about.

Call for Help

Sometimes only a friendly voice can help allay your fears and worries, or can ask all the right questions to get to the bottom of an issue, and that's why companies offer telephone support. No matter how brilliant and user friendly computers and the Internet become, no matter how wonderful and easy technology and automation are or will be, human contact and intellect is the ultimate form of communication, never to be supplanted by any manmade construct. That's also the reason that books made of good ol' paper (like this one) will never completely go away; people want that feel of contact, that intimacy, you have with the author of the book, if only until the last page is turned. But I digress…

Having stated the latter, it should be known that the order of support should be as follows:

1. Read the manual! Users guides, built-in help like that in Mac OS X, and documentation that came with your software or hardware should always be the first stop in your troubleshooting mission.

2. Check the support website for the product in question. As previously mentioned in this chapter, Apple's support site is a stellar example of just how good these kinds of resources can be. Certainly some companies support sites leave much to be desired, but those are becoming the exception as the Internet matures as a standard means of communications.

3. Finally, call the telephone support lines for the product. You must understand, however, that the level of satisfaction you receive through this means of support will vary greatly from company to company. Apple is annually recognized as the best of the best when it comes to telephone support in their particular industry.

A few hints and tips when it comes to calling technical support:

■ *Give the technician a reasonable chance to resolve the problem.* Before you call, write down the symptoms of the problem and try to formulate a concise description of it before calling.

■ *Don't be a jerk to the technician and you will receive much better help.* Sometimes we may get frustrated about a problem, but taking it out on the person who you are calling and asking for help from may not be the best course of action. Some people subscribe to the theory that if they scream loudly enough they will get help more quickly. Believe me, that's not always the case by any means; quite often the opposite effect is achieved.

A Potential Support Aggravation

Unfortunately, some companies have decided that saving labor costs outsourcing or moving their support to a foreign country is more important than keeping their customers satisfied by providing higher-quality domestic support at a higher cost. This decision prioritizes short-term profits over the potentially much higher future profits resulting from having satisfied repeat customers who also recommend the company's products to other potential customers.

Understand that the problem does not lie with opening support offices in foreign countries; the problem is with opening these offices in countries that do not natively speak the language of the customers who will be calling them. How can a native English-speaker hope to properly convey the problem to someone who doesn't speak English well at all? Their chances of accurately solving the problem with little to no stress are virtually nil. While the problem may eventually get resolved, by that time both the customer and the technician have pulled half of their respective hair out. Likewise, how can a customer from Japan who speaks very little English explain to a technician born and raised in Iowa, with no training whatsoever in the Japanese language, the extent of his problem, much less have a real hope for a resolution before hanging up the phone?

If you run into this kind of situation, my advice is to complain, complain, complain, and then complain some more! You paid for the product, and you should get proper support for it, too! This stance may not endear me to these companies that shall remain nameless here, but someone's got to say something, whether they will listen or not.

- *Be cooperative.* Don't jump all over the place performing tasks totally different from one the technician is asking you to do.

- *Remember, the technician is not hiding the answer from you.* If they have the answer they will give it to you. Their job performance is often judged by how quickly they can resolve problems, so rest assured they aren't trying to give you a runaround because they have to ask a few questions of you.

- *Call the right people!* Try to narrow down your problem as best you can, and if it looks like the issue may indeed lie with a third-party application you installed yesterday, contact the maker of that application first before contacting Apple. Likewise, if you're having a problem printing from one Mac on your network but the other 60 Macs can print fine to the same printer, the issue most likely rests with the single Mac, meaning you should probably first call Apple and not the printer manufacturer.

Keep these tips in mind and you will find that calling tech support isn't so bad after all. As a matter of fact, it can be downright pleasant if both parties attempt to make it that way. And if you do have a good service experience, make someone else's day a bit brighter by being nice and saying so!

Find Helpful Mac Sites on the Web

The number of sites on the Web dedicated to all things Mac is astounding! Perform a search on Google for Mac sites and you will find a seemingly endless parade of hits, from old standbys to the newest blogs. I've saved you the trouble of searching for some of the best sites by including them here for your perusal, even separating them by their expertise.

Troubleshooting and Repair Sites

The Internet is chock full of sites offering advice on resolving problems with your Mac and sites selling parts for your Mac, but the following are some of the most reliable:

- **MacFixIt (www.macfixit.com)**   The links at the top of the MacFixIt home page, shown in the next illustration, tell the story of this site. It has a ton to offer, such as tutorials, reports of common problems, discussion forums, archives of old articles, and much more.

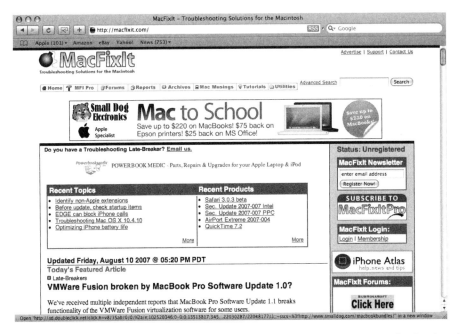

- **Accelerate Your Mac (www.xlr8yourmac.com)** This site offers great in-depth articles on how to get your Mac's motor running.

- **AllMac (www.allmac.com)** This site is great for finding parts for your Mac.

- **iFixit (www.ifixit.com)** These folks specialize in parts and repair for both Macs and iPods.

Information and News Sites

There is an embarrassment of wealth when it comes to Mac news and information sites on the Web. There are so many, in fact, that I am only going to list a few of the truly iconic Mac news and info sites:

- **Macworld (www.macworld.com)** The official site of *Macworld* magazine and a great place for the latest news and reviews of Apple products.

■ **MacInTouch (www.macintouch.com)**   Get the scoop on the latest products from Apple as well as releases for Mac-compatible software and hardware.

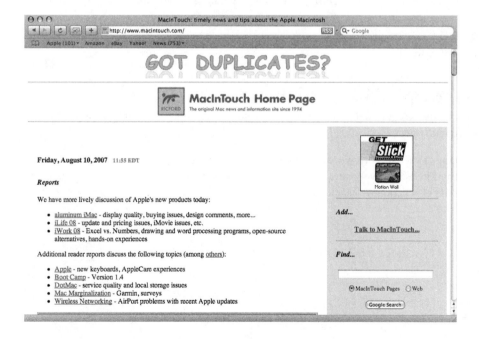

You're Not Really a Mac Fan Until…

…you've started checking out the Apple rumor sites. There is a little game of cat and mouse that Apple and its most ardent fans like to play with one another when it comes to guessing what great new products Steve Jobs is going to grace us with next. You will have officially arrived as a bona-fide Mac geek only after you've visited the following sites to find out all the latest rumors and gossip regarding all things Apple:

- Think Secret (www.thinksecret.com)
- AppleInsider (www.appleinsider.com)
- MacRumors (www.macrumors.com)

- **The Mac Observer (www.macobserver.com)**   I've long enjoyed this site for its articles as well as its live coverage of key Mac events like Steve Jobs' Macworld Expo and WWDC (Worldwide Developers Conference) keynote speeches.
- **MacNN (www.macnn.com)**   Mac news you can use.
- **TidBITS (www.tidbits.com)**   This news site has been around since 1990! An oldie but very goodie.
- **MacNewsWorld (www.macnewsworld.com)**   Mac news aimed at the IT/enterprise professional.

Sites for Tips, Tricks, and Hints

The sites in this category help you learn to use your Mac. Some of the tips are very basic while others are *really* deep.

- **Mac OS X Hints (www.macosxhints.com)**   This is one of my favorite sites of its type. This site is relatively new but became extremely popular not long after its inception due to its excellent articles and advice.

■ **Macinstruct (www.macinstruct.com)**   Macinstruct is run entirely by volunteers who love to help others learn to use the Mac.

■ **My First Mac (www.myfirstmac.com)**   I've only recently discovered this great site. It has lots of useful information for new Mac users, especially those who have come over from "the dark side," aka Microsoft Windows.

Software Sites

If you've ever heard a Windows nerd trying to defend his "operating system" against Mac OS X, he may have said something like "There's no software available for the Mac!" Well, as a user of both Mac- and Windows-based computers dating back to the late 1980s, I can personally confirm for you that he is a buffoon. There is more software available for the Mac than you could ever possibly need, and in every category as well. Don't believe me? Check out these sites, and prepare to grovel for my forgiveness:

■ **MacUpdate (www.macupdate.com)**   Simply the best Mac-only software site on the planet.

■ **VersionTracker (www.versiontracker.com)**   Hundreds of titles just waiting for you to give them a go.

■ **Open Source Mac (www.opensourcemac.org)**   Shows you the latest and greatest (and free!) open source software for your Mac.

Fun Stuff!

What's the point of a computer if you can't have any fun with it? There are hundreds of games available for the Mac, and these two sites will set your gaming senses to tingling:

■ **Apple's Games site (www.apple.com/games)** Apple has provided a great site for Mac users who want to "get their game on." This site tells you everything you need to know about playing games on your Mac, and yes, has all the best and popular titles available for the Mac (notice the Starcraft II trailer in this screenshot?).

■ **Macgamefiles.com(www.macgamefiles.com)** Download a slew of game demos, upgrades, and even free titles from here.

Summary

There is absolutely no shame in needing help. Every so-called expert had to start somewhere, and most of the real experts are always more than willing to lend a helping hand to someone eager to learn. This overview of the help resources available to you will hopefully point you in the right direction the next time you need help, want to learn more about your Mac, or simply want to find a cool game with which to while away a few hours.

Know this: the only stupid question is the one you don't ask!

Part VII

Change the Silicon Every Three Thousand Miles: Maintaining Your Mac

Chapter 22
Keeping the Engine Tuned

How to ...

- Keep your system and applications updated
- Give your Mac a tune-up
- Avoid potential problems
- Keep your Mac nice and clean

There seems to be an intrinsic bond between computers and automobiles, at least when it comes to analogies, and I'm about to spring one on you.

Your beautiful, shiny new car runs like a top, purrs like a kitten, rides smoother than silk, and is responsive to your every touch. At least for the first few thousand miles, that is. Eventually the tires wear or become misaligned, you feel more play in the brakes and they squeal loudly when the pedal is pressed, the ride is a little bumpier than it was a couple of months ago, and the engine is starting to seem a little sluggish. What would you do if this were your car? If you are a responsible owner, you will have the tires changed and balanced and have the alignment checked, have the brake pads replaced, have the shocks inspected, and check the oil, filters, and plugs. All of these tasks are normal maintenance items that your ride needs and deserves to prevent breakdowns at the least opportune times. You spent a lot of money on your car, so you're going to take good care to see that it performs to the best of its ability.

Think of your Mac in the same vain. You spent several pockets-full of change on this purchase, too, and if you're like most computer users, some of your most important data and information resides on it. Keeping your Mac maintained and updated is as important to its functionality as is the maintenance you provide your other high-dollar devices, including your automobile.

Check for Updates with Software Update

Apple is very good about releasing timely updates to Mac OS X and its other software offerings (Safari, iTunes, iPhoto, and so forth). These updates resolve problems that weren't discovered at the time the operating system or application was first released. If you are new to computing, don't worry; these kinds of updates are common from all software makers. Problems, better known as "bugs" by geekery worldwide, are an inevitable part of computers and their software. Thankfully Apple is a very proactive and reactive company and works to rectify these problems as soon as it can. Truthfully speaking, most updates you see are preventative measures for most users, because usually only a relatively small handful of people have experienced the issues fixed by the update.

Run Software Update Manually

Mac OS X uses a utility program, fittingly called Software Update, to help you keep your software versions up to par. Open Software Update by choosing Apple | Software Update, and it automatically begins querying Apple's servers for information about new software.

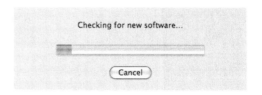

Apple's servers respond to Software Update with a list of updated software, which Software Update compares to the versions you already have installed. If there are newer versions available, you see a list of the new software and should click the Install button in the bottom-right corner to continue the update process.

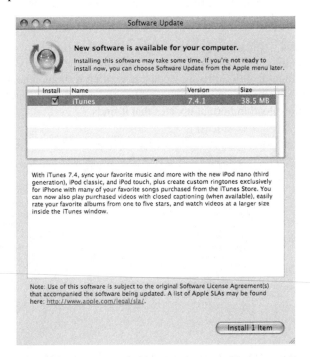

Once the new updates are applied, Software Update checks the servers again to see if there are updates to your updates! This happens because one of the updates you've downloaded may cause your Mac to need another update.

If Software Update didn't find any new software, you see this message:

Click Quit to close the Software Update application.

Sometimes you are prompted to restart your Mac after you've upgraded certain kinds of software. Software Update notifies you if a restart is necessary to install some upgrades; you can cancel the updates if you aren't ready to restart your Mac. After you reboot, the changes take effect and your Mac thanks you for an update well done.

Configure Software Update Preferences

Like other applications in Mac OS X, Software Update has preferences that help you customize it to work the way you think it should. Open these preferences by choosing either Software Update | Preferences or Apple | System Preferences | Software Update. The Software Update preferences pane has two tabs:

■ **Scheduled Check** Software Update is set by Apple to periodically check for new software via the Internet. You can force it to check for updates at any time by clicking the Check Now button. Tell Software Update how often it should check for updates (I recommend Daily if you have a broadband Internet connection) and whether to automatically download important updates that it finds.

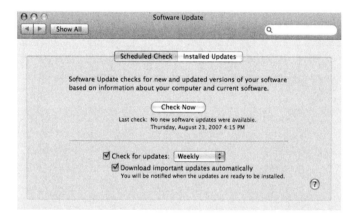

■ **Installed Updates** This is simply a list of updates that your Mac has downloaded and installed via the Software Update utility.

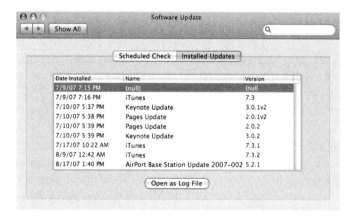

What Is an "Important" Update?

Aren't all updates important? Yes, but some updates are *more* important than others. Some updates simply add small features to an application, or fix a little-used function of it, and other updates fix major problems that could cause disruptions in usage or, much worse, loss of data. Important updates may even close "holes" in programs, especially those that access the Internet for their functionality (Safari, Mail, and so forth), which could potentially allow malicious hackers to gain control of your system. I'd say those kinds of updates merit being termed "important" over the others.

Keep Your Third-Party Applications Updated

Third-party apps need love too! Very few Mac users (or any other computer user, for that matter) stick to just the applications their computer originally came with, so chances are good that at some point you will own a third-party program, if you don't already. Programs such as Adobe Reader, Microsoft Office for Mac, and Quicken tend to find their way onto a lot of Macs.

From time to time, such third-party programs have updates available from their developers, and those updates can be very important to how the programs perform. Updating third-party applications is as necessary to the health of your Mac as is keeping current with its original applications.

Some developers, especially those of popular commercial applications such as Microsoft Office and Adobe Photoshop, have utilities built into their programs that work much like Software Update. These utilities check the servers of the developer to see if any new versions of the software have been released. If so, you can usually decide to download the updates and install them either now or at a later time. These utilities are certainly the easiest and most consumer-friendly way to keep programs up to speed.

However, some developers haven't seen it necessary to incorporate these kinds of utilities into their applications, so you may have to peruse their websites for updates from time to time. Often a developer will send an email to customers who have registered their software that keeps them informed on the product's comings and goings, which is essentially the same as using a utility to check the developer's servers but without the added convenience of automatically downloading and installing any available updates.

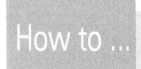

Easily Keep Up to Date

Browsing the Internet for the individual websites of every developer who made the applications you own can be a downright hassle. There has to be an easier way…

There is! Thank your lucky stars for a little website known as VersionTracker. This website keeps track of third-party updates so you only have to worry about checking 1 site instead of 15. VersionTracker also offers lots of freeware and shareware programs that you may have never heard of, along with reviews from people who have actually used the software before. This is a must-visit site! Check it out at www.versiontracker.com/macosx/.

Follow Simple Mac Maintenance Procedures

Because Mac OS X is a UNIX-based operating system, most UNIX functions are built right into it, including the UNIX maintenance scripts. These scripts remove system logs and temporary files, cleaning out the old data to make way for the new data. The scripts also make backups of crucial databases that are necessary for Mac OS X's smooth operation.

Did you know?

What Is UNIX?

UNIX is an operating system developed in the late 1960s that has gained a well-deserved reputation for stability and security. There are many versions, or variants, of UNIX. Mac OS X and Linux are variants of UNIX, and use many of UNIX's commands and internal underpinnings, using its legendary stability as a base to build on.

There are three script types, and each one has its own set of tasks it needs to accomplish. These three script types are separated by when they run: daily, weekly, and monthly. The scripts are designed to run in the background, which means you should never really notice that they are working. To tell the truth, unless you are an extreme night owl or a vampire, the chances of you seeing these scripts run, or even using your Mac while they are running, are slim to none. The reason for this is simple: by default they are scheduled to run between 3:15 and 5:30 A.M. local time. These scripts can't run when your Mac is turned off or is asleep, but they do need to be run to ensure that your system is running efficiently.

To make these scripts run while the world is awake, you're going to get the distinct pleasure of working with one of the oldest tools of the computing trade: the Terminal application. Terminal is simply a program that lets you access the command line of Mac OS X in a window. If you used a computer in the 1970s or 1980s, you probably know first-hand the sheer pleasure of running a purely text-based operating system with no graphical interface to speak of, so Terminal shouldn't scare you at all. However, it can be daunting for some first-timers. My suggestion to those in the latter category is to follow every single step verbatim:

1. Open Terminal by choosing Hard Drive | Applications | Utilities (or Finder | Go | Utilities) and double-clicking its icon, at which time you are greeted by this modest little window:

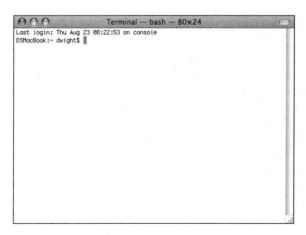

How to ...   **Use a Third-Party Graphical Maintenance Utility**

If you don't like working in Terminal, there are lots of third-party utilities out there that help you run the maintenance procedures just described via a graphical user interface. Some of the most popular are OnyX and MacJanitor. I suggest you go to VersionTracker's site and search the System/Utilities section to find the latest and greatest of these utilities. If you decide to go with one of these programs, be certain that it is compatible with the version of Mac OS X you are running!

2. In the interest of saving you from typing three different commands, you're going to run all three scripts at once. At the command prompt, type the following *exactly as you see here*:

```
sudo periodic daily weekly monthly
```

3. Read the warning if you must, but then proceed by pressing the RETURN key, typing your admin password, and pressing RETURN again.

You will not have any visual clues that anything is happening because all the magic is occurring behind the scenes. Your command prompt returns when the scripts have completed their heroic deeds.

Optionally, you can run the scripts one at a time if you like. To do so, just type

```
sudo periodic daily
```

and press RETURN. To run the other scripts, substitute `weekly` or `monthly` for `daily`.

A Clean Mac Is a Happy Mac!

Again with the car analogies…

Nobody wants to ride around in a car that's caked in mud on the outside and cheese sticks, corn chips, and fountain drinks on the inside, right? And guess what? Nobody wants to use a computer whose mouse buttons stick because of the icing you get on it from eating your morning doughnut while checking email. They also don't want to look at a screen that's had spittle rained on it every day since its last cleaning five weeks ago. Who wants to type on a keyboard that has little pieces of Hershey's Kisses stuck between the keys? Okay, maybe some of you, so let me rephrase that—with *someone else's* Hershey's Kisses stuck between the keys? (If you still raised your hand after I rephrased the question you should be buying psychology books, not computer how-to's.)

Before you ever begin cleaning your computer, unplug it from its power source. That also means to remove the battery if the Mac is a laptop.

Since you want your Mac to look its best, be sure to never use any common household cleaning products on it like a window cleaner, aerosol, or abrasives. Any product containing ammonia, acetone, or alcohol is an instant no-no! Also, never spray a liquid onto the Mac, because it can be difficult to control the amount of flow; the liquid may drip into cracks and crevices and wreak all kinds of unholy havoc on your innocent Mac.

"Well, good grief! What am I supposed to use—harsh language?"

The first tool in your cleaning kit should be a very soft, lint-free cloth. Some Macs even come with a cleaning cloth in the box. Item number two? A little dash of clean, crisp water! Barely dampen the cloth and gently wipe the surfaces of the Mac, as well as its screen, to make it look like new again.

If you just *have* to use a cleaning product, Apple recommends iKlear by Meridrew Enterprises. You can see more about the product at the company's website, www.klearscreen.com.

Summary

After this chapter, you should be a pro at maintaining your Mac's overall health and attitude, but don't be lulled into thinking you're forever and always safe from potential mishaps. While you will certainly minimize your chances of running into problems by following these maintenance tips, it's good to know what to do if something does arise. That's the very reason for the existence of the next chapter, called (and here we go with the car thing again) "Getting Under the Hood."

Chapter 23

Getting Under the Hood

How to ...

- Open Disk Utility from the Mac OS X installation disc
- Use Disk Utility to search for and resolve problems
- Format and partition disks
- Burn CDs or DVDs of disk images

Sometimes to resolve problems, you just can't avoid getting your hands dirty. If your car is having problems starting up, you may have to get under the hood to check things out if you've already tried and failed to start it by turning the ignition switch over and over again. Getting under your Mac's "hood" usually means bringing out the Disk Utility program to examine your hard drives and repair any problems that may be found.

Get Familiar with Disk Utility

Disk Utility is Mac OS X's Swiss army knife. When it comes to working with disks of any type, even virtual ones, Disk Utility is the tool to use. This utility is such an important part of Mac OS X's maintenance and repair functions that it warrants a chapter all to itself. Disk Utility isn't just

What Are Partitions and Disk Images?

Partitioning a hard drive is the process of dividing the disk into multiple sections, or *partitions*, each of which appears to your system as a separate hard drive. You can use these partitions as if they were separate hard drives, installing whatever you like on each one, even having multiple Mac OS X installations on one physical hard drive. I use partitions on my Mac in just this way; notice the drives listed in the Finder in this illustration.

There are three icons for hard drives but there is only one physical drive on my Mac. I've partitioned the drive, installing Mac OS X 10.5 on "Leopard," Mac OS X 10.4 on "Tiger," and keeping personal files and folders on "Stuff." With this setup I can boot my Mac in either version of Mac OS X and still retain access to my personal files on the Stuff partition. Pretty slick if I say so myself.

Disk images are files that contain the exact contents and file structures of a physical disk, like a hard drive or CD/DVD. These kinds of disk images are exact carbon copies of the disks they are made from, making them great for archiving disks. A second type is a blank disk image, which acts like a physical disk that you can copy files and folders to. Disk Utility can easily burn disk images to physical disks.

a repair tool, though. Use it to format your disks, create partitions on your disks, make custom disk images, or burn CDs and DVDs of disk images.

Open Disk Utility by choosing Hard Drive | Applications | Utilities | Disk Utility. Figure 23-1 shows Disk Utility's default interface.

Work with the Disk Utility Toolbar

The standard toolbar functions give quick access to common tasks, as described next:

- **Verify** Select a disk or disk image from the sources list on the right and then click this button to have Disk Utility examine it for any problems.

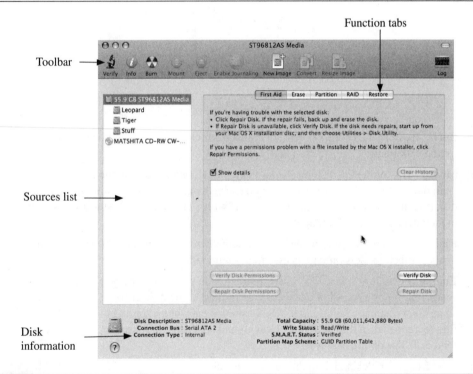

FIGURE 23-1 Disk Utility is ready for action!

■ **Info**   Clicking the Info button provides much more detailed and technical information than most Mac users need.

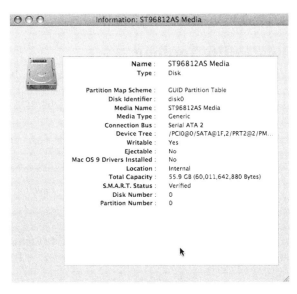

■ **Burn**   To burn a CD or DVD of a disk image, click this button and browse your Mac for the disk image.

■ **Mount**   To "mount" a disk means to make it available for use by the Mac, and to "unmount" obviously performs the reverse. You cannot mount or unmount your startup disk (the disk your Mac is using to run itself with). The Mac OS X startup disk is always mounted, and cannot be unmounted.

■ **Eject**   Clicking this button ejects only ejectable media, such as CDs, DVDs, and disk images. Ejecting a disk image is essentially unmounting it.

■ **Enable Journaling**   Mac OS X uses Journaling to protect the integrity of its file systems. Journaling keeps a record of changes made to files on the disk. If there is a power failure or some other traumatic failure, Mac OS X can look back at the journal to restore the Mac's files to a time when they were in a known-good condition. If Journaling is already enabled for a disk, this option is grayed out.

■ **New Image**   Click a disk in the sources list and then click the New Image button to create a new disk image from the selected disk. Title your disk image, choose where to store it, choose the compression and encryption options, and then click Save to save the disk image.

- **Convert** Clicking this button enables you to change the disk image from one type to another. For example, if you create a disk image that can be read and written to, but later decide you don't want the information to be changed, you can convert the disk image to read-only.

- **Resize Image** Clicking this button allows you to resize a disk image to your liking. If you have a disk that you want to add more information to, but it is filled to capacity, you can resize the disk image to a size necessary to contain the new information.

- **Log** Clicking this button opens the Disk Utility Log, which lists all the sordid details of Disk Utility's activities.

Work with the Disk Utility Tabs

Select a disk from the sources list on the right and you will be able to choose one of the function tabs so you can work with the disk. The following sections describe what functionality these tabs provide.

You cannot make changes to your startup volume. Some functions, such as verifying the disk, can be performed, but if any errors are found, you cannot repair them. To repair or format your startup volume, you must reboot the Mac using the Mac OS X installation disc and run Disk Utility from it.

First Aid

Disks sometimes need repairing, and the First Aid tab can quite adequately render the service its name suggests. Click the disk you want to use in the sources list, and then click the First Aid tab to see the available options. The repairs effected by First Aid are not physical, but rather are logical, meaning that the actual physical disk itself is not mechanically repaired, but the data on the disk is corrected.

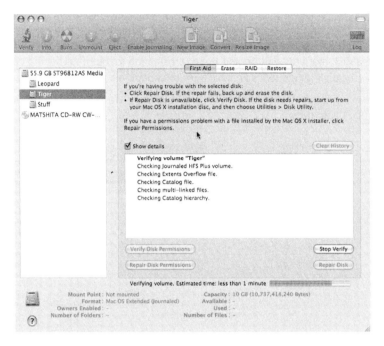

The following are the options on the First Aid tab:

■ **Show Details** Check this box to see the progress of the requested task.

■ **Verify Disk/Repair Disk** Click Verify Disk (shown as Stop Verify in the preceding illustration because it has been clicked) to have Disk Utility examine the file system structure of your disk. If any problems are found, click the Repair Disk button to resolve them. Clicking Repair Disk first instead of Verify Disk runs both a verification and a repair session at once.

■ **Verify Disk Permissions/Repair Disk Permissions** Click Verify Disk Permissions to make sure the access permissions for each file are valid. If errors are present, click Repair Disk Permissions to fix them. Again, clicking Repair Disk Permissions first instead of Verify Disk Permissions invokes both tasks.

TIP *Most hard drives incorporate Self-Monitoring, Analysis, and Reporting Technology (S.M.A.R.T.), which is hardware developed by IBM to allow drives to examine themselves for any possible failures. Disk Utility is able to utilize S.M.A.R.T., displaying the S.M.A.R.T. status of a drive in the disk information section at the bottom of the Disk Utility window. If the S.M.A.R.T. status is verified, the drive is fine, but if it says "About to fail" you need to back up your system pronto!*

Erase

The Erase tab offers options for formatting your disk or a partition on your disk.

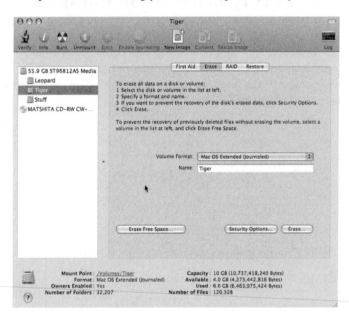

Choose the Volume Format, assign a name to the disk, and then click Erase to format the disk or partition.

Partition

Select a hard drive from the sources list to see the Partition tab.

To partition a disk, choose a Volume Scheme, which is a description of how you want to partition the disk, and then set the size of each partition. Click Apply to create the partitions or click Revert to start the process over. Partitioning a disk erases all the data it contains.

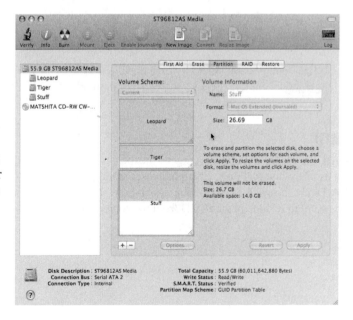

 **Securely Erase Disks and Partitions**

Even after you have formatted a disk, the data on the disk is still readable and recoverable by most disk recovery applications. Disk Utility provides options for making certain the data that was on your disk cannot be retrieved. To use these features, click the Security Options button on the Erase tab, which opens this window:

Each option is satisfactorily explained in the dialog box. The better security you use the longer the formatting process, so keep that in mind if time is a factor.

RAID

RAID stands for Redundant Array of Inexpensive Disks. A RAID is a set of multiple disks that act as one individual disk, which increases storage capacity and increases disk performance. The RAID tab, shown in the following illustration, allows you to create a RAID by dragging disks you want to include in the RAID from the sources list to the RAID list.

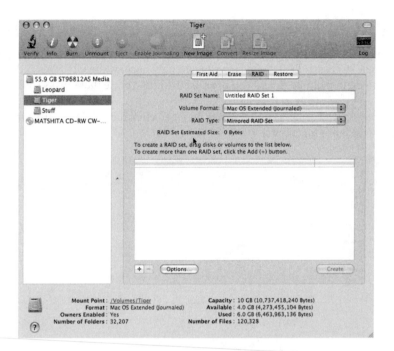

This is one of those techniques that only a geek can love. If you don't know what a RAID is already, you probably don't need to create one.

Restore

The Restore tab allows you to copy or restore a disk or disk image to another disk. Select the disk or disk image you want to copy or restore, choose a destination disk to be copied or restored to, and then click Restore.

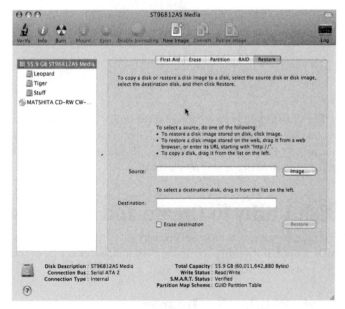

Use Disc Utility to Erase Rewriteable CDs and DVDs

Using rewriteable CDs and DVDs (aka CD-RWs and DVD-RWs) is a great way to temporarily store data. "Regular" CDs and DVDs can be written to only once, while CD-RWs and DVD-RWs can be rewritten to multiple times. You use Disk Utility to erase these disks so that you can reuse them.

Insert a rewriteable CD or DVD into the Mac and then click the CD/DVD drive in the sources list to see the erase functions.

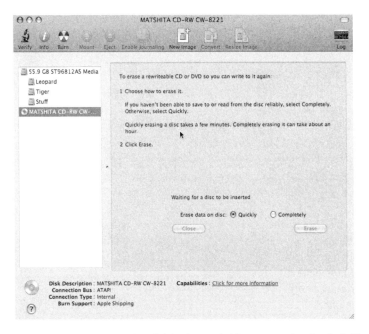

The options you have are to erase the disk's data quickly or completely. Quickly erasing only takes a few minutes (DVDs take longer than CDs since they are much larger in terms of capacity), whereas completely erasing can take an hour or so. When the erasure is finished, you can use your disk like it was new again.

Use Disk Utility to Create and Burn Disk Images

Creating disk images is an excellent way to archive data or make backup copies of CDs and DVDs. Disk Utility helps you create disk images, either from scratch or from another disk, and helps you to burn your disk images to a CD or DVD.

Create Blank Disk Images

To create a custom blank disk image, click the New Image button in the toolbar of Disk Utility. Create your disk image using these options:

- **Save As and Where**   Give the disk image a descriptive name and choose a location to save it to from the Where menu.

- **Volume Name, Volume Size, and Volume Format**   The name of the volume doesn't have to be the same name as the disk image, but it may help alleviate confusion about what the disk image contains. Choose a size for your disk image and a volume format, which is Mac OS X Extended (Journaled) by default.

- **Encryption**   Encrypting your disk image is a security feature designed to prevent unauthorized viewers from accessing the data on it.

- **Partitions**   Choose a partition type from the options available. Choose the best option to suit your intentions for the data. For instance, if you plan to burn the data to a CD or DVD, choose CD/DVD as the Partitions option.

- **Image Format**   Choose which format to use for your disk image.

Once you've determined the settings for your new disk image, click the Create button. The new disk image appears in the directory you saved it to, as well as in the source list of Disk Utility, as shown here.

The disk image also appears on your desktop, but notice that there are two icons! "What's up with that? I only created one disk image!" The icon for the disk image itself looks like a piece of paper with a hard drive icon on it, as is illustrated by diskimage.dmg in Figure 23-2. When a disk image is opened, or mounted, it displays its volume icon, which looks like a slot-loading drive of sorts (see Disk Image, also in Figure 23-2).

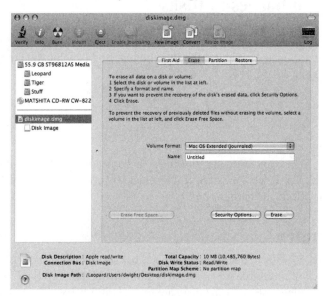

FIGURE 23-2   Icons for a disk image (top) and for the mounted volume of the disk image (bottom)

Create a Disk Image from an Existing Disk

My favorite thing about Disk Utility is being able to make perfect copies of my CDs, ensuring that if the original is scratched beyond recognition or smashed with a hammer by the little "angels" in my house, I can simply burn a new identical copy of the original to a blank CD.

To create an image from any disk, whether a hard drive, CD, or DVD, click the disk in the sources list and choose File | New | Disk Image from *disk name*.

Make your choices from the Image Format and Encryption menus, and then click Save.

Burn Images to Disks

This job couldn't be much simpler.

Choose Images | Burn, browse your hard drive for the disk image you want to burn, choose the disk image, and click the Burn button. At this point you are prompted to insert a disc.

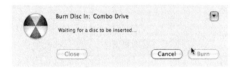

When you do so, the disk image is burned to the physical disk, whether it be a CD or DVD. Disk Utility lets you know if it foresees any problems, such as the disk not having enough space to perform the burn.

Summary

You're ready to handle most of your disk maintenance and repair needs. Disk Utility is one heck of a versatile program and is probably the best utility of its kind to ship as part of a major operating system. While there are several third-party disk utility programs out there, for the average Mac user, Disk Utility more than holds its own.

Chapter 24

Back 'er Up: Using Time Machine

How to . . .

- Set preferences for how Time Machine works
- Back up your Mac using Time Machine
- Use Time Machine to restore files and folders

Your files are precious to you, right? I don't mean they're Gollum from *Lord of the Rings* "precioussssssss," but they mean a great deal to you: photos of kids, friends, grandparents, and once-in-a-lifetime vacations; songs that you can't hear on the radio any more; tax returns, budgets, and bill statements that are critical to your financial outlook; emails from friends far, far away; home movies of your now-grown children that you were able to move to digital from old 8mm film, using iMovie to create beautiful memories that can be passed down to your great grandkids.

Imagine all of that is on your Mac, and then one day—POOF!—it's all gone. A lightning bolt zapped it away, or your three-year-old child thought your Mac needed a bath so she put it in the sink and turned the water on, or your laptop was crushed beneath a cast-iron set of dumbbells.

This sounds like a nightmare to most folks, but not to you. Oh, that's right! Not to you! Why not? Because you're smart enough to back up your system, so at most you may have lost a few e-mails containing bad jokes or profane spam messages. You had the foresight to keep copies of all your most important files in a safe place. You thought ahead, remembering to back up your Mac on a regular basis or whenever you made big changes to it. You understand that bad things can happen to good people, so it's best to be prepared. You are a smart computer user.

If your Mac has crashed, and the statements in the prior paragraph don't sound like they describe you, you're possibly up a creek without the proverbial paddle. Is your data recoverable? The best answer I can give you is "maybe," but you'll have to pay (sometimes dearly) to get it back. Some third-party disk recovery software may be able to salvage some or all of your data, or you can take it to a computer professional who will charge you big bucks to attempt a retrieval of your material.

Please, please, please heed my plea: BACK UP YOUR MAC!

Apple has provided a great new tool for backing up a Mac: Time Machine.

Back Up with Time Machine

Time Machine is the latest and greatest technology from Apple, and is an integral part of Mac OS X as of version 10.5. Time Machine is best used to back up entire systems, but that's not its claim to fame. Lots of third-party utilities out there can handle basic backups, but Time Machine literally lets you go back in time to retrieve copies of files, folders, and even entire drives, whether they've been recently deleted or not. Time Machine not only performs this feat, but also offers eye candy (a geek term for really neat-looking graphics) to convey the retrieval that is so fun to watch you'll want to restore files all day long.

To use Time Machine, you need an external or internal hard drive with enough space to back up your entire system (and then some), or a volume attached to a server on your network.

NOTE   *The trick with backup volumes in Time Machine is that the volume must be formatted in the Mac OS Extended format (see Chapter 23 for details about using Disk Utility to format drives). It's best if the disk is solely dedicated to Time Machine. The more space you have taken up by other files on the disk, the less there is for Time Machine to use.*

The first time you connect the drive, your Mac asks if you want to use this drive with Time Machine. If you answer Yes, Time Machine handles all of its configuration needs in the background and performs a backup automatically. Time Machine also sets up a backup schedule so that it can always keep your backups up to date. But what if you want to make changes to the way Time Machine works with the drive, or you just want to set up the drive yourself? Do it the old-fashioned way, that's what, by setting the Time Machine's preferences.

Set Time Machine's Preferences

The first thing you need to do when using Time Machine is to set up its preferences. Access these settings by choosing Apple | System Preferences | Time Machine.

From the Time Machine preferences pane, follow these steps:

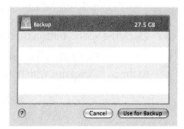

1. Time Machine is turned off by default, so turn it on by clicking the slider switch to ON.

2. Click the Choose Backup Disk button to choose a hard drive to use for your backups.

3. Choose the disk you want to use and click the Use for Backup button. Your disk (called Backup in my case) shows up in the Time Machine preferences pane as the backup destination. The amount of space available on the drive is given, as well as the previous backup dates, if any.

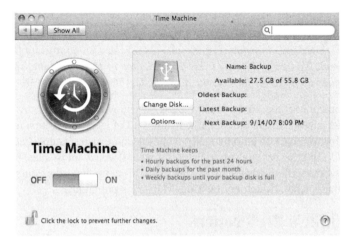

4. Click the Options button in the preferences pane. The dialog box that opens shows which volumes you've chosen to *not* back up.

NOTE *This does work against normal conventions for backup utilities; in most of them you select which volumes you do want to back up, but it's just the opposite in Time Machine.*

5. Click the + or – button to, respectively, add or remove volumes from the list.

6. Click the Done button when you're finished and Time Machine will begin its countdown to the next backup, which happens in 120 seconds.

There are two ways to view Time Machine's progress: you can watch the status in the Time Machine preferences pane, or minimize the preferences pane and just watch the bar in the small Time Machine progress window.

When the backup is finished, the Time Machine preferences pane tells you when the last backup was performed, as well as when the next backup is scheduled. When the slider switch is set to ON, Time Machine performs a backup every hour.

To pause a backup, just click the slide switch to OFF, and to resume it, slide it back to ON.

Use the WABAC Machine

Those of you who are familiar with the *Rocky and Bullwinkle Show* no doubt caught the reference in the title of this section. The WABAC (pronounced "wayback") Machine was a device used by Mr. Peabody (a brilliant dog) and Sherman (Mr. Peabody's owner), two characters who had their own series of shorts on the *Rocky and Bullwinkle Show*, to travel back into time and come back again. Time Machine is Apple's Mac OS X equivalent of the WABAC Machine, going back into your Mac's history to find data that it brings back to the present. (I believe I've just exposed the depth of my intellect by referring to *Rocky and Bullwinkle* as opposed to the great literary giant, Jules Verne…)

Open Time Machine by clicking its icon in the Dock or by choosing Hard Drive | Applications | Time Machine from within the Finder, and you will be transported into a time warp!

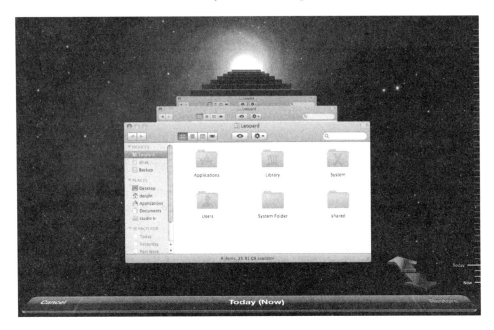

The interface for Time Machine is so simple it's almost surprising:

- The timeline is on the right side of the window, denoted by the light and dark gray dashes. Run your mouse cursor up and down the timeline to see previous dates in which the system was backed up.

- The directional arrows speed you through the windows in reverse or forward motion.

- The toolbar at the bottom of the window gives the option to Cancel your trip through history, and allows you to Restore a file, folder, or an entire disk.

To restore a file that has been deleted or to revert back to a previous version of the file, first open the directory on your Mac in which the file was or is stored (the Finder windows in Time Machine work exactly as they normally do in other programs). Once you're in the proper directory, use the forward and reverse arrows to browse through your backups, or go directly to a specific date by scrolling through the timeline. Find the file you need, click it once to highlight it, and then click the Restore button to move an exact copy of the file to the present directory.

Here's an example: Let's say I've accidentally deleted a file called "tech edit progress" and I need to get it back from a previous backup. The directory I stored "tech edit progress" in is called HTDEWYM. I proceed as follows:

1. I open the HTDEWYM directory in the Finder and click the Time Machine icon in the Dock, at which point I'm presented with this window:

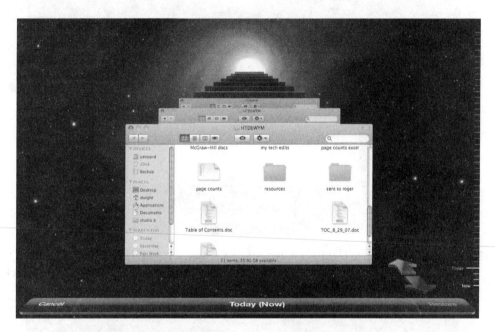

2. I scroll through the past using either the arrows or the timeline.

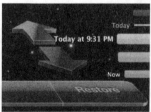

There's what looks like my file! Notice the time changed from Now to the time the file was backed up.

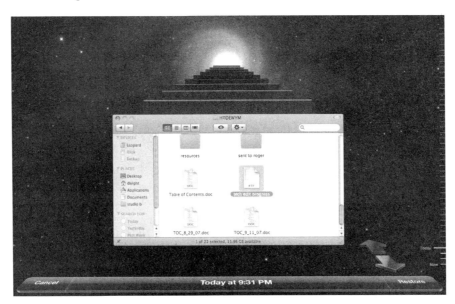

3. I click the file once to highlight it, but before I restore it I'd like to check it to make certain that it is indeed the file I'm looking for. To get a peek at the file, I click the Quick Look icon in the Finder toolbar and see the following:

How to ...   **Restore an Entire Disk with Time Machine**

God forbid your entire hard disk drive should ever crash, but if it does, and you've regularly backed up your Mac, at worst you may only lose a few days of information.

To restore a disk back to its former glory:

1. Reboot your Mac using the Mac OS X installation disc that came with it.
2. Run Disk Utility to reformat the drive, giving the drive exactly the same name it used before the crash.
3. Reinstall Mac OS X.
4. Open your Time Machine preferences to set your backup volume.
5. Open Time Machine, click the disk you want to recover, and then click the Restore button.

The restoration may take quite a bit of time, but by the time it's finished, you should have most, if not all, of your Mac's previous life back.

4. Yep, that's it! That's my file! I close the Quick Look window by clicking the Close button, which looks like a circle with an "x" in the middle.
5. I click the Restore button, and my file is *WHOOSHED* through time and space to the present.

It doesn't get any easier, better, or cooler than that!

Summary

Now that you know how to back up, the next step is to actually do it. As terrible a feeling as having computer troubles can be, it's a million times worse when you think you may have lost months' or years' worth of work forever. Whether you like Time Machine, or even some other third-party backup utility, do yourself a favor by actually using it. You'll thank me later for being so insistent.

Index